THE DESIGN OF
EXPERIMENTS IN NEUROSCIENCE
SECOND EDITION

THE DESIGN OF
EXPERIMENTS IN NEUROSCIENCE
SECOND EDITION

MARY HARRINGTON
Smith College

Los Angeles | London | New Delhi
Singapore | Washington DC

For information:

SAGE Publications, Inc.
2455 Teller Road
Thousand Oaks, California 91320
E-mail: order@sagepub.com

SAGE Publications India Pvt. Ltd.
B 1/I 1 Mohan Cooperative Industrial Area
Mathura Road, New Delhi 110 044
India

SAGE Publications Ltd.
1 Oliver's Yard
55 City Road
London EC1Y 1SP
United Kingdom

SAGE Publications Asia-Pacific Pte. Ltd.
33 Pekin Street #02-01
Far East Square
Singapore 048763

Printed in the United States of America

Library of Congress Cataloging-in-Publication Data

Harrington, Mary.
The design of experiments in neuroscience/Mary Harrington.—2nd ed.
 p. ; cm.
Includes bibliographical references and index.
ISBN 978-1-4129-7432-5 (pbk. : alk. paper)
 1. Neurosciences—Research—Methodology. I. Title.
 [DNLM: 1. Neurosciences. 2. Research Design. WL 20 H311d 2011]

RC337.H38 2011
612.8072—dc22   2010020000

This book is printed on acid-free paper.

10 11 12 13 14 10 9 8 7 6 5 4 3 2 1

Acquisitions Editor:	Vicki Knight
Associate Editor:	Lauren Habib
Editorial Assistant:	Ashley Dodd
Production Editor:	Eric Garner
Copy Editor:	Jovey Stewart
Typesetter:	C&M Digitals (P) Ltd.
Proofreader:	Joyce Li
Indexer:	Terri Corry
Cover Designer:	Edgar Abarca
Marketing Manager:	Stephanie Adams

Brief Contents

Detailed Contents

Preface

You are about to start on a great adventure. You are going to transition from reading about science to becoming a scientist. Most students I know are both excited and doubtful as they approach this transition. They may be thinking, "It sounds pretty cool to be a neuroscientist, but am I really able to think of my own experiments?" For many, their idea of a scientist is a creature totally unlike themselves. In this book, I will address your self-doubt by explaining the basics of how this whole enterprise works. You will be able to start off on your adventure with an understanding of how to go about selecting a topic, designing an experiment, analyzing the results, and publishing a paper. I love to give advice, so be confident that you will also get many suggestions on how to find a mentor, what to focus on in your training, and common traps to avoid. I have watched many students apply this background immediately as they take on internships in neuroscience research labs and launch their own careers. Whether they end up as research scientists, physicians, public health workers, or simply well-informed citizens, the hands-on experience of producing new scientific knowledge is one I think they all enjoy reflecting on.

One of the additions to the second edition of this book is a new chapter on becoming an independent investigator. I have extensively quoted from a small book by Santiago Ramón y Cajal, *Advice to a Young Investigator*, written more than 100 years ago. You will see that some of this advice has not changed. Ramón y Cajal was writing from the perspective of a Spanish scientist at a time when no one expected brilliant science coming from the lab of a Spaniard. I expect that some of the readers of this book may encounter similar disbelief from those around them. Yet your unique background might guide you to ask new questions or to see old questions from a new angle. I hope you will use my book as an enticement to read Ramón y Cajal's entire book and take to heart the important role of persistence and dedication in leading to success in science.

The bare bones of the subject matter covered in this book appear in many other books; what sets this book apart is the use of examples from neuroscientific research. Nearly every example is from a published study, and these range across the broad expanse of diverse studies that are encompassed by the field of neuroscience. The material progresses from general to specific. Ethical issues are covered first, in Chapter 2; they are critical to design considerations for neuroscientists. Whether you will work with human or nonhuman animals, you must thoughtfully incorporate ethical guidelines at every stage of the project. The choice of a hypothesis is discussed next, in Chapter 3. This is obviously the starting point of a research project, and it can be the most difficult for a young scientist. Guidelines for choosing a question, shaping a hypothesis, finding a mentor, and accessing reports of previous studies on the topic are described. Chapter 4 covers the basics of experimental design in the context of a simple study with a treatment group and a control group. Chapter 5 describes in depth controlling extraneous variables. This is truly the heart of experimental design, and there are many fundamental research design issues related to control of variables. Chapter 6 discusses factorial designs, introducing complex research designs, while Chapter 7 explores simple correlational designs, providing the beginning student access to a more realistic level of complexity that will be encountered in the research literature. Chapter 8 summarizes the entire process of taking a research project from start to finish and offers general advice for shaping your education and your work as a scientist. Much is left for a course in advanced research design, but a student completing study of this text should be well-equipped for guided readings of the primary research literature and mentored investigations in a neuroscience research laboratory.

Statistical concepts that shape research design are covered within the main body of the text. Students who need a review of basic concepts can refer to Appendix A at the back of the book. This appendix material is sufficient to guide a student with no prior background in statistics as they complete beginning laboratory exercises and analyses of data sets. It becomes apparent to all beginning students that this level of knowledge is ultimately insufficient, and further instruction in probability and statistics is fundamental to their training in neuroscience.

I have adopted what I call the "12-step program for reading journal articles," and I hope you will adopt this approach as your own. This list of 12 questions, which can be applied to any journal article (from Locke, Silverman, & Spirduso, 1998), guide you to focus on the important elements of the paper. To help you master this approach, I have provided several examples of answers for these questions for selected articles. One article is provided as a reprint in Appendix C, along with sample answers to the 12 questions. To help you transition from reading journal articles to publishing your own journal articles, Appendix B provides guidelines for writing papers for publication. The general structure of a research report and overall writing style hints are described. The appendix also gives specific format guidelines for the *Journal of Neuroscience* and for journals sponsored by the American Psychological Association. Going a step further, Appendix C demonstrates a paper both in the form of a publication as well as in the format to be submitted to the journal for consideration for publication.

A glossary in Appendix E provides concise definitions of terms used throughout the text. You can check your grasp of fundamental concepts through completion of end-of-chapter questions, the answers to which are provided in Appendix F. I hope you will be stimulated to investigate some of the topics covered in this book in more detail and to help you do that, I provide suggestions for further reading at the end of each chapter.

ACKNOWLEDGMENTS

There are many people to acknowledge for their help in shaping this book. I owe special thanks to Adam Hall, my colleague and friend, who developed the *Experimental Methods in Neuroscience* course with me (see Hall & Harrington, 2003). His frank comments on drafts of this book helped enormously. I also owe thanks to my colleagues at Smith College who encouraged us in this direction and granted us the freedom and funds to create this addition to our curriculum. Joanne Huyler patiently explained the U.S. animal care regulatory structure. Students in the course also provided feedback on drafts, and Sophie Kerszberg wrote much of the text in Appendix F, the answers to end-of-chapter questions. Penny Molyneux helped in the initial stages of planning this book and read final drafts with a careful eye; during the time that I was writing the second edition, she kept my lab running smoothly and tried to keep me this side of sanity.

My editor, Vicki Knight, guided me in this project with wise advice. Her experience and patience were instrumental in helping me complete this project, as were her deadlines. The reviewers that Vicki selected to read early drafts were invaluable, and I thank them earnestly for their comments. These include Josephine F. Wilson, Wittenberg University; Sharon Thompson-Schill, University of Pennsylvania; Harriett Amster, University of Texas at Arlington; George Spilich, Washington College; Gary Klatsky, SUNY at Oswego; Joel Voss, Northwestern University; Patti Simone, Santa Clara University; Katherine Cameron, Washington College; Craig Howard Kinsley, University of Richmond; Hewlet McFarlane, Kenyon College; Lynne Weber, Knox College; N. Bradley Keele, Baylor University; German Torres, NYCOM/ NYIT; Eric Corp, University of Massachusetts; Lynda Honour, California State University, Northridge; Julio Ramirez, Davidson College; and Joseph Dien, Tulane University. The second edition was revised with guidance and advice from both faculty members who had adopted the first edition as well as some who were new to the book. I thank

Cindy M. Bukach
University of Richmond

Joshua C. Brumberg
Queens College, CUNY

Cindy Gibson
Washington College

Stephen C. Maxson
The University of Connecticut

Kathy Stansbury
Michigan State University

Beth Wee
Tulane University

My good friends Jeff Radel and Gail Eskes gave suggestions that greatly improved this book, and I thank them for their time and effort. Nicholas Horton somehow found the time to read my entire first draft while teaching his first semester of courses at Smith College. His suggestions were among the best I received and definitely among the most difficult to address.

My parents were consistently encouraging and provided several opportunities that allowed me to write in a quiet setting. My brother-in-law, Bill Ravenhurst, read an entire draft and gave feedback from the perspective of a scientist unfamiliar with neuroscience. My deepest gratitude goes to my spouse, Casey, and my children, Johanna, Gretchen, and Daniel, for their love and support.

I started writing this book soon after the personally devastating death of my very close friend Robyn Zimmerman. Robyn died from glioblastoma, a brain cancer, leaving her spouse and four young children, as well as her many friends. There is no cure for glioblastoma, and prognosis is dismal. Writing this book helped me through the bleak years around Robyn's death. I hope that the next generation of neuroscientists will find cures for this and other debilitating brain disorders. They will touch the lives of all future generations, a richly deserved form of immortality.

About the Author

Mary Harrington is the Tippit Professor in Life Sciences at Smith College in Northampton, Massachusetts. She teaches courses in experimental methods and in neuroscience. Her research laboratory— largely staffed by undergraduate students—has contributed to understanding circadian rhythms and the neural pathways that synchronize our internal rhythms to environmental cycles. Drawn into research by the irresistible examples of Paul Cornwell, Herschel Leibowitz, and Robert B. Post (at Pennsylvania State University), she completed a PhD with Benjamin Rusak (Dalhousie University), an inspiring mentor and role model. She has supported her research laboratory via multiple grants from the National Institutes of Health (NIH), National Science Foundation (NSF), and Pfizer Inc., including a generous Research Career Development Award from NIH. She lives with her husband, three children, three cats, and 56 chickens in Hatfield, Massachusetts.

The Varieties of Scientific Experience

Only in the past few decades has neuroscience solidified as a distinct field. The interdisciplinary nature of neuroscience means that you as a student entering this area face the daunting prospect of having to learn biology, psychology, chemistry, physics, computer science, and mathematics just to be able to converse with other members of your own field. Not only does a student of neuroscience need to learn the language and basic foundations of all these other sciences, but an acquaintance with the fundamental laboratory techniques of these disparate areas is necessary as well.

It may be difficult to learn all the background information that helps to make you a neuroscientist, but fortunately it is not so difficult to get started conducting research in neuroscience. If you choose a simple question and a few laboratory techniques as a first focus, you can begin independent research in neuroscience. You may conduct research on a wide variety of questions, ranging from robotic models of artificial intelligence to the molecular basis of learning in the fruit fly, *Drosophila*. Common to all of these topics are the general underpinnings to any scientific investigation. Understanding the general structure of a scientific investigation will aid your research no matter what flavor of neuroscience you prefer. If you continue in research and have a career as an experimental neuroscientist, you will be learning new techniques throughout your lifetime; you will probably end your career using techniques not yet dreamed of. Nevertheless, how you design and analyze your experiments will still follow the principles introduced in this book.

THE SAVVY RESEARCH STUDENT

To help you understand how this course may influence you, let me tell you about a recent experience of a student of mine. Stephanie had arranged for a summer internship after her second year of college. She was going to work in a laboratory studying Alzheimer's disease using a molecular approach. We discussed material that the head of the lab had given her, the honors thesis of a student who had just completed his research in that lab. As we talked, I realized that Stephanie needed to sort out what was measured by a Western versus a Southern versus a Northern blot (protein, DNA, and RNA, respectively). She needed help finding the protocol books that give step-by-step directions for everything from making a stock solution to running a gel (I recommended Kathy Barker's (2004) *At the Bench: A Laboratory Navigator;* see the end of this chapter for further information). Nevertheless, she was doing fine without understanding some of the laboratory techniques and protocols, because her experimental methods course had given her a good understanding of the scientific process. She was reading the previous student's thesis with a critical eye. She had absorbed the basic working model the lab was testing and focused her efforts on discovering what aspects of that model were not yet firmly supported by experimental evidence. She understood the relative strengths of correlative versus experimental designs, and she quickly grasped the reports from statistical tests. Stephanie was well prepared for this wonderful internship opportunity. She would learn many new techniques, and the fundamental understanding of experimental design and analysis from her prior course would help her plan her summer experiments to contribute to scientific knowledge.

This text will prepare you for success if you join a neuroscience research laboratory as an apprentice, an experience essential to scientific training.

THE SKEPTICAL CONSUMER

A research laboratory is not the only context in which you will apply the concepts discussed in this book. When you read the newspaper or browse the web, you will often encounter reports about scientific studies with results that are relevant to your life. You will also find that it is rare that all scientists agree on the bottom line. What are you to think if the experts disagree? Here is an example: If you are having trouble cramming for your final exam, should you consider taking a drug to help you stay awake longer and learn more material? One drug that students sometimes suggest is modafinil (Provigil). This drug is approved for the treatment of the sleep disorder narcolepsy, but news reports suggest some people are using it as a "cognitive enhancer" or "smart drug." From most of the research on this drug, it appeared that it was not addictive; the U.S. Food and Drug Administration (FDA) classified it as "Schedule IV" or a controlled substance with low potential for abuse. A recent report (see Figure 1.1a) indicates modafinil could have addictive properties, contradicting earlier findings. Does this mean those early studies were wrong?

Figure 1.1a | Article From Bloomberg.com

NARCOLEPSY PILL USED AS SMART DRUG MAY BE ADDICTIVE

By Marilyn Chase

March 17 (Bloomberg)—Cephalon's narcolepsy drug Provigil, increasingly used as a so-called "smart drug" by students and professionals looking to boost their mental skills, may have a risk for addiction, a study found.

Researchers at the National Institute on Drug Abuse found the drug affects the same brain chemicals as stimulants like Ritalin and amphetamines. PET or positron emission tomography scans of the brain activity in 10 healthy volunteers who took the drug showed it boosted the level of dopamine circulating in the part of the brain involved in pleasure, reward and addiction, according to the study published today in the *Journal of the American Medical Association*.

The anti-drowsiness drug is being taken to help people stay more alert and sharpen their thinking at school and work, said Patrick Finley, professor of clinical pharmacy at the University of California, San Francisco. "Provigil is catching on," he said, as an augmenting agent added to antidepressants Prozac or Zoloft to offset grogginess.

The increase of dopamine seen with the medicine is "the signature for drugs that have the potential for producing addiction," said Nora Volkow, lead author of the study and director of the National Institute on Drug Abuse, in a telephone interview yesterday.

Physicians prescribing Provigil should "be alert to the possibility that it could produce addiction," Volkow said. Consumers also should be aware the drug "may have more abuse potential than originally believed," she said.

Nonmedical Use

The study noted that Provigil, known generically as modafinil, is being used by people who want to boost their mental ability. "Modafinil is increasingly being diverted for nonmedical use by healthy individuals with the expectation that it will improve cognitive performance," the authors wrote.

A decade-old drug approved to treat sleepiness caused by narcolepsy, obstructive sleep apnea, and shift-work sleep disorder, Provigil is Cephalon's biggest-selling product with $988 million in 2008 sales.

A longer-acting version called Nuvigil, known as armodafinil, is scheduled to be sold beginning in the third quarter of 2009, the Frazer, Pennsylvania-based company said. Cephalon said earlier today that a study of Nuvigil showed it improved depressive symptoms of bipolar disorder when added to drugs that stabilize mood swings.

The Nuvigil study sent Cephalon to its biggest single-day gain since Oct. 13. Cephalon rose $5.87, or 9.3 percent, to $69.06 at 4 p.m. New York time in Nasdaq Stock Market composite trading.

"Different" From Stimulants

Cephalon management praised the research report on Provigil but insisted the drug's risk for addiction is marginal.

"It's a good study," said Jeffry Vaught, chief scientific officer of Cephalon, in a phone interview yesterday. Vaught said Provigil's effect on dopamine is "weak," adding it is "very different from amphetamines and its abuse potential is very low."

(Continued)

(Continued)

Provigil is classified as a Schedule 4 drug under the U.S. Controlled Substances Act. That system ranks drugs' abuse potential in descending order from the highest (Schedule 1 drugs, such as heroin) to lowest (Schedule 5 drugs such as certain cough medicines).

Provigil's label materials, approved by the Food and Drug Administration, contain cautionary statements addressing the drug's potential for misuse or abuse.

Data Sought

Volkow said she isn't seeking stronger product warnings for the Provigil label at this time. She said she hoped to strengthen the institute's annual survey of high school drug use by adding questions about the sleep drug.

Some doctors cautioned against taking the report as the last word.

The new research is "basically a pilot study," said Clete Kushida, associate professor of psychiatry and acting director of the Stanford University Sleep Disorder Clinic, where the drug is used to treat narcolepsy and other approved indications. "Most centers including ours are very judicious in how we prescribe modafinil."

A legal expert said growing interest in drugs for cognitive enhancement calls for further study of whether they can be used safely and ethically.

"It's illegal. I wouldn't advise anyone to do anything that's illegal," said Henry Greely, Stanford law professor and Director of the Center for Law and the Biosciences. "Whether it should be illegal, that involves issues of safety when used by healthy people, for which we could use more data."

Casual nonmedical use of Provigil to sharpen thinking isn't limited to students, said Finley, of UCSF. "I've had interesting conversations with physicians who take it at lunchtime to increase their alertness," he said.

With no background in scientific method, it might be tempting to either give up, disgusted that scientists cannot seem to get the story straight, or turn to a respected authority and ask that person to make a judgment. With a background in scientific methods, you will be able to analyze the studies even from the bare-bones description in the web page report. Did the original reports include dopamine measures? Did the studies all assess addiction in the same manner? Was the dose of modafinil similar? You may feel compelled to post a comment or you may examine the details of the original primary source from which the first article was based (see Figure 1.1b for a copy of the lead page of the original article). You will be a more competent consumer of scientific information, and given the dramatic impact scientific information has on our lives, this is an important component of educated citizenship.

Figure 1.1b | Lead Page From Article in *JAMA*

Effects of Modafinil on Dopamine and Dopamine Transporters in the Male Human Brain
Clinical Implications

Nora D. Volkow, MD

Joanna S. Fowler, PhD

Jean Logan, PhD

David Alexoff, BSE

Wei Zhu, PhD

Frank Telang, MD

Gene-Jack Wang, MD

Millard Jayne, RN

Jacob M. Hooker, PhD

Christopher Wong, BA

Barbara Hubbard, RN

Pauline Carter, RN

Donald Warner, AA

Payton King, BA

Colleen Shea, MS

Youwen Xu, MS

Lisa Muench, BA

Karen Apelskog-Torres, AA

Context Modafinil, a wake-promoting drug used to treat narcolepsy, is increasingly being used as a cognitive enhancer. Although initially launched as distinct from stimulants that increase extracellular dopamine by targeting dopamine transporters, recent preclinical studies suggest otherwise.

Objective To measure the acute effects of modafinil at doses used therapeutically (200 mg and 400 mg given orally) on extracellular dopamine and on dopamine transporters in the male human brain.

Design, Setting, and Participants Positron emission tomography with [^{11}C]raclopride (D_2/D_3 radioligand sensitive to changes in endogenous dopamine) and [^{11}C]cocaine (dopamine transporter radioligand) was used to measure the effects of modafinil on extracellular dopamine and on dopamine transporters in 10 healthy male participants. The study took place over an 8-month period (2007-2008) at Brookhaven National Laboratory.

Main Outcome Measures Primary outcomes were changes in dopamine D_2/D_3 receptor and dopamine transporter availability (measured by changes in binding potential) after modafinil when compared with after placebo.

Results Modafinil decreased mean (SD) [^{11}C]raclopride binding potential in caudate (6.1% [6.5%]; 95% confidence interval [CI], 1.5% to 10.8%; $P = .02$), putamen (6.7% [4.9%]; 95% CI, 3.2% to 10.3%; $P = .002$), and nucleus accumbens (19.4% [20%]; 95% CI, 5% to 35%; $P = .02$), reflecting increases in extracellular dopamine. Modafinil also decreased [^{11}C]cocaine binding potential in caudate (53.8% [13.8%]; 95% CI, 43.9% to 63.6%; $P < .001$), putamen (47.2% [11.4%]; 95% CI, 39.1% to 55.4%; $P < .001$), and nucleus accumbens (39.3% [10%]; 95% CI, 30% to 49%; $P = .001$), reflecting occupancy of dopamine transporters.

Conclusions In this pilot study, modafinil blocked dopamine transporters and increased dopamine in the human brain (including the nucleus accumbens). Because drugs that increase dopamine in the nucleus accumbens have the potential for abuse, and considering the increasing use of modafinil, these results highlight the need for heightened awareness for potential abuse of and dependence on modafinil in vulnerable populations.

JAMA. 2009;301(11):1148-1154   www.jama.com

MODAFINIL IS A WAKE-promoting medication used in the treatment of narcolepsy and other sleep disorders. Modafinil may enhance cognition and is used off-label for the treatment of cognitive dysfunction in some psychiatric disorders (ie, schizophrenia, attention-deficit/hyperactivity disorder [ADHD]).[1] Moreover, modafinil is increasingly being diverted for nonmedical use by healthy individuals with the expectation that it will improve cognitive performance.[2] Although modafinil apparently has very low abuse liability (low reinforcing effects) in non–drug abusing individuals, the *Physicians' Desk Reference* cautions that it can produce psychoactive and euphoric effects typical of central nervous system stimulant drugs,[3] and there is debate surrounding its potential for abuse.[4,5]

The mechanisms of action of modafinil are not well understood but are believed to differ from those of stimulant

Author Affiliations are listed at the end of this article.
Corresponding Author: Nora D. Volkow, MD, National Institute on Drug Abuse, 6001 Executive Blvd, Room 5274, MSC 9581, Bethesda, MD 20892 (nvolkow@nida.nih.gov).

SOURCE: Volkow, Fowler, Logan, Alexoff, Zhu, Telang, et al., 2009.

WHAT IS SCIENCE?

Before we begin exploring the process of scientific discovery, we should first define our subject. What is science? It is often hardest to define the simple terms that we use in everyday life. Can you give a definition of science? Even science majors in their senior year of college find this difficult. Is science a collection of facts? How can you distinguish science from history, which also involves a collection of facts? Is science a collection of facts arising from laboratory experimentation? What about astronomy or taxonomic classifications?

I prefer this definition of **science:** "An interconnected series of concepts and conceptual schemes that have developed as a result of experimentation and observation and are fruitful of further experimentation and observation" (Conant, 1951, p. 5). This definition stresses the important role of conceptual schemes, such as theories or models, which guide the development of scientific understanding. Both experimentation and observation are included as techniques for gaining new understanding. Scientific understanding is never static. The definition highlights this idea by stressing that scientific models are fruitful and lead to further experimentation and observation.

The process of science has three general phases. First, there is a period of observation or experimentation. Results from these observations and experiments must be replicable; that is, other observers must be able to be repeat the observations and experiments and get the same results. Second, scientists compare the new evidence from these observations and experients with current scientific theories. If necessary, scientists revise theories to take into account the new results. Third, scientists test these refined scientific theories by further experimentation or observations. This is a spiraling process, leading to theories that are ever more sophisticated.

RECOGNIZING PSEUDOSCIENCE

Sometimes a body of knowledge looks like science and sounds like science, but it is not science. A trained scientist recognizes it as **pseudoscience,** unscientific information masquerading as science. How can you recognize pseudoscience and distinguish it from real science? Now that you have a clear understanding of the definition of science, this is not too difficult. Whereas pseudoscience consists of a system of ideas that either do not change or change randomly, science consists of ideas that change based on observations or experiments. Whereas pseudoscience lacks organized skepticism and the mechanisms for acquiring new knowledge are vague, the basis of science is organized skepticism through replicable experiments and observations, and there is agreement on the techniques for acquisition of new knowledge. In pseudoscience, established findings are often disregarded, whereas a new theory in science must always take into account previously established facts. Pseudoscientific writings often stress the personal characteristics of the writer, commonly suggesting that the scientific establishment is conspiring against the writer's ideas for dubious reasons; however, this cloak-and-dagger mentality is rarely present in scientific writing (see Box 1.1 for more hints).

BOX 1.1	**TOOLS OF THE TRADE**
	Rules to Help You Recognize Pseudoscience

1. Read the references. Many sources of pseudoscientific information will not provide references, and that is a dead giveaway of the unsubstantiated nature of the claims. The sources that worry me are the ones that *do* give references. Be sure you actually read those references yourself to determine if the authors of the source referenced actually support the claims.

2. Be alert for illogical leaps. Even if your brain waves show similarities to those from people with slight memory loss, this does not inevitably lead to the conclusion that you require a nutritional supplement to correct the "abnormality."

3. Do not be impressed by an idea's longevity. Just because an idea has been around for centuries does not indicate that the idea is valid. Pseudoscientists love to draw on "ancient wisdom," even if scientists have long ago discarded the ideas. Scientists look for evidence to support or falsify the idea and therefore make progress beyond ancient ideas. An example here is phrenology—a long-discredited idea that the pattern of bumps on the skull indicated an individual's personality. I was surprised to discover that there are people today who ascribe to the beliefs of phrenology.

4. Do not be swayed by the degrees and awards claimed by the person promoting the pseudoscience. A person can be trained as a scientist and lapse from that training. Diplomas or awards do not make a person a scientist—a skeptical, evidence-based approach makes someone a scientist. That "Most Esteemed Medical Researcher of the Year" award may be from a pseudoscience organization. Similarly, the "Nobel Prize nominee" may have been nominated by his or her mother.

5. Nearly every pseudoscientist will offer to sell you something. Whether it is a nutritional supplement, a book that will change your life, tapes that help you breathe correctly, or electrical devices that balance your hormones, you can be sure there is some merchandise.

NEUROSCIENCE IN THE SERVICE OF PSEUDOSCIENCE

I am appalled by uses of legitimate neuroscientific research in the service of pseudoscientific claims. They can give a patina of legitimacy to quack medical advice.

An example that intrigues me is "cranial electrostimulation." There are companies quite happy to sell you little devices that will apply an electrical current to your earlobes to electrically stimulate your brain. They claim that as you dial up the frequency of stimulation, you can achieve any desired brain wave frequency and thus an altered mental state. How will this help you? It will improve your life in countless ways—decrease anxiety, increase intelligence, improve sleep quality, lessen headaches, alleviate cancer pain . . . you get the picture. The companies promoting these devices suggest they would be helpful in treating headaches, anxiety, and stress—predictably, these are vague, widely reported symptoms. They also point to the ancient history of using electrical currents for therapy, even going back to when the most reliable source for electrical stimulation was electric eels.

But does it really work? A scientist cannot declare an idea wrong simply based on what I have told you so far. Look for well-controlled studies on this topic to find out. These studies should be conducted with the patient, therapist, and researcher unaware of whether the patient is receiving true cranial electrical stimulation or is actually in the untreated control group. Levels of stress and anxiety are rather subjective to measure, and it is important that the measurements are collected in an unbiased manner. Such symptoms do improve spontaneously, so it is important to test a large enough sample so that you are not fooled by improvement due to chance. It would be necessary to have a control group that followed the same procedure, applying electrodes to the earlobes, experiencing a tickling sensation indicating current is being delivered, sitting quietly for an hour or two each day while treatment is delivered, and so on. This is an essential control group. Obviously, stress and anxiety might be reduced simply by relaxing for several hours each day or by the assurance that you are receiving treatment for the anxiety. One of my favorite books—*The Monkey Gland Affair* by David Hamilton (1986)—describes the history of testicular implant treatments for the loss of libido in aging men. We now know that the body immediately rejects and destroys such implants of foreign tissues. The medical establishment was fooled into accepting these treatments as legitimate, in part because of the strength of reported positive effects. Several weeks of rest and abstaining from alcohol, receiving healthy food and solicitous care from young women, were followed by an expensive operation promised to restore libido. Can you guess why the elderly male patients reported increased sexual drive?

WHAT IS THE SCIENTIFIC METHOD?

In this book you will learn to apply the scientific method to questions of interest. But what exactly is the scientific method? Actually, there is not one scientific method. Rather, **scientific methodology** is a collection of logical rules, experimental designs, theoretical approaches, and laboratory techniques that have accumulated throughout history. Each field of science has its own history; thus, each field has slightly different scientific methods. Scientific methods are not fixed. In fact, the idea of the **experiment,** where the investigator gains new information by observing results after changing one variable with all other variables held constant, is a relatively new idea made popular in the 16th and 17th centuries. Scientists before that time largely relied on one of the important tools of modern scientists, careful observation. With the addition of the experiment, a new logical analysis was possible. Because the only difference between the groups in an experiment is the one variable of interest, we presume that the variable is the cause of any difference between the groups in the outcome measures. Given the power of the logical analysis of results that an experiment makes possible, many scientific studies are experiments; however, scientists have more methods in their repertoires. In this book, we initially focus on the experiment, but we will also cover other, nonexperimental, scientific approaches such as case studies, correlational studies, and observational studies.

EPISTEMOLOGY FOR SCIENTISTS

How do we know that our scientific methods are valid and our interpretations correct? Why should we even assume that we could understand nature at all? There is a long history of philosophers considering these questions, and much to gain from a consideration of their thoughts. This branch of philosophy, **epistemology,** is the study of how we know what we know.

Some of the things we accept as known we know based on **authority.** In the long period of the Middle Ages (5th–14th centuries), the church was the ultimate authority in Western culture. Church authorities had to approve new theories of the brain, which could not conflict with other church teachings. As an example, consider how the teachings of the church influenced the understanding of the ventricles, the fluid-filled caverns within the brain. Scientists thought that there were three ventricles; the first ventricle was where sensations were taken in, the second ventricle was responsible for perception, and the third ventricle was the site of reason. Why were the ventricles so important? The religious authorities taught that the soul was immaterial, so scientists of the time searched for a place in the brain where immaterial spirits could reside. The halls of the ventricles seemed ideal for a spacious home for spirits.

Empiricism, the idea that all knowledge arises from experience through the senses, grew in popularity in the 15th and 16th centuries. Instead of relying on the power of authority, such as the authority of the church, one could learn by observation and careful study of nature. Leonardo da Vinci's study of the ventricles is an example of the empirical approach. The human body fascinated da Vinci, a masterful observer. To better understand the ventricles of the brain, da Vinci borrowed a technique used by artists, making a mold from molten wax. He poured hot wax into the ventricles of an ox brain, let the wax cool and harden, and then dissected away the brain tissue to discover the true shape of the ventricles. As Figure 1.2 shows, da Vinci discovered by empirical observation that the ventricles were not shaped as three caverns, but had a more complex architecture.

Figure 1.2 | Early Depictions of the Brain

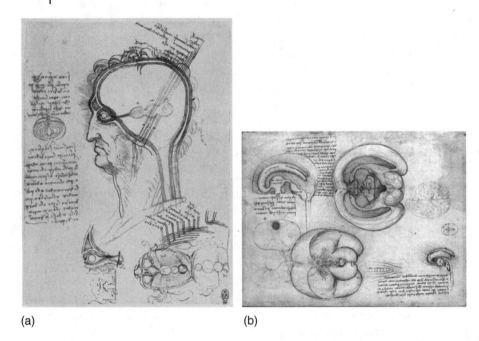

(a)   (b)

This early drawing (a) by Leonardo da Vinci represents the ancient understanding of the ventricular system of the brain as three caverns. Compare it with his drawing (b) after making a wax cast of the ox ventricular system. The drawings from the wax cast are much more realistic.

SOURCE: ©Alinari Archives/Corbis.

One problem with empiricism is that we cannot totally trust our senses. Sensory perception necessarily involves active construction of theories. Thus, observed "facts" are already constructs, and our theories influence them. Examine the drawing in Figure 1.3. The schematic shows which areas of the drawing have equal gray colors, but because we infer a box shape and a shadow, we interpret those equiluminant grays as very different intensities. Visual illusions such as this one teach us that it is impossible to observe nature to learn the truths of nature without imposing our active perceptual processes. The ideal of an unbiased objective observer faithfully detecting nature is an ideal that is impossible to achieve. For example, look at Figure 1.4. This is an early drawing of the human cerebral cortex. Early writers described the cortex as similar to the intestines. It is obvious that this descriptive metaphor has so influenced the artist that the cortex actually resembles the intestines more than it does the true cerebral cortex (Gross, 1999; contrast with the photograph in Figure 1.5). What metaphors might we be using today that blind us to the reality before our eyes?

Figure 1.3 A Perceptual Illusion, Where Grays Appear to Be Lighter in the Area That Is in Shadow

 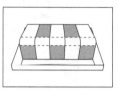

The inset shows the areas of the figure where the grays are actually physically identical.

SOURCE: Purves & Lotto, 2003, Fig. 3.9.

Figure 1.4 Drawing of the Human Cerebral Cortex by Raymond de Vieussens, a Leading Neuroanatomist in the Late 17th Century

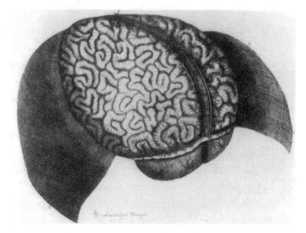

Note that the convolutions resemble intestines. Contrast this with Figure 1.5.

SOURCE: From History & Special Collections Division, Louise M. Darling Biomedical Library, UCLA.

Figure 1.5 | Photograph of the Human Cerebral Cortex

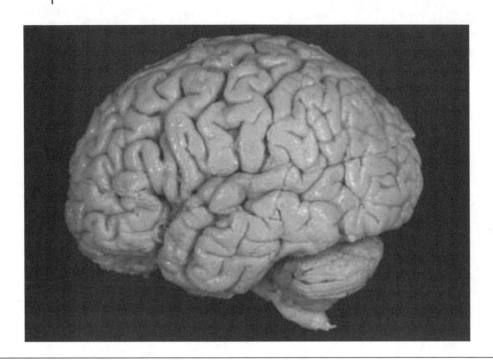

SOURCE: Dr. Fred Hossler/Visuals Unlimited/Getty Images.

In the 17th century, René Descartes suggested that truth and knowledge are attainable through reason, not experience. This philosophy, **rationalism,** encouraged less observation of nature and less reliance on knowledge gained through the senses. Instead, careful logical analysis would lead to a truth you could trust. Descartes was particularly interested in the question of how the immaterial soul could reside in the material body, a question that continues to fascinate many. He reasoned that the soul must consist of immaterial spirits located in the head. There must be a unitary structure associated with the soul, because the soul is unitary. Most structures in the brain are duplicated in each hemisphere; there are very few unitary structures. The pineal gland stands out as a unitary structure, and at that time, the pineal gland had no other function assigned to it. Although Descartes was probably aware that in other animals the pineal gland is located on the dorsal or topmost surface of the brain, he placed it within the ventricles of the human, so that the pineal gland might move and alter the spirits residing in the ventricles.

As you work as a scientist, the sources of your knowledge will have roots in both the empirical and rational approach. The currently accepted form of scientific inquiry is a product of our culture and history. In neuroscience, much of our research can be conceptualized as describing connections between phenomena described with the techniques of one field—say, chemistry—to the same phenomena described with the techniques of another field—say, psychology. Each of these disciplines must consider the others as they build explanations. E. O. Wilson (1998) describes this in a small book, *Consilience: The Unity of Knowledge*. Consilience is the linking together of knowledge from different disciplines to create a common explanation (Wilson, p. 8). An explanation of a psychological phenomenon must be consilient with (or connected and consistent with) biological findings. Similarly, biological explanations must be consilient with chemistry. An interdisciplinary field such as neuroscience may be fundamentally different in approach than more classical fields of science, such as physics. It is helpful to apply Darden and Maull's (1977) conception of **interfield theories,** theories that bridge two fields of science. In neuroscience, we explain phenomena by building a web of links between descriptions at different levels of explanation. Our goal is to answer questions that cannot be answered using only one level of explanation or to describe a mechanism that links the various fields we draw on. Some of the phenomena we seek to explain may be unobservable, and we generally accept that we can study unobservable concepts as long as we identify observable manifestations of that concept. For example, we can study learning, using behavioral changes or alterations in synaptic efficacy as the observable manifestations of the process of learning. A neuroscientific explanation of a phenomenon in the best cases is one that incorporates all of the levels of explanation, with theories bridging the many encompassed fields, such as anatomy, physiology, physics, chemistry, biology, and psychology.

Thomas Kuhn (1975) described the accepted facts and approaches in a scientific field at any one time in history as a **paradigm.** For instance, the current paradigm in neuroscience does not include questions about how the spirits move within the ventricular system; those questions belong to an earlier paradigm. Questions of that sort no longer make sense within our current shared understanding. The current paradigm is based upon several key theories; for example, Ramón y Cajal's "neuron doctrine" is a key tenet in neuroscience today (Shepherd, 1991). The **neuron doctrine** is the belief that the neuron is the fundamental unit of the nervous system. Kuhn described how the paradigm for a field of science is usually rather stable, with scientists working within the same set of shared beliefs, conducting experiments to refine their theories. At other times, the paradigm appears to shift in a sudden "scientific revolution." When Copernicus proposed that the Earth revolves around the sun, challenging the understanding of the cosmos as centered on the Earth, the suggestion of heliocentrism was profoundly revolutionary. A scientific revolution comes about when findings accumulate that are incompatible with the previously accepted paradigm. As these antagonistic findings accumulate, the scientists working with the current paradigm initially passionately resist them. Now, just because current scientists are actively resisting some radical claims, this is not proof that those claims are heralding a new scientific paradigm. When one paradigm is overthrown, it is replaced by a new paradigm. Note that it is not wrong to work within the current paradigm; in fact, that is generally what each scientist should do. Only when an overwhelming weight of evidence indicates the current paradigm is incorrect or requires expansion should scientists work to change the paradigm in a scientific revolution.

Your role as a scientist is to be skeptical and question everything. Ask for the evidence for the scientific "facts" your teachers present. Scrutinize that evidence with a critical eye. I can guarantee that some of these "facts" are incorrect and that scientists in your generation will correct them. Beyond the smaller "facts," perhaps there is a fundamental flaw in our current paradigm. Kuhn (1975) suggested that students training in science often accept the problems their teachers hand them, without questioning or even noticing the hidden assumptions underlying the research programs. It is worthwhile to question the ground rules, to ask for the evidence, so that you start your career in neuroscience aware of both the strengths and the potential weaknesses in our fundamental tenets, such as the neuron doctrine.

This book is designed to help you begin your career with the analytic tools you will require to be such a skeptical scientist. Although laboratory skills will not be covered explicitly, references are given below for good sources that will help you gain these essential bench skills. In this text, you will learn to analyze experimental designs, to determine when an experiment has an elemental flaw, and to design a well-controlled experiment. You will also learn nonexperimental approaches and will appreciate what these can do for your understanding. There is advice about analyzing your data using statistical techniques. I have assumed that you have some background in statistics, but if you are a bit rusty, Appendix A covers the basics. Appendix B gives you instructions for preparing a report for publication. To begin, however, we will first consider ethical questions because ethical constraints underlie many issues of experimental design in neuroscience.

✓ CHECK YOUR UNDERSTANDING

True or False?

1. Scientists keep changing their minds about what they believe, whereas areas of pseudoscience keep true to ancient and eternal wisdom. This indicates a basic weakness in science.

2. Nonexperimental approaches do not belong in modern science but are important for historical interest.

3. The study of how we know what we know is called epistemology.

4. The activity of interdisciplinary scientists building a web of connections between different levels of explanation is called creating "outfield explanations."

5. The "neuron doctrine" is a good example of a portion of our paradigm in current neuroscience.

Select the best answer

1. Empiricism is the idea that all knowledge arises from _____, and rationalism is the idea that knowledge comes from _____.

   a. Authority, investigation

   b. Metaphysical experience, physical experience

   c. Experience, logic

2. A scientific revolution is:

   a. When the king of science is deposed.

   b. A sudden shift in the paradigm.

   c. A response to lack of funding for science.

   d. An abrupt change in interfield relationships.

   e. All of the above.

3. Pseudoscience can be recognized by:

   a. Observations of unscientific behavior.

   b. Vague mechanisms for acquiring new knowledge.

   c. Cranial electrostimulation.

   d. Studies of patients unaware of the details of their therapy.

   e. All of the above.

THINK ABOUT IT

1. It is currently common to use a computer metaphor to describe the brain. In what ways might this metaphor influence our understanding of the brain?

2. We keep learning more about the important roles of glial cells in the nervous system. One study indicates that some glial cells respond to visual stimuli like neurons, with details of the responses organized in a map across the cerebral cortex (Schummers, Yu, & Sur, 2008). Furthermore, much of the change in blood flood activity detected during noninvasive brain imaging is eliminated when glial cell activity is blocked. Does this finding challenge the neuron doctrine? Why or why not?

SUGGESTIONS FOR FURTHER READING

Barker, K. (2005). *At the bench: A laboratory navigator* (Updated ed.). Woodbury, NY: Cold Spring Harbor Laboratory Press.

Carter, M., & Shieh, J. (2010). *Guide to research techniques in neuroscience.* New York: Academic Press.

Darden, L. (2006). *Reasoning in biological discoveries: Essays on mechanisms, interfield relations and anomaly resolution (Cambridge studies in philosophy and biology).* New York: Cambridge University Press.

Finger, S. (2000). *Minds behind the brain: A history of the pioneers and their discoveries.* New York: Oxford University Press.

Gross, C. G. (2010). *A hole in the head: More tales in the history of neuroscience.* Cambridge, MA: MIT Press.

Kandel, E. R. (2007). *In search of memory: The emergence of a new science of mind.* New York: W. W. Norton.

Kuhn, T. S. (1975). *The structure of scientific revolutions.* Chicago: University of Chicago Press.

Shepherd, G. M. (2010). *Creating modern neuroscience: The revolutionary 1950s.* New York: Oxford University Press.

Wilson, E. O. (1998). *Consilience: The unity of knowledge.* New York: Knopf.

ON THE WEB

Good source for up-to date lab protocols:

Current protocols in neuroscience (Online ed.). New York: John Wiley & Sons. Available at http://www.currentprotocols.com

Ethics

As a scientist, you must maintain the highest ethical standards when conducting your research. There are multiple arenas where your ethical behavior will come into play (Bolton, 2002). Later in this chapter, I will discuss in detail ethical guidelines for the use of nonhuman animals and for human participants. For many of these guidelines, following them is a matter of compliance to federal laws, with careful oversight by local committees to ensure your compliance. Your use of hazardous chemicals and radioactive materials are governed in similar ways. Other ethical guidelines are taught by mentors and training programs, and following them is largely a matter of personal integrity. Following the best possible experimental methods should be a matter of personal pride in that you have an obligation to the scientific community to contribute only findings that are as reliable as possible. Timely correction of errors and balanced discussions of the implications of your data are expected from all scientists. But what about deliberately deceptive forms of scientific misconduct? In this chapter, we will first briefly consider production of fraudulent data and plagiarism, serious scientific misconduct that is regulated both at the institutional and federal levels.

RESEARCH ETHICS

Fraud

You should not produce fraudulent data. That may seem obvious to you, as a basic tenet of honesty and personal integrity, but there are often enormous pressures on scientists that may sway susceptible people to produce fraudulent results. For example, you may feel pressure from the principal investigator of the lab who is depending on you to produce the results that can be used as the basis for a grant application. You may feel internal pressure, a drive to get the results that could lead to publication in a prestigious journal, thus advancing your career. You may feel simple competitive spirit, hoping to achieve better results than a scientific competitor does. There is a long history of fraud in science (Erwin, Gendin, & Kleiman, 1994). Some instances of fraud involve the outright **fabrication** of data or making up results; in other cases, researchers have not taken precautions against expected sources of error in data, have changed or omitted results, or have altered equipment used in the experiment to achieve the desired results. For example, most mathematical errors that are not corrected lead to results that support the experimenter's hypothesis. You can imagine why this might happen. If, on your first analysis of the data set, you come up with results that support your hypothesis, you are unlikely to worry over detailed double-checking of the numbers. If, on the other hand, your first analysis does not lead to results that support your hypothesis, you are more likely to go back to the original data and double-check the numbers. An interesting example of this is described in Stephen Gould's (1981) book *The Mismeasure of Man* where he describes his own sleuth work in reanalyzing the data collected by the influential American scientist Samuel George Morton on cranial capacity measured from skulls of people from various races. Morton wished to test his hypothesis that people of different races could be objectively rank-ordered using physical characteristics of the brain. He endeavored to measure brain size by assessing cranial capacity, and by the end of his life in 1851, he had amassed a collection of more than 1,000 human skulls. He carefully measured cranial capacity and published several tables of data, often reprinted, providing "objective" data for a rank-ordering of human races, with Caucasians top-ranked with the largest cranial capacity. Morton had published all his raw data and apparently was not conscious of any miscalculation. Yet Gould discovered many miscalculations and omissions, all of which led to results that were supportive of Morton's hypothesis that Caucasians had larger brains than people from other groups. Gould's reanalysis of the same data set, correcting these mathematical errors, found no evidence of support for Morton's hypothesis.

How can you protect yourself from fraud? First, acknowledge the sources of pressure that lead you to desire particular results from your experiment. Given this acknowledged bias, set up your data handling procedures to protect yourself from temptation. Analyze data without knowing the conditions of treatment of the cases you are analyzing ("blind" to the conditions). Make it a habit to double-check all numbers before analyzing the results. Automate data handling as much as possible, with checks to make sure the analyses were done properly. As you become part of a research team, protect yourself from the possibility of using fraudulent data collected by another member of the team. Good habits in maintaining laboratory notebooks can be critical. Write your notes in laboratory notebooks in pen, with pages numbered and dated. The principal investigator should regularly check them and understand them. Different members of the team should be able to replicate results. When preparing figures for publications, know the standards of the field as to what manipulations of the images are acceptable and which ones are considering fraudulent (see the article by Rossner & Yamada, 2004, cited at the end of this chapter; also see Box 2.1).

BOX 2.1	**MORE, PLEASE!**
	Some Ways to Avoid Problems With Fraud

- Correct and analyze data blind to experimental conditions when possible.
- Double-check *all* numbers.
- Automate data handling.
- Keep detailed lab books in pen with pages numbered and dated.
- Maintain files with your raw data at the institution where you collected it. For research conducted with U.S. federal funding, these files must be stored for at least 3 years after the final grant report submission.

Review for Quiz

What should you do if you suspect fraud? As a student, you should speak directly to the principal investigator or the person responsible for managing the laboratory. You should not snoop around, looking into other team members' laboratory notebooks. Lab notebooks are the property of the lab and are open to inspection by the head of the laboratory; they are otherwise private documents, and you should have the permission of the person keeping the lab book before you read any part of it. Note that allegations of fraud should not be made lightly. Just because you cannot replicate someone else's work does not mean it is fraudulent. Address concerns about fraud at the lowest organizational levels possible to avoid damaging the reputation of an innocent scientist. An excellent book on this topic is *The Baltimore Case: A Trial of Politics, Science, and Character* by Daniel Kevles (1998).

The issue of fabricated or falsified data is a very serious one for science. Although science will eventually correct for such instances, due to independent replication of observations, many studies are not replicated immediately, and most are not replicated in exact detail. Future scientific studies will build upon previous ones, and fraudulent data will mislead future studies. Scientific misconduct cases related to scientists receiving funding from the U. S. Public Health Service are summarized on the website for the federal Office of Research Integrity (available at http://ori.dhhs.gov), with 14 cases summarized for the year 2009 alone. A recent report suggests about 2% of scientists admit to having fabricated or altered data to improve the results at least once in their career (Fanelli, 2009). This is surprisingly common, given the devastating effect a charge of scientific misconduct will have on a research career.

Aside from taking the steps outlined above to protect yourself from collecting fraudulent data, if you detect an error in one of your published reports, it is important to correct that error as soon as possible. Journals will publish a brief correction or even a full retraction if necessary. An interesting case of a retracted paper occurred in 2002. A study published in *Science* indicated that the recreational drug Ecstasy induced Parkinson's-like symptoms in nonhuman primates (Ricaurte, Yuan, Hatzidimitriou, Cord, & McCann, 2002). Widely read and reported, *Science* is one of the most prominent places to publish research. This work was later retracted, also in *Science* (Ricaurte, Yuan, Hatzidimitriou, Cord, & McCann, 2003). It was important that the retraction was published as prominently as the original article, so that many people were able to read that the original work was flawed. On the other hand, it is likely that some people will see the original report and not see the retraction. In the instance of the Ecstasy papers, the original article may have influenced the passage of anti-rave legislation that was being debated at the time of publication (the Illicit Drug Anti-Proliferation Act passed on April 30, 2003). The potential for societal damage from publishing flawed research is obvious. Yet the researchers are to be commended for their persistent sleuth work in discovering and fully reporting the flaws in the original work.

Plagiarism

Your writing should be in your own words. This means entirely in your own words; even a sentence or two lifted from another source without quotation marks and citation of that source is considered an unethical use of someone else's words. This can be difficult to accomplish, particularly if you are writing about a subject that you do not fully understand. It can help to avoid writing your description immediately after reading another source. After reading the source, describe to someone else the content of what you read. Describe the finding or idea in several ways. Only then should you try to write your own description. Of course, you can use specific words or phrases that are necessary to define a phenomenon. Science often requires a very specific vocabulary to retain precision. If the cells in the brain area you are studying are described as having "Gray Type 2 synapses," you should use this phrase too, because it is the precise phrase always used to describe such synapses. You might have some difficulty distinguishing such phrases from less stereo-typed phrases. Check a glossary of neuroscience terms, such as those available in the back of your neuroscience textbooks, to determine if a particular phrase is standard.

Your writing should cite sources for ideas or findings that are not your own. If several adjacent sentences describe the same idea, one citation to the source is sufficient, as long as it is clear that all sentences describe informa-tion from that source. You are not required to cite a source for general knowl-edge. It can be difficult to determine what is considered "general knowledge" in a field that is new to you. One way to determine this is to look for multi-ple other sources that refer to this finding, and do not cite a source. Readers are often interested in where they can find more information on a topic, so even a generally accepted idea developed over the years from multiple sources could have a source listed. In this case, a review article summarizing the years of research and citing all the individual papers would be the proper citation for you to use. Note that you are expected to have read the sources you are citing. Just skimming the abstract can get you into trouble, where you may end up citing a source as support for an idea that the source actually does not sup-port. If you read about a finding described in a secondary source, and you can-not access the original source, you should cite this as "the original source" as cited by "the secondary source": for example, "Lee (2008) as cited by Fong (2010)." Appendix B on writing a manuscript provides specific guidelines for citation style.

Close paraphrasing is considered plagiarism (see Figure 2.1), so be very careful in how you collect notes on readings and compile a manuscript. Put your notes in your own words and then revise them into different words. Change the sentence structure, start in different places within the text, and write from memory, not while looking at the original. Do not take notes by copying a passage directly from another source, because this is too commonly the source of major problems with plagiarism. Organize your writing with an outline generated after reading multiple sources, trying to find your own approach to the material.

Figure 2.1 | An Example of Plagiarism Involving Close Paraphrasing

Original source (Yannielli, McKinley Brewer, & Harrington, 2004):

"Circadian rhythms are daily physiological cycles that are internally generated and reset each day by external cues to maintain a 24 h rhythm synchronized to the environment. The main resetting cue is light. Photic input has access to the hypothalamic suprachiasmatic nuclei (SCN), which functions as an endogenous circadian pacemaker in mammals, through a direct projection from retinal ganglion cells (Ebling, 1996), and resets circadian rhythm phase during the subjective night mainly through glutamate release."

Paraphrasing that is too close to the original source and would be considered plagiarism:

"Circadian rhythms cycle on a daily basis from internal generation and are reset every day by external signals to keep a 24 h rhythm synchronized to the environment. Light is a major synchronizing signal. Light input comes into the suprachiasmatic nuclei (SCN) of the hypothalamus, the pacemaker in mammals, from direct retinal pathways (Ebling, 1996), and adjusts the phase of circadian rhythms during the night time though glutamate release (Yannielli, McKinley, & Harrington, 2004)."

Summary of the source that would not be considered plagiarism:

"Light synchronizes daily or circadian rhythms by resetting the internal rhythm during the subjective night. The neural signal by which light resets circadian rhythms is through glutamate release from retinal ganglion cell axons onto cells in the suprachiasmatic nuclei (SCN) of the hypothalamus (Ebling, 1996; as cited in Yannielli, McKinley & Harrington, 2004)."

The best way to avoid plagiarism is to understand the material about which you are writing. When you try to describe in your own words a finding that you do not fully understand, it can become a temptation to use long phrases from the original source. It would be better to strive for complete comprehension of the material before trying to write about it. If you are struggling to comprehend your source material, look for simpler sources, for example, moving from primary research articles to more general textbooks. Similarly, some students may try to write a manuscript before they have read enough to be able to think about the phenomena independently, which makes it difficult to organize the manuscript according to their own ideas.

ETHICS OF ANIMAL USE

Neuroscience has made great progress as a field in part because of the ability to test hypotheses in experiments using animals. The use of animals in research is an important topic for a student to consider carefully. You have two important topics to clarify. First, what do you personally think is proper public policy regarding animal use? Your decision should be informed by current public policy and by consideration of arguments proposed for changes to our policy. As you consider this important topic, you will want to read widely and should discuss your ideas with people with diverse opinions about animal use in research. Second, you will also need to learn how to employ animals in research in a humane and responsible manner. You should be familiar with established regulations and guidelines as you begin your training.

Unfortunately, I doubt that you will find it simple to answer the ethical questions that arise surrounding the use of animals in research. Your answer will probably lie between the two extreme answers: (1) Animal use is never justified in any situation, or (2) all animal use is absolutely justified. I expect that the vast majority of us cannot accept these simpler extremes and must find our way through the complexity of the middle ground. There are many aspects to consider.

What kinds of animals? Do you think that the same ethical guidelines apply to all animals, or do you somehow rank-order animals? We can try to assess the mental capacity of various species, with an eye for determining if that species might be capable of sensing pain, suffering mental anguish, remembering past freedom, or anticipating an event in the future. Although all of this is impossible to determine unambiguously, we can make our best judgments given the current status of knowledge, and we may well want to specify procedures that we consider ethical to perform using a cockroach but not with a mouse, or procedures that are fine for a hamster but not for a nonhuman primate.

What kinds of uses? Some experiments involve the death of an animal by **euthanasia,** a "gentle death," generally by overdose with an anesthetic or some other approved humane means. If no invasive procedure occurs prior to death, when perhaps tissue is collected for further study, then are we free from concerns about the ethics of animal use? No. Even in this scenario, there are animal welfare concerns, such as determining if the housing conditions in the animal care facility were optimal for that animal. When conducting an experiment that requires the animal to experience a surgical procedure from which the animal will recover, there is a real possibility of pain and suffering. Attention should be devoted to the use of anesthetics and analgesic, sterile surgical techniques, and careful monitoring of the animal following surgery. The advice of a consulting veterinarian is essential. Whether such a procedure is ethically justified depends not only on it being carried out competently, but also on the potential benefits from the experiment.

Many more considerations are sure to arise as you consider this complex topic. A guiding principle is summarized by the **three Rs: refine, reduce, and replace** (Russell & Burch, 1959). You should strive to **refine** your procedures to ensure the animals are treated as humanely as possible, **reduce** the number of animals used to the minimum necessary to achieve statistically meaningful results, and whenever possible, **replace** animals. Computer simulations are one nonanimal alternative. Alternatively, you could replace "higher" animals, such as nonhuman primates, with those from "lower" orders, such as invertebrates.

If you are involved with the use of laboratory animals in a class or in research, you should be aware that some people are adamantly opposed to such work. You may have heard of People for the Ethical Treatment of Animals (PETA) or other groups with strong principles against the use of nonhuman animals in research. Some of these groups are willing to adopt extreme strategies to achieve publicity for their cause. These strategies could endanger the animals, the people involved with animal research, or the physical facilities. You may find their arguments interesting, and you should seriously consider these arguments as you make up your own mind about your beliefs on this ethical issue. However, you should never allow access to the animal facility to someone who is not authorized to enter the area. You should also be careful about how, and where, you discuss animal use with friends and family. Discussing your use of animals in research at the local pub might lead to less well-reasoned responses. Remember to inform others about the regulations surrounding the use of the animals and the factors that contribute to their humane care; often, people are surprised to learn about the regulatory structure controlling animal use in research (also see Box 2.2).

opposing animal research

BOX 2.2	**MORE, PLEASE!**
	Just the Facts: Animal Research in the United States

- From 17 to 23 million animals are used annually for research in the United States.
- About 95% of the animals used in research are rats and mice. Of the remaining 5% of research animals, less than one half of 1% are composed of dogs, cats, and nonhuman primates considered together.
- In 2007, there were 72,037 dogs and 22,687 cats used in research. The number of dogs and cats used in research has declined by more than 50% since 1979.
- It is estimated that each year more than 5,000,000 unclaimed cats and dogs are put to death in pounds or shelters.
- Most animals used in research do not experience significant pain or distress.

SOURCE: Bartlett, Bartlett, Walshaw, & Halstead, 2005; USDA Animal Care Annual Report, 2008; Foundation for Biomedical Research, 2008.

Sometimes an experimenter becomes sentimentally attached to a lab animal. There can be a strong bond between humans and animals, and you may find yourself in an awkward position of wanting to adopt the lab animal at the end of the experiment. This is awkward because regulations are strict regarding such adoptions. Can you ensure that the animal will be cared for in accordance with the high standards set by the federal regulations? Students may have the additional complication of living in dormitories where pets are not permitted.

REGULATION OF ANIMAL USE

The regulation of animal use in research has increased steadily. Because specific regulations vary across countries, it is difficult to summarize all the regulations relevant to every student. Here I provide a brief summary of the current regulatory structure in the United States as an example of the levels of control and the types of principles guiding regulation.

Up until the middle of the 20th century, responsibility for the humane care and treatment of animals in the United States was in the hands of the researchers themselves. As you can imagine, conditions varied widely. A group of veterinarians working with researchers in the Chicago area met in 1961 to begin drafting guidelines for animal care and use. In 1963, they published the first edition of the *Guide for the Care and Use of Laboratory Animals,* which has been updated several times. The United States **Animal Welfare Act,** written in 1966 (Public Law 89-544) and updated several times since, was the first legislation to set standards for the use of animals in laboratories in this country. The Animal Welfare Act covers all warm-blooded animals used in research, with the exception of birds, rats, and mice that are bred for use in research, and farm animals used in agricultural research. The regulations are enforced by inspections from the U.S. Department of Agriculture (USDA). The USDA inspectors, who often arrive unannounced, will examine the quantity of air exchanges, control of room temperature levels, sanitation standards, housing conditions, and a multitude of other factors covered in the regulations. Any research conducted or supported by the Public Health Service (PHS) follows additional regulations that cover all vertebrate animals. These regulations are summarized in the *PHS Policy on Humane Care and Use of Laboratory Animals.* Each institution must assure the PHS that it is meeting these regulations prior to carrying out any activity using animals. In general, this is accomplished not by visits from inspectors but by the institution submitting regular reports to PHS detailing its compliance with the regulations. Although two different federal agencies regulate animal use, the USDA and PHS offices keep each other informed about any concerns. One very important aspect of compliance with these regulations is to establish an Institutional Animal Care and Use Committee (IACUC) to oversee the facility and the use of animals at your institution.

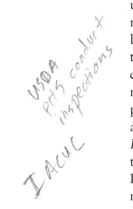

The **Institutional Animal Care and Use Committee (IACUC)** is a group of individuals who review any proposed use of vertebrate animals at a U.S. institution. An investigator wishing to carry out animal research must first submit a detailed proposal to the IACUC. This proposal will vary with the institution, but all will include several key items. You should provide justification for the use of animals in terms of potential educational or research benefit and, if applicable, how this research will impact human health. You should justify the choice of species and explain why this is the most suitable animal for this study. Take care to consider if a less sentient animal species might be able to be used, or if an animal available from large populations might be used in place of a species with more limited abundance. To demonstrate that there are no nonanimal alternatives to answer the question, consider the possibility of computer simulations or similar approaches and describe why they cannot be used to answer your research question. You should include information on databases searched, including the terms used for searching and the date the search was conducted, as you provide background to demonstrate that you have thoroughly explored alternative approaches and to convince members that the research you propose does not unnecessarily duplicate previous research. Consult with a statistician if needed to justify the number of animals proposed, remembering that proposals can be turned down both for proposing too few as well as too many animals. You should explain why the number of animals you propose to use is the minimum number needed to achieve statistically reliable results. Whereas the justifications and background to your project should be written in a style that can be understood easily by a lay person, with all scientific terms explained clearly, when describing the research procedures to be used try to include all details even if this makes the reading a bit more difficult for the lay members of your IACUC. Describe the exact procedures used, the housing conditions, plans for care of the animals, and training of the people involved. Of particular emphasis are the methods used to minimize pain and distress of the animals. Generally researchers consult with their institution's veterinarian before submitting a proposal to the IACUC to be sure they are aware of the latest procedures applicable to their project.

Who sits on the IACUC committee and reviews these proposals? Federal regulations define the makeup of the committee that includes scientists, nonscientists, a lab animal veterinarian, and most importantly, a nonaffiliate member, representing general public concern. The chief executive officer of the institution appoints the members of this committee. The IACUC inspects the animal facility at least twice a year. It has the power and authority to suspend noncompliant animal research programs.

Some institutions strive for membership in the **Association for Assessment and Accreditation of Laboratory Animal Care (AAALAC)**. This organization developed from the same group of veterinarians working in Chicago to produce the

Guide for the Care and Use of Laboratory Animals in 1963. Membership in AAALAC is voluntary and accreditation is challenging. In 2009, more than 790 institutions in 32 countries were accredited. Achieving and maintaining AAALAC accreditation status requires very intensive inspection and documentation. Few institutions are able to achieve this, but when accomplished, this certifies that the very highest standards of animal care are being applied to all vertebrate animal use in teaching and research.

Occupational health and safety is another important concern. You probably will be asked to supply information about your tetanus and tuberculosis vaccination status before being allowed access to the animal facility. Many institutions screen for immune deficiencies, asthma, and allergies and ask medical practitioners to advise prospective animal handlers. How do we protect ourselves from allergens? Standard procedure is to use a designated lab coat and to use disposable gloves when handling the animals. Animals have bacteria and viruses that might cause disease in humans—these are called **zoonotic** diseases. Always wash your hands after handling animals. If you are scratched or injured when working around animals, be extra careful to clean the area and report the injury to the proper authorities. Do not eat, drink, smoke, or apply makeup when working in the animal facility. Extra precautions and training are necessary for people working with nonhuman primates. Concerns about health and safety provide another reason never to bring a friend or relative along when you enter the animal facility.

If you have concerns about animal use, be sure to discuss these with the proper authorities. Every institution must post guidelines for reporting concerns. The first person to discuss your concerns with is the person training you, your teaching assistant or instructor. If you continue to have concerns, bring them up to the director of the animal facility. If you would like to remain anonymous, this can be possible. For example, it is likely that the director would be happy to listen to concerns voiced in a phone call and would be able to respond via a follow-up call that you place at a designated time. If you have concerns that should be voiced to the highest levels, each institution has an institutional officer whom the IACUC reports to and who is ultimately responsible for ensuring the federal regulations are followed.

HUMAN PARTICIPANTS

Ethical guidelines for the study of humans in research have been developed in response to several instances of blatantly unethical research. For example, starting in 1932 and continuing until 1972, the U.S. Public Health Service conducted a study in Tuskegee of the natural course of the disease syphilis. About

400 poor rural African American men with syphilis and 200 men without the disease were enrolled in the **Tuskegee Study**. They were offered free medical care but were not informed that they had syphilis, were not asked for their consent to participate in a research study, and were not informed that this research was of no benefit to them. In the 1940s, after penicillin was established as an effective treatment for syphilis, the men in this study were neither informed of the potential for treatment nor offered treatment. When reports of this study came out in the national press in 1972, the public outrage led to the appointment of a panel to advise the government on steps to take to ensure such an experiment was never conducted again.

This panel considered the **Nuremberg Code,** drafted in 1947 by the judges of the Nazi war criminals who conducted horrendous "medical experiments" on concentration camp prisoners during World War II. They considered other international agreements, such as the United Nations' 1948 "Universal Declaration on Human Rights" and the World Medical Association's guidelines for physicians, "Declaration of Helsinki" (first drafted in 1964). The United States has had some federal guidelines covering the study of humans in research since 1953, with suggestions for a mechanism for a review of proposed studies by disinterested third parties. The recommendations from this and other panels led to increased federal regulations, culminating in 1991 with a policy termed the **Common Rule.** The Common Rule governs the study of humans in research across a wide range of U.S. federal agencies.

When, in 1993, it became known that the U.S. government had conducted thousands of human radiation experiments, exposing people to radiation without their knowledge or consent (research conducted between 1944 and 1974), public attention was again focused on this issue. In 2000, the **Office for Human Research Protections (OHRP)** was established within the U.S. Department of Health and Human Services. The OHRP is concerned with the protection of human participants in research and the oversight of **institutional review boards (IRBs)**.

The IRB is a committee of at least five members established at each institution by federal mandate. This committee is responsible for reviewing the research conducted with human participants at that institution. The members should be qualified to evaluate the research, but not directly involved in the research, so they can serve as disinterested parties. If some of the research involves especially vulnerable populations, such as children, at least one member of the committee should be experienced with working with that population.

Another outcome from the panel appointed in 1972 following revelation of the Tuskegee study was the **Belmont Report**. This report, titled *Ethical Principles and Guidelines for the Protection of Human Subjects of Research,* was published in 1979. It provides the foundation for current ethical guidelines and appears on

Belmont Report
(critical guideline)

the National Institutes of Health, OHRP, website (see the On the Web section at the end of this chapter). The Belmont Report suggests three major principles:

1. Respect for persons

2. Beneficence

3. Justice

Respect for Persons

A person must be fully informed of the risks and benefits of the proposed research before beginning participation. This is referred to as getting **informed consent** and is generally documented by a signed form. Participants must be informed of the purposes of the study, the exact procedures involved and their anticipated risks and benefits, as well as any reasonable alternatives to these procedures. Participants must not be coerced to participate, with special effort made to be sure they do not participate in an effort to please a researcher who is in some position of authority over them (their professor or physician, for example). They must be given ample time to decide if they will choose to participate. The researcher should make special effort to be sure participants understand the information provided. If participants are unable to make this decision on their own, as in the case of children or people with cognitive impairments, permission must be secured from the parents or legal guardians. Even after agreeing to participate in a research study, participants must be informed that they are free to withdraw from the study at any time. If you are conducting a study and a participant indicates that he or she would like to withdraw, you should immediately allow that, making no effort to convince the person to continue, unless there are risks to the participant associated with withdrawal.

As a neuroscientist, you might find yourself testing patients with cognitive impairments, either from brain damage or from a disease such as Alzheimer's disease. You will need to follow the legal and regulatory guidelines for your research site to ensure that the patient is competent to give informed consent for your procedure.

Beneficence

The principle of beneficence is that the research participant should be protected from harm. The researcher should not directly harm the participant and should make an effort to maximize the benefits from the research while minimizing the risk. A *risk-benefit* analysis attempts to determine what the potential risks and benefits of the research project are. You may suspect that your research study involves minimal risk to the participants, but you must leave this judgment to the IRB that evaluates each proposal for research involving human participants. **Minimal risk** means a level of risk that does not exceed that expected from ordinary daily life or routine physical or psychological examinations or tests. If there are risks inherent in participation in the research, these must be weighed against the potential benefits. No individual should be harmed simply for the potential of societal benefit.

In medical settings, you may need to take particular care to ensure that patients understand that participation in a research study may promise no particular personal benefit. The benefit of increased scientific knowledge is a general benefit to society, but patients may misunderstand and assume that the study has some promise of directly benefiting them. Be sure to stress that whether or not the patient decides to participate in the study will not affect the quality of the medical care provided.

In rare cases, deception or withholding information must be used because informing participants of the intended procedures or purpose of the study would invalidate the results. The IRB will carefully screen these cases to determine if deception is necessary. In all cases, participants must be told all information that might be reasonably expected to influence their decision to participate in the study. If some information must be withheld, the participants should receive it during a **debriefing** session, where the experiment is fully explained to the participant after they have completed the study.

One risk that you may forget is the risk of loss of privacy and the protection of confidentiality. You must be aware of the legal regulations governing privacy rights applicable to your site of research. There are situations when the data should be kept confidential, and other times when it should be collected in an anonymous manner. The researcher is responsible for ensuring that identifying information is collected only as necessary and that information identifying the participant be kept separate from the data. Generally, this occurs by maintaining a separate sheet of unique codes linked to the identifying information. Data sheets are then identified by the code only, with the primary investigator keeping the identifying information in a secure location. Note that even if you are proposing research on tissue or blood samples, if those samples can be identified, then your research project involves human participants and you must secure approval of your IRB before conducting the experiment.

You also will have to consider issues of liability related to conducting research with human participants. For example, one risk in a study involving brain scans of normal subjects is that you might detect an abnormality in the scan. Before beginning the study, you should determine, in consultation with regulatory boards such as the IRB, who will examine the brain scans for potential abnormalities and how the participant will be informed. Addressing these concerns would involve working closely with a lawyer familiar with the regulations specific to the site of research.

Justice

The risks and benefits from the research should be distributed fairly. Do not select the study population because it is easily available or likely to participate; choose the population that will benefit from the research most.

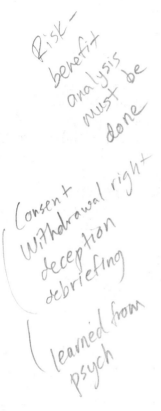

GENERAL ETHICAL CONSIDERATIONS

In any report of your research, you should fully describe your sources of funding or any financial interest you or your coauthors may have in the research. The Society for Neuroscience has published clear guidelines: "Responsible Conduct Regarding Scientific Communication" (available through the Society's website at http://www.sfn.org/index.aspx?pagename= responsibleConduct).

The costs of developing a new drug or medical device and testing it to the point that it is ready for the market are astronomical. The average cost of developing one new prescription medicine is estimated as millions of dollars (DiMasi, Hansen, & Grabowski, 2003; also see Riggs, 2004). Pharmaceutical or medical device companies are appropriately concerned about protecting their investment in a new compound or instrument, and they may want to control what is published regarding research on these topics. However, the scientific process requires the open exchange of information. Disclosure of financial contributions and any potential conflict of interest is given in the "Acknowledgments" section of a manuscript. Figure 2.2 shows this section from the paper describing the modafinil study discussed in Chapter 1 (Volkow et al., 2009).

Figure 2.2	Financial Disclosure Section of Article

Author Affiliations: National Institute on Alcohol Abuse and Alcoholism, Bethesda, Maryland (Drs Volkow and Telang, Mr Jayne, and Ms Muench); National Institute on Drug Abuse, Bethesda (Dr Volkow); Brookhaven National Laboratory, Upton, New York (Drs Fowler, Logan, Wang, and Hooker; Messrs Alexoff, Wong, Warner, and King; and Mss Hubbard, Carter, King, Shea, Xu, and Apelskog-Torres); Mount Sinai School of Medicine, New York, New York (Drs Fowler and Wang); and Departments of Chemistry (Dr Fowler) and Applied Mathematics and Statistics (Dr Zhu), State University of New York at Stony Brook.

Author Contributions: Dr Volkow had full access to all of the data in the study and takes full responsibility for the integrity of the data and the accuracy of the data analysis. Drs Volkow and Fowler contributed equally to this work.

Study concept and design: Volkow, Fowler, Wang.

Acquisition of data: Telang, Wang, Jayne, Hubbard, Carter, Warner, King, Shea, Xu, Muench, Apelskog-Torres.

Analysis and interpretation of data: Volkow, Fowler, Logan, Alexoff, Zhu, Hooker, Wong.

Drafting of the manuscript: Volkow, Fowler, Alexoff, Telang, Wang, Jayne, Hooker, Wong, Hubbard, Carter, Warner, King, Shea, Xu, Muench, Apelskog-Torres.

Critical revision of the manuscript for important intellectual content: Volkow, Fowler, Logan, Zhu.

Statistical analysis: Zhu.

(Continued)

(Continued)

Obtained funding: Volkow, Fowler.

Administrative, technical, or material support: Telang, Wang, Jayne, Hubbard, Carter, Apelskog-Torres.

Study supervision: Volkow, Fowler, Wang.

Financial Disclosures: None reported.

Funding/Support: This research was carried out at Brookhaven National Laboratory under contract DE-AC02-98CH10886 with the US Department of Energy with infrastructure support from its Office of Biological and Environmental Research. Support was also provided by grant K05DA020001 (J.S.F.) from the National Institutes of Health, the National Institute on Alcohol Abuse and Alcoholism Intramural research program, grant F32EB997320 (J.M.H.) from the National Institute of Biomedical Imaging and Bioengineering, and grant MO1RR10710 from the General Research Clinical Centers. A Goldhaber distinguished fellowship provided support for Dr Hooker.

Role of the Sponsor: The funding agencies had no role in the design and conduct of the study; in the collection, analysis, and interpretation of the data; or in the preparation, review, or approval of the manuscript.

Previous Presentation: Presented at the 55th Annual Society of Nuclear Medicine meeting; June 16, 2008; New Orleans, Louisiana.

Additional Contributions: David Schlyer, PhD, and Michael Schueller, PhD, Brookhaven National Laboratory, assisted with cyclotron operations. Joan Terry, and Hai-Dee Lee, MS, Brookhaven National Laboratory, assisted with clinical research center operations. Nikhil Pujari, BS, State University of New York at Stony Brook, helped with the image analysis, and Linda Thomas, BS, National Institutes of Health, provided editorial assistance. None received compensation outside of their salaries. We thank the individuals who volunteered for these studies, who each received a volunteer fee.

SOURCE: Volkow et al., 2009.

By full disclosure of potential sources of conflict of interest, outside mentors can help you determine the best course of action. For example, others might assume you are under pressure to report results helpful to a company if you depend on that company for financial support. The disclosure reprinted in Figure 2.2 describes the independence of the scientists from the funding agencies in conducting this study. How else might researchers protect themselves from a conflict of interest hurting their scientific research?

A primary ethic should be to conduct the strongest, smartest, best-designed experiment possible. Neuroscience experiments directly affect our lives. A poorly designed experiment could lead to false conclusions and potentially harmful practical applications. A well-designed experiment could lead to the next biomedical breakthrough.

✓ CHECK YOUR UNDERSTANDING

1. Ways you can reduce fraud are:
   a. Collect data blind to the condition.
   b. Automate data handling.
   c. Double-check all numbers.
   d. Write in ink in your lab book.
   e. All of the above

2. If you read a paper by Jones, Smith, and Lee published in 2010 that refers to a paper by Lee, Smith, and Jones published in Swahili in 2005, and you cannot read Swahili but you would like to refer to the findings of the 2005 paper, you should:
   a. Not cite it—you cannot cite a source you have not read.
   b. Cite it as "Jones et al., 2010."
   c. Cite it as "Lee et al., 2005, as cited in Jones et al., 2010."
   d. Cite it as "Lee et al., 2005."

3. Two different federal agencies regulate laboratory animal use. These are:
   a. IACUC and AAALAC
   b. USDA and PHS
   c. IACUC and IRB
   d. CIA and FBI
   e. OHRP and IRB

4. Members of the IACUC include:
   a. The chief executive officer of the institution
   b. All scientists at the institution that use laboratory animals
   c. Community members with an active interest in animal welfare
   d. A lawyer
   e. All of the above

5. The three principles of the Belmont Report are:
   a. _____
   b. _____
   c. _____

6. Read the passage below.

 a. Write in one or two sentences, in your own words, the major findings, and cite the source, using the guidelines in Appendix B.

 b. Write a close paraphrase of several sentences and include a citation of the source. Would this be considered plagiarism?

 Men are generally more interested in and responsive to visual sexually arousing stimuli than are women. Here we used functional magnetic resonance imaging (fMRI) to show that the amygdala and hypothalamus are more strongly activated in men than in women when viewing identical sexual stimuli. This was true even when women reported greater arousal. Sex differences were specific to the sexual nature of the stimuli, were restricted primarily to limbic regions, and were larger in the left amygdala than the right amygdala. Men and women showed similar activation patterns across multiple brain regions, including ventral striatal regions involved in reward. Our findings indicate that the amygdala mediates sex differences in responsiveness to appetitive and biologically salient stimuli; the human amygdala may also mediate the reportedly greater role of visual stimuli in male sexual behavior, paralleling prior animal findings. (Hamann, Herman, Nolan, & Wallen, 2004).

7. The IRB must approve proposals for research using human participants in the United States. What does "IRB" stand for? Who sits on this committee?

8. The revelation of the Tuskegee study to the public lead to development of the "Common Rule" and the "Belmont Report." What was unethical about the Tuskegee Study? Should the data resulting from this study be used?

9. What types of information about your study must you provide to a participant before getting informed consent?

10. You will furnish the IRB or similar body a risk-benefit analysis of your study. If your study involves more than minimal risks to the participants, and even potential harm to the participants, what types of benefits might outweigh such risks?

11. Describe the "three Rs" used to evaluate proposals for animal research.

12. Would a Public Health Service–funded research project involving the use of mice be covered by regulations in the Animal Welfare Act, enforced by USDA inspectors? Would it require the approval of your IACUC?

13. Who are the members of the IACUC?

14. What should you do if you have concerns about the use of animals in the research with which you are involved?

THINK ABOUT IT

1. In the 1960s, prisoners participated in more medical research than most other healthy populations (Hornblum, 1997). Why do you think prisoners elected to participate in such research? Why do you think researchers wanted to study them? What sort of safeguards would you suggest to ensure that we distribute the risks of such research equitably across our society? What sorts of studies would be appropriate for such populations?

2. You have the opportunity to conduct a controlled study to determine if institutionalizing children in the early years of development will produce significant cognitive deficits. You will do this study in a country where young children are routinely institutionalized, and your control group will be a sample of randomly selected children who will be removed from the institution and placed in home-based foster care. What are some of your concerns in collecting "informed consent"? Do you have other ethical concerns?

3. One of the 10 principles of the Nuremberg Code is that research questions should be investigated using animal subjects prior to conducting research using humans. In what way might a member of PETA argue against this principle? How might a biomedical researcher defend it? In what cases might animal research not be appropriate before studying human participants?

4. A recent study reports on patterns of brain activity while people are lying (Greene & Paxton, 2009). Participants were not instructed to lie, but some of them did. Patterns of brain activity were different between the groups of participants in the "Honest Group" versus those in the "Dishonest Group." What ethical issues might be raised in debriefing these participants?

5. Private companies can use scans of brain activity to attempt to determine if people are lying. An editorial in the journal *Nature Neuroscience* ("The ethical neuroscientist," March, 2008) questions the regulation of such companies. These companies are not required to follow the ethical guidelines of the Belmont Report. Do you think it is allowable for a neuroscientist to follow a different ethical guidelines when working in an academic versus commercial setting?

SUGGESTIONS FOR FURTHER READING

Bolton, P. A. (2002). Scientific ethics. In *Management benchmark study* (chap. 16). Washington, DC: U.S. Department of Energy, Office of Science, Office of Planning & Analysis.

Rossner, M., & Yamada, K. M. (2004). What's in a picture? The temptation of image manipulation. *Journal of Cell Biology, 166*, 11–15.

ON THE WEB

Committee on Science, Engineering, & Public Policy [COSEPUP]. (1995). *On being a scientist: Responsible conduct in research* (2nd ed.). Washington, DC: National Academy Press. Retrieved February 8, 2010, from http://books.nap.edu/catalog/4917.html

National Institutes of Health. (1979). *The Belmont Report: Ethical principles and guidelines for the protection of human subjects of research.* Retrieved February 8, 2010, from http://ohsr.od.nih.gov/guidelines/belmont.html

National Research Council. (1996). *Guide for the care and use of laboratory animals* (7th ed.). Washington, DC: National Academy Press. Office of Laboratory Animal Welfare. Available at http://www.nap.edu/openbook.php?record_id=5140

Office of Laboratory Animal Welfare. (2002). *PHS policy on humane care and use of laboratory animals.* Retrieved April 26, 2010, from National Institutes of Health website: http://grants.nih.gov/grants/olaw/references/phspol.htm

Society for Neuroscience. (1998). *Guidelines: Responsible conduct for scientific communication.* Retrieved April 26, 2010, from http://www.sfn.org/skins/main/pdf/Guidelines/ResponsibleConduct.pdf

These sites provide quizzes and guidelines that will help you avoid problems with plagiarism:

https://www.indiana.edu/~istd/index.html

http://owl.english.purdue.edu/owl/resource/589/01/

http://www.lib.usm.edu/legacy/plag/plagiarismtutorial.php

http://ori.hhs.gov/education/products/plagiarism/plagiarism.pdf

Getting Started

CHAPTER
3

This chapter will cover how you select a research question and form a hypothesis. Selecting a strong research hypothesis will have major repercussions for the future success of your research project. I will discuss details of research design in later chapters, but your first concern is always, "What is my question?"

PICKING A QUESTION

The first step in conducting an experiment is to decide what topic you will investigate. You will first select a broad topic, then progressively narrow and refine your focus until you arrive at the one testable hypothesis that you will confirm or reject in your research. How will you get from your current interest in neuroscience to the point where you have a testable hypothesis?

What Are the Big Questions?

In science one is often forced to choose between providing precise answers to piffling questions (how many cones are there in a human eye) or vague answers to big questions (what is the self), but every now and then you come up with a precise answer to a big question (such as the link between deoxyribonucleic acid [DNA] and heredity) and you hit the jackpot. (Ramachandran & Blakeslee, 1998, p. 81)

What are the big questions in neuroscience? Ask a neuroscientist! In my opinion, figuring out how mind arises from brain is the largest and most enduring question in neuroscience. "Mind" encompasses perception, sensation, action, memory, emotion, thought, and language. Consciousness (in some circles referred to as the "c-word") may be the most intractable but alluring component of mind to explain in terms of neuroscience. Understanding the development of the nervous system fascinates many scientists. To understand the complicated wiring of the adult nervous system, it is helpful to study a simpler nervous system, as you can in a young developing organism. Knowledge of the mechanisms by which this amazingly complicated system is put together can give insight into many developmental nervous system disorders, such as autism or schizophrenia.

It is not only neuroscientists who have opinions on what questions are the most important for a young neuroscientist to tackle. Most people have had their lives touched by one of the major neurodegenerative disorders—Alzheimer's disease affects approximately one in eight persons aged 65 years or older (Alzhemier's Association, 2010). Parkinson's disease affects up to 4.5 million people in the United States alone (Hebert, Scherr, Bienias, Bennett, & Evans, 2003). Perhaps you know someone living with epilepsy or heard Christopher Reeve speak about the great need for further research into the regenerative capabilities of nervous system tissue, in the hopes of clinical benefits to people with damage to the brain or spinal cord. What causes neurodegenerative disorders and how we can treat or perhaps cure disorders of the nervous system are very important questions.

Look within yourself. What questions appeal most to you? Do you lean toward the philosophical mind/brain questions? Are you more interested in curing or developing better treatments for a disease or medical condition? Are you fascinated by mechanistic explanations of brain function? You will also want to ponder what approaches suit you best. Do you see yourself in a slick lab using the most current molecular genetics approaches, or do you see yourself providing therapy to patients suffering from a neurodegenerative disorder? Be aware, however, that the desire to answer a specific question motivates most neuroscientists; that question can lead them to use an incredible diversity of laboratory and clinical approaches.

Influence of Dogma or Bias on Selecting Your Research Question

Science is completely objective, right? Wrong! Science is a human activity and suffers from all the human frailties. The scientific method provides many safeguards that protect us from those common failings, but this methodical approach comes *after* we have selected the research question. Bias can occur before that. Current neuroscience uses a mixture of rationalism and empiricism, and our biases can have strong influence on our rationalistic thinking, as we saw in the example of Descartes (see Chapter 1).

Unfortunately, detecting bias in past research conducted by others is easier than identifying the biases affecting your own research. In Chapter 1, we saw how the metaphor used to describe the cerebral cortex influenced drawings of the brain, so that the cortex looked more like the intestines than the surface of the brain. Our current use of the computer as a metaphor for the brain may similarly shape our thinking. As briefly discussed in Chapter 2, in the 18th century and early 19th century, racist biases strongly affected the research conducted by many Europeans and European Americans on the relationship between brain shape and size and human intelligence (see Figure 3.1; for an engaging summary, also see *The Mismeasure of Man,* by Stephen J. Gould, 1981). Do researchers with a political belief in the basic equality of humans find it difficult to accept evidence for immutable biological differences? (You might find that *The Blank Slate,* by Steven Pinker, 2002, influences your thinking on this issue.)

If your introductory course professor tells you that the central nervous system has no neural regenerative capabilities, are you likely to look further? In fact, such dogma slowed research for years; only when scientists set this aside did they begin to discover

Figure 3.1 | Relationship Between Brain Weight and Body Weight in Several Mammal Species

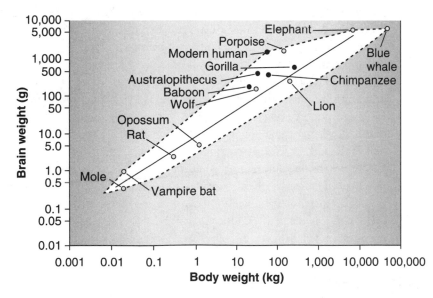

Even though brain weight is highly correlated with body weight, scientists did not control for body weight when searching for race differences in the cranial capacity of humans.

SOURCE: Rosenzweig, Leiman, & Breedlove, 1999, Fig. 6.11a, p. 151. Reprinted by permission of Sinauer Associates, Inc.

ways to encourage central neural regeneration. When picking your research question, be aware that dogma or bias may be unconsciously limiting your choices.

Questions to Avoid

Not all questions can be approached using the scientific method. "What is the meaning of life?" is a good example of one such question. Note that the similar question, "What is life?" is a perfectly good scientific question, and a famous small book with that title was important for the eventual development of the field of molecular biology. Is your question suitable for an empirical approach?

Sometimes a question is a perfectly good empirical question, but it is ahead of its time. Consider the state of technology: Will you be able to test this question given the technology currently available or potentially developed within the near future? The development of the electron microscope was necessary to settle the extensive dispute between Ramón y Cajal and Camillo Golgi over whether neurons were individual cells separated by gaps or connected in a vast continuous neural web. Ultimately, technology allowed neuroscientists to see the gap that exists between neurons, establishing Ramón y Cajal's theory as correct.

On the other hand, I want to encourage you to push the boundaries of what is currently thought of as the domain of the scientific approach. When I began my training as a neuroscientist, my professors said that consciousness was not a suitable topic for scientific investigation. Now many creative and productive neuroscientists are working on just that topic. Often technology has been developed that can be brought to bear on a previously unapproachable question. If your interests are broad enough, you might have the advantage of being the first person to apply technology developed in another field to a question in neuroscience. Thus, it is to your advantage to read widely, browsing a variety of fields and journals. Discuss your ideas with others, but be aware that some may discourage you. Seymour Benzer (2004), noted for his groundbreaking investigations into the neurogenetics of behavior, comments that if all your colleagues tell you that you are crazy, you probably are, but if only half of them think you are crazy, you should take that as encouragement.

As you begin your training, you may not immediately start research on the question that will most deeply capture you, but I encourage you now to attempt to identify such a question. You will soon discover the hours of monotony associated with the day-to-day life in a scientific laboratory; a personal obsession with solving your big question will help you discover the persistence to keep going through the tedium.

FORMING A HYPOTHESIS

For the next few steps, you cannot be lying on your bed, contemplating the ceiling, pondering which hypothesis to test. Science is a social activity. Your research must be a part of the larger context of research on that topic.

Work With a Mentor

Finding a mentor is critical for your early training. A good mentor will be someone who has expert knowledge in the topic of interest to you and is interested in sharing that knowledge with you. Your mentor will guide you to conduct an experiment that addresses cutting-edge issues, something that would be difficult for you to accomplish as a novice working alone. A mentor will not just tell you what to do. A good mentor also will spend a lot of time listening to you, probing for your interests as well as for your strengths and weaknesses. You should feel an equal obligation to get to know your mentor. Your research project should interest both you and your mentor. Finding this topic requires finding the intersection between your interests.

Recently a student, Dora, asked if she could gain some research experience in my laboratory. As I discussed this with her, I described my research interests and current projects ongoing in my lab. I suggested she get to know the other students, find out more about their projects, and talk with me more after she had an idea of what she would like to work on. When we spoke later, Dora told me that she had always been fascinated by endocrinology, the study of hormonal regulation. In particular, she was interested in what made male and female brains differ. Well, to tell the truth, I find this interesting as well, but my research expertise is in the study of circadian rhythms. If another faculty member at our college were an expert in sexual differentiation of the brain, I would have suggested to Dora that she work with that faculty member, but, unfortunately, this was not an option. So Dora and I worked together to find a topic of mutual interest. We eventually decided we might both be interested in the effects of estrogen on circadian rhythms.

Read, Read, Read!

Once you have selected your research question, you will need to narrow your focus to a testable hypothesis. How will you do this? Start by reading as much as you can on what previous researchers have discovered. Your mentor will have good suggestions for where to start. Reading research reports will train you in many ways. You will learn what aspects of this topic are firmly established. You will discover gray areas where current researchers are not yet certain of how to interpret their findings, or available results are contradictory. Textbooks are a good place to start for locating a research area and gaining a basic background. However, as a rule, textbooks do not highlight such areas of ambiguity—you must be reading the primary research literature to discover the inconsistencies that might be worth exploring further (see Box 3.1).

BOX 3.1	**MORE, PLEASE!**
	Primary Versus Secondary Sources

Scientists do not give equal weight to all journals. You will want to focus your research on **primary research articles,** direct reports of experiments conducted by the authors. You should learn to distinguish primary research articles from **secondary sources,** reviews of research in which the primary report is published elsewhere. There are several distinguishing features.

Primary journal articles are peer reviewed. This means that the author submits the article to the journal and the journal editor in turn sends the article to two or three experts in that topic. The experts read the manuscript and determine if the research is well done, if the conclusions are merited based on the evidence presented, and if the authors provide all the details necessary to allow replication of the studies by other scientists. They often send detailed suggestions for further experiments or revisions that the authors are required to address before the paper is published. Figure 3.2 shows examples of peer-reviewed journals in neuroscience. You may want to check with your instructor if you are unsure about a particular journal.

The information in a primary journal article is about one or several experiments on a specific focused topic. You will find a section devoted to the methods that describes in detail the procedures used to conduct the experiment. The results section describes both the major findings as well as any small inconsistencies.

Some journals will also publish "reviews," summaries of recent research on a chosen topic. Review articles can be useful as you try to understand the state of current knowledge on your topic, but you will want to be sure to read primary articles presenting results of individual experiments, because the review article gives one person's interpretation of those primary articles.

Figure 3.2	Assortment of Peer-Reviewed Journals in Neuroscience

SOURCE: *Journal of Neuroscience, 25*(7), 2005, reprinted with permission from The Society for Neuroscience. *Nature Neuroscience, 8*(2), 2005, reprinted with permission from the Nature Publishing Group. *Neuron, 45*(4), 2005. reprinted with permission from Elsevier. *Journal of Neurophysiology, 93,* 2005, published by the American Physiological Society.

You will find PubMed an essential resource. This is a searchable database of biomedical research reports. You can access PubMed through the U.S. National Library of Medicine (http://www.nlm.nih.gov), and an online tutorial will get you started searching for journal articles. Some articles will be publicly accessible or accessible through your institution's library subscription. You may be able to order other articles through InterLibrary Loan. Do not overlook the resources often available on the home page of an investigator working on a topic of interest to you. Sometimes it is profitable to conduct a search on an investigator's name using a common search engine such as Google or Google Scholar (see Box 3.2).

BOX 3.2

TOOLS OF THE TRADE

Using Web Searches in Your Research

Before you begin your web searches, jot down a list of keywords you might use, and be ready to modify these as you get results. Often the breakthrough in your online searches comes when you discover the best keywords to use. You are probably quite used to using Google as a search engine. For your scientific research, Google Scholar might offer a better result. This will provide scientific articles, as well as links to articles that cite the article of focus. It will link you to articles that are available for free and, if your library has arranged for this, will also link you to articles that have full-text available to you through your library subscriptions. I am more likely to use PubMed than any other search engine, but I know that it can produce results that are too detailed for many students. The PubMed search page also allows you to change your search database from PubMed journals to books, a resource that might be especially helpful as you begin your research (http://www.ncbi.nlm.nih.gov/books). If you are searching for journal articles on your research topic, try adding terms to your search on PubMed; i.e., instead of searching on "anxiety," search on "anxiety mice elevated plus GABA" or whatever constellation of terms might bring you closer to your focused topic. Look for the link to "MeSH" which will help you find the vocabulary the Library of Medicine uses for indexing information. You can add the term "review" or select results that are flagged as review articles to get an initial overview of the topic and then use the papers cited in the review article to begin reading primary journal articles. You have many other options to limit your searches, for example, you can limit by the journal name, the year of publication, or the type of article. PubMed will also offer links to related articles, so once you find one very appropriate article, you might find others using these options. You can click on the name of the author to find further research by that person, which is often on closely related topics. When you begin longer-term research, sign up for a free account with the National Center for Biotechnology Information (NCBI) on PubMed to receive e-mail alerts when new articles on your research topic are published.

A key resource is your science librarian. Make an appointment to get help with identifying other search engines available at your institution. There are many possibilities for search tools that require a paid subscription. You can also get tips on better use of Google and PubMed, as well as information on your institution's policy regarding ordering articles through InterLibrary Loan.

Read at least three primary research articles on a narrowly focused topic (see Box 3.1). Read the entire paper; skimming the abstract is not going to give you the information you need. If you must skim, skim the figures, not the abstract. The figures should illustrate the main points of the article, and you can get a sense of the magnitude of the effects and the extent of the investigation undertaken. Study the introduction and discussion sections of each paper. Explore the limits of current knowledge. You probably first read the articles trying to understand what was done; now reread the articles with an eye for what has *not* been done. You will find it helpful to follow what I call the "12-step" program for reading journal articles (Locke, Silverman, & Spirduso, 1998). Write brief answers to each of the 12 questions posed in Table 3.1 after reading a journal article. You can use the article in Appendix C as an example; see the sample answers to the 12 questions following the article (see Table 3.1).

Table 3.1	Twelve Questions to Answer After Reading a Journal Article Describing Experimental Studies

1. What report is this? (Use full reference citation, *Journal of Neuroscience* or APA format.)

2. What was the "big question" of the study? What were the specific research questions of this study?

3. What was previously known about this question? How does answering the research question(s) add something new to what is already known?

4. Who or what was studied? (Cite number and key characteristics.) What was the experimental design (see Chapter 8 for a list)?

5. In sequential order, what were the major steps in performing the study? (Record these in a flowchart.) Do not just repeat details from Items 1–4 and 6–9. Create an explanatory sketch that a year from now would help you recall how the study was done.

6. What data were recorded and used for analysis?

7. What kinds of data analysis were used?

8. What were the results? (Refer to figures.) (After analysis, what do the data from Item 6 say about the questions addressed in Item 2?)

9. What does the author conclude? (In light of both Item 8 and the entire study experience, what is said about Item 2?)

10. What cautions does the author raise about interpreting the study?

11. Were there any flaws in this study? How could the experimental design be improved?

12. What particularly interesting or valuable things did you learn from reading the report? (Consider results, method, discussion, references, and so on.)

Narrow Your Focus

How can you answer your question with the resources available to you? Get to know the laboratory facilities available to you before you get your heart set on an experiment that will not be possible at your institution. Although the resources available may limit the scope of your initial studies somewhat, try to keep your focus on the research question that most interests you. Your mentor will help define the approaches that suit the laboratory resources and expertise available. Often an institution will hold a research day, where students currently working with faculty members present their research results. You should attend these presentations to talk to those students. Find out what they were able to do and what they accomplished. This will both serve to inform you on the research capabilities of your institution as well as the general amount of progress a student can make on a project given the time you have available.

Study the descriptions of the results of the experiments covered in the journal articles you have read. The results section contains ideas for many future experiments. Was there a small inconsistency in one study? For example, did the results indicate that blocking GABA receptors led to a specific response, except for one particular GABA antagonist (receptor blocker)? A small inconsistency might be worth exploring in future studies and might form the basis for your initial research. Do the reported results fall short of addressing the bigger question to which they are directed? Often authors will point out near the end of their paper what next steps should occur before the line of research addresses the bigger question.

Your goal is to formulate a clever study that builds on previous research, a study that you will be able to carry out. Although you probably will not be able to carry out a study of the magnitude and importance you eventually hope for, there is no reason to set your sights too low at this stage. Discuss your ideas with experts, asking for critical feedback. Criticism of your ideas should be something you crave at this point, because it could save you from spending a lot of time in the future testing a weak hypothesis.

When Dora and I read primary journal articles about estrogen and circadian rhythms, we discovered that at that time there were several well-characterized effects of estrogen on circadian rhythms of rats and hamsters. No one seemed to be sure how estrogen induced these effects. Did estrogen directly affect the neurons of the circadian pacemaker in the suprachiasmatic nucleus of the hypothalamus? Estrogen receptors were reported in the human suprachiasmatic nucleus, but it was unclear if estrogen receptors were present in rat and hamster suprachiasmatic nuclei.

We noted that research studies in other fields used mice deficient in specific estrogen receptors, but to our knowledge, no one had yet studied these mice to determine the effects of estrogen on circadian rhythms. Perhaps we could use these mice to determine which estrogen receptor was important in these effects of estrogen. A big initial question was whether estrogen would alter circadian rhythms in mice. Previous work had used rats or hamsters, never mice. Dora planned her first research study to measure circadian rhythms of activity in mice with or without estrogen treatment. I supported this study in part because a colleague with more experience in the techniques necessary for it was interested in collaborating, and this project fit into the time frame Dora had available. Another colleague with more expertise in this specific topic verified that, to his awareness, no one had yet conducted this particular experiment and it was, in his opinion, a worthwhile and interesting study. It is important to check that you are not unknowingly replicating a previous study. Because publications often appear several years after the experiment, word of mouth is an important resource.

WHAT MAKES A GOOD HYPOTHESIS?

As described in Chapter 1, science proceeds by gathering information, constructing a model, conducting experiments that test that model, and revising the model according to the results of the experiments (see Figure 3.3). Look over the journal articles you have read. What is the model the scientists are testing (see Box 3.3)? A good model will make testable predictions or hypotheses. Some predictions are more important than others are. The most critical predictions determine if the model is valid or invalid. There must be some specific predictions that, if verified, will demonstrate that the model is wrong. This is the criterion of **falsifiability**, important because of a peculiar asymmetry in our logic. While many instances of correct predictions will support the model, it is impossible to prove definitively that the model is true. On the other hand, only one instance of an incorrect prediction demonstrates that the model is false and needs to be modified. Thus, efforts directed toward falsification of the current models might move knowledge ahead faster than efforts directed toward garnering support for the model. Can you think of any predictions of the model that you could test in your experiment?

Do not test an obvious hypothesis. If you think there is absolutely no chance of any outcome but one, why do the research? Do not confuse exercises used in teaching laboratories, often demonstrations of known phenomena, with real research. State your hypothesis as an "If . . . then" statement. For instance, Dora might state her hypothesis this way: "If I find that mice deficient in the beta subtype of estrogen receptors do not show circadian rhythm changes induced by estrogen, and control mice do show these changes, then it is possible that estrogen alters circadian rhythms by action on the beta subtype of estrogen receptor." Always consider what you will conclude given the other possible outcome, the **alternative hypothesis.** Here, Dora is less conclusive: "If I do not find differences between control mice and mice deficient in the beta subtype of estrogen receptor, then estrogen may not act on this receptor subtype to alter circadian rhythms or another receptor subtype might also be able to mediate this effect of estrogen."

| **Figure 3.3** | Scientific Process by Which Models Are Continually Under Revision |

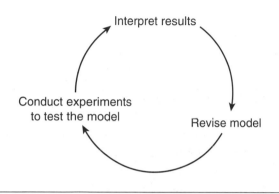

If you do not confirm your **experimental hypothesis,** will that support an alternative explanation? Some research studies are conclusive no matter what the outcome, because the study is designed to test multiple competing hypotheses (Platt, 1964). Designing a study with this characteristic should be your goal, but this is not always possible. In some cases your alternative hypothesis may be a **straw-man hypothesis,** an implausible assumption that no one would really support. For example, if your research hypothesis was that people getting a fMRI brain scan after reading a scenario that induces feelings of envy would show increased activation of a certain brain region (the dorsal anterior cingulate cortex; Takahashi, Kato, Matsuura, Mobbs, Suhara, & Okubo, 2009), then a straw-man hypothesis would be that envious people would not show increased brain activity in any region. This is a straw-man hypothesis because it is so implausible; most scientists would expect some change in brain activity associated with a change in emotion. Your goal in designing an experiment to test a hypothesis is to differentiate between two or more *real* hypotheses.

Your hypothesis should be falsifiable. This means that it should be possible to demonstrate that the hypothesis is false. If Dora had decided she wanted to test the hypothesis that estrogen administration made a mouse "better" in some way, would she ever be able to demonstrate that this hypothesis was false? She might find many examples of ways in which the estrogen-treated mice were not better than the controls, but there would continue to remain the possibility that they were better in some way she had not yet tested. I would discourage her from following this research line. This hypothesis is too vague and slippery to demonstrate that it is wrong.

Your hypothesis might ask a "how" question, in which case it might be a hypothesis related to the **proximate causation** of the phenomena. This is in contrast to a "why" question related to what we call the **ultimate causation** (see Box 3.3). For example, Dora's question about which receptor subtype mediates effects of estrogen on circadian rhythms is a "how" question. She is interested in determining exactly how estrogen acts on brain tissue to change this behavior. If she were to ask a question about the importance of such effects of estrogen in an experiment where animals are in a reproductive competition, then she would be asking a "why" question. She would be interested in determining why natural selection has apparently favored animals with these effects of estrogen

---

BOX 3.3	**MORE, PLEASE!**
	Model Versus Theory?

A **model** is mechanistic, a description of a process or phenomenon. At a higher conceptual level, scientists form theories to explain a process. A **theory** incorporates diverse phenomena and describes general organizing principles. A theory attempts a much more general explanation than a model does. Although the line between theory and model is sometimes fuzzy, it is useful to recognize our ultimate goal of more and more generalizable explanations. Theories are scarce in the field of neuroscience (Stevens, 2000). What makes a good theory?

1. A theory that explains more is better than one that explains less.

2. A simpler theory is preferred to a more complex theory if both have equal explanatory power.

3. Theories are also assessed by their fertility—do they lead to new ideas, new applications, and/or new connections? Does the theory predict unforeseen results? Does it lead to testable predictions?

Note that neuroscientists also use the term "model" to refer to a specific experimental preparation that is used to study a particular phenomenon. For example, animals treated with the neurotoxin MPTP suffer degeneration of substantia nigra neurons, the same neurons that die over the years in Parkinson's disease. MPTP-treated animals are used as research "models" of aspects of Parkinson's disease, with the caution that these animals do not have true Parkinson's disease.

Operationalizing Your Hypothesis

Your hypothesis will need to move from general language to an **operationalized hypothesis.** This means that you will need to define your hypothesis in terms of the operations or procedures you will perform to test that hypothesis. Let us consider how Dora operationalized her hypothesis. Recall that her initial study asked the question, "Will estrogen alter circadian rhythms of mice?" "Estrogen" was operationalized as "administration of a subcutaneous implant of 20% crystalline estradiol benzoate in a silastic tubing capsule 2 cm long." Note that once we have operationalized the hypothesis in this way, we are open to new critiques. If Dora does not see effects of estrogen on circadian rhythms in mice, can she conclude that estrogen does not alter circadian rhythms of mice? No, she can only conclude that administration of a subcutaneous implant of 20% crystalline estradiol benzoate in a silastic tubing capsule 2 cm long does not alter circadian rhythms of mice. In fact, because she operationally defined "mice" as "c57 strain female mice, ovariectomized [with the ovaries surgically removed], two months of age," this is what we should say the experiment refers to, not the more general "mice." Of course, we would hope that our results generalized to mice of other strains and ages, but that remains to be demonstrated. A similar process of defining "alters circadian rhythms" completes the operationalization of the hypothesis. In the end, Dora has moved from the original hypothesis, "Estrogen will alter circadian rhythms in mice," to the operationalized hypothesis, "Administration of a subcutaneous implant of 20% crystalline estradiol benzoate in a silastic tubing capsule 2 cm long will change the length of the free-running period of the circadian wheel-running activity rhythm in c57 strain female ovariectomized two-month-old mice."

Note that you will soon be forming a hypothesis using more than published papers. After your first observations or experiments on this topic, you will not necessarily be reading journal articles to form new hypotheses—you will be mulling over the results of your own studies. You will also be mulling over results you heard about at scientific meetings, such as the annual meeting of the Society for Neuroscience. (See Figure 3.4 for a typical student presentation at a scientific meeting.) You should

Figure 3.4 | Student Presenting a Poster at a Science Convention

be cautious as you incorporate these results into your thinking because, although they are cutting edge, they are also not peer reviewed and often are preliminary. After further study and critique, the authors of those reports might draw very different conclusions.

EXTERNAL VALIDITY AND INTERNAL VALIDITY

You will assess every research project for two attributes: internal validity and external validity. **Internal validity** is how well the research study allows conclusions about the causal relationship between the variables, or how reliable and replicable the results are. This is a reflection of the quality of the research design and the success of the experimenter in controlling extraneous variables. A **reliable** measurement gives similar results each time it is repeated under the same conditions. A **replicable** result is seen when the entire experiment is repeated and similar results are obtained. A study with high internal validity will have high reliability and replicability.

External validity is how well the research study addresses the problem you would ultimately like to solve or how well the research study generalizes to other populations or other settings. Generalizability of your findings could eventually be determined by varying test conditions across different experiments to determine if results are comparable across different contexts. **Ecological validity** is how well your research mirrors the conditions in the natural world. For example, if you were interested in testing how steroid hormones alter risk-taking behaviors, testing financial traders as they work on the trading floor of a London firm, as was done in a recent study (Coates & Herbert, 2008), would provide measures with high ecological validity. To determine how well your study addresses the problem you would ultimately like to solve, you could consider the **predictive validity** of your approach, or how well these measures can predict outcomes of key importance. For example, an animal model of a human disease might not in all ways mirror the appearance of that disease in humans, but it may have great predictive validity in assessing the potential of various therapies.

For example, consider the hypothesis that depression may lead to neuronal cell death and that antidepressants may work by encouraging *neurogenesis,* the birth of new neurons. One study designed to test this hypothesis used mice (Santarelli et al., 2003). Measuring depression in mice is difficult, but researchers used a standard test, called the "novelty-suppressed feeding" test. This is a measure of how much a hungry mouse will eat when placed in a brightly lit, unfamiliar arena with food in the center. Taking longer to venture into the center to eat the food is a measure of depression. Treatment with the antidepressant fluoxetine (better known as Prozac) caused mice to approach the food and begin eating more quickly than controls. A marker that labels newborn neurons was administered to mice treated with fluoxetine, and their brains were examined. The hippocampus showed increased numbers of new neurons in fluoxetine-treated mice as compared to control mice. Fluoxetine improves this behavioral measure of depression and also increases neurogenesis. The researchers then used x-radiation to kill the stem cells in the hippocampus that give rise to new neurons. Mice without the hippocampal stem cell population no longer responded to antidepressant treatment with reduced latencies in the novelty-suppressed feeding test, and they no longer showed increased numbers of new neurons in the hippocampus. The therapeutic action of antidepressants in mice appears to depend upon neurogenesis.

The study with mice was a well-controlled experiment. Mice were randomly assigned to treatment groups. They were all from similar environments, with housing variables well controlled. They were from an inbred strain and were similar genetically. The mice all received the drug in identical doses, administered in identical ways, with control mice receiving vehicle injections. The measure of depression was a precisely quantified measure in a well-controlled test. The measure of neurogenesis was direct; researchers labeled and counted newborn neurons. This experiment has high internal validity. What about the external validity? One important aspect of external validity is whether the dependent variable measures what you mean to measure. The test used here of novelty-suppressed feeding has high predictive validity in that treatment with Prozac changed the behavior as predicted, but we might have some concerns about this as a completely valid model for human depressive disorder.

Our hopes that this well-controlled laboratory study might generalize to the diversity of humans experiencing depression are strengthened by the results of a study conducted with human participants. Researchers studied 38 women suffering from depression and estimated how many days they had been severely depressed and how many days they had taken antidepressant medication for depression. They measured the size of the hippocampus from brain scans of the women suffering from depression and compared the results with similar measurements taken from brains of women who were not depressed (Sheline, Gado, & Kraemer, 2003). Participants with depression had smaller hippocampi than controls, and those with the most days of untreated depression had the smallest hippocampi.

However, this study has many potential problems. One concern is about the dependent variable. The measurements may be unreliable. Depression is an altered mood state and is therefore difficult to measure precisely. Depression was measured in days, but the severity of depression may vary, and this is not assessed. What if people took different types of medication or different doses? Another concern is about the independent variable. What if the samples of depressed women and control women differed in more than the presence or absence of depression? There are many possible confounding variables. The authors matched the participants for age, education, and height, but what if the participants differed in other ways? They may have different levels of stress in their lives, they may have different socioeconomic status, or they may vary in the support they derive from their close interpersonal relationships. Measurements of hippocampal volume are estimates from a brain scan; obviously, removing the hippocampus and weighing it would provide a more precise measurement of volume. But volume may not even be the appropriate measure to take because the hypothesis refers to neurogenesis. This study did not even measure neurogenesis. You can probably think of other points to raise in a critique of this study. This study has low internal validity when compared to a true experiment.

The best strategy is to conduct both highly controlled laboratory experiments as well as studies under more naturalistic settings, using convergent methods.

What if I do not test a hypothesis? Sometimes a student is so eager to get going on their research they will go through the preliminary stages of selecting a question, finding a mentor, and reading on a focused topic, at which point they discover something that has never been done before and they declare, "I will do that!" If the sole rationale for the experiment is that no one has ever done it, this is not hypothesis-based research. As Chapter 1 noted, often our work in neuroscience is a process of building a web of connections between different levels of explanation, that is, building "interfield theories." In some cases, your research is based on an effort to identify and describe these interfield connections. For example, you may want to identify the neurochemical changes that are associated with changes in cognitive abilities and memory in Parkinson's disease. This descriptive research is important as we increase our understanding of the nervous system using the approaches of multiple fields. But even descriptive research can test a hypothesis. For example, you might test the hypothesis that loss of "executive function" cognitive abilities in Parkinson's disease patients is associated with neurochemical changes in the prefrontal cortex, whereas deficits in memory are associated with neurochemical changes in the hippocampus.

You will very likely feel frustrated during your efforts to come up with a good hypothesis for your first study. Perhaps you envisioned yourself in a laboratory carrying out exotic procedures—and here you are, in front of your computer, searching databases. But you should spend as much time choosing your hypothesis and designing your experiment as necessary. The effort you put in will be richly rewarded at the end. No amount of sophisticated statistical analysis can rescue a poorly conceived experiment. In the next chapter, we will begin to consider the essential elements of a good experiment.

✓ CHECK YOUR UNDERSTANDING

1. For each hypothesis below, say whether it is a good hypothesis and explain why or why not:

   a. I would like to know if animals behave oddly when I administer a recreational dose of the drug called "Ecstasy" (MDMA). I have not read any published research articles on this topic, but I am curious and would like to just try it.

   b. Based on current models of synaptic release and the known biochemical properties of Compound Z, I predict that Compound Z will cause increased neurotransmitter release. If it does not cause increased release, then I will conclude that either the current models are wrong or the compound does not act as thought.

   c. All published reports indicate that neurons in the visual cortex should respond to light. I would like to see this for myself. My hypothesis is that if I expose an animal to light, then I will see increased activity in visual cortex neurons.

   d. Two competing theories might explain responses to seasonally changing day lengths, the internal coincidence model or the external coincidence model. My experiment will test between these competing theories. In my experiment (details of which need not concern us here), if Group A shows a greater response than Group B, then I will conclude that the external coincidence model is correct. However, if Group B shows a greater response than Group A, then I will conclude the internal coincidence model is correct.

2. Recall that in her initial study, Dora was looking for effects of estrogen on circadian rhythms of mice. If she conducted her study and found no effects of estrogen on circadian rhythms of mice, explain how this might be due to the way she operationalized her hypothesis. Suggest a different operational definition of the same hypothesis.

3. In a recent study using a mouse strain that develops Alzheimer's disease (AD), researchers tested the theory that loss of neurons accounts for memory loss associated with AD. To test this hypothesis, instead of studying neurons they did a study of glial cells, measuring gial cell activity in the AD mouse brain to look for problems in glial cell function. They are best described as working towards:

   a. A straw-man hypothesis

   b. Falsification of the hypothesis

   c. An operational definition

   d. A case control study

THINK ABOUT IT

1. Let us say you had some interest in the brain pathways by which sleep deprivation alters learning and memory. In searching for a research mentor, you talked to three professors. Describe a possible research hypothesis to propose to each professor, incorporating both your interests and your mentor's. Professor 1: This professor has an interest in the consolidation of memory and the effects of stress, conducting most research using college students. Professor 2: This professor studies neural plasticity using the rat hippocampal slice preparation, with a particular interest in the role of GABA in altering synaptic strength. Professor 3: This professor studies fruit flies (*Drosophila*) and is fascinated by effects of experience on synapses, using anatomical and biochemical techniques to measure synapse properties in fly brains.

SUGGESTIONS FOR FURTHER READING

Bernard, A., Sorensen, S. A., & Lein, E. S. (2009). Shifting the paradigm: New approaches for characterizing and classifying neurons. *Current Opinion in Neurobiology, 19,* 530–536.

Chiao, J. (2009). *Cultural neuroscience: Cultural influences on brain function,* Vol. 178 (Progress in brain research series). New York: Elsevier.

Geschwind, D. H., & Konopka, G. (2009). Neuroscience in the era of functional genomics and systems biology. *Nature, 461,* 908–915.

Lindvall, O., & Kokaia, Z. (2010). Stem cells in human neurodegenerative disorders: Time for clinical translation? *Journal of Clinical Investigation, 120,* 29–40.

NIH Blueprint for Neuroscience Research website: http://www.neuroscienceblueprint.nih.gov

Owen, A. M., Schiff, N. D., & Laureys, S. (2009). A new era of coma and consciousness science. *Progress in Brain Research, 177,* 399–411.

Platt, J. R. (1964). Strong inference. *Science, 146,* 347–353.

Raizada, R. D. S., & Kishiyama, M. M. (2010). Effects of socioeconomic status on brain development, and how cognitive neuroscience may contribute to leveling the playing field. *Frontiers in Human Neuroscience, 4,* 1–11 (doi:10.3389/neur0.09.003.2010).

Basic Research Designs | CHAPTER 4

One day, when conducting an experiment with a new drug, one that activates a specific neuropeptide Y receptor, I noticed that the hamsters given the drug seemed less nervous than untreated hamsters. They ambled around their cages, even while under an extremely bright light. My initial interest was in the effect of this drug on the hamster's daily rhythm in activity, but I became intrigued by this potential effect of the drug in decreasing anxiety (an *anxiolytic* effect). How could I test the idea that the neuropeptide Y receptor agonist had an anxiolytic effect?

In general, I use all sorts of methods to test my ideas: I might discuss the idea with others and ask if they agree with the idea; I might "sleep on it" and see if I continue to agree with myself; I might try to think of anecdotal reports of instances that are pertinent to my question. However, anecdotes are often influenced by our biases, and simply consulting prevailing belief limits my understanding to the boundaries of our current thinking. To be more scientific in my investigations, I could use an observational approach, measuring anxiety-related behaviors in a careful and precise manner. This is necessary if I am interested in a hamster's experience of anxiety, because hamsters are notoriously unlikely to complete self-report surveys about their feelings. Careful behavioral observations might provide helpful insights, presumably insights anyone else could replicate, if they were willing to carry out observations under similar conditions. Based upon my careful observational studies, I would design an experiment to test my hypotheses.

OBSERVATIONAL STUDIES

Once you have a narrowly focused topic of study, you often begin by making careful observations. In fact, many studies in neuroscience are simply observations of a phenomenon. A careful description of one particular instance can be enough to establish a point. As Ramachandran and Blakeslee (1998) have pointed out, a single demonstration of a talking pig is enough to establish the point that pigs can talk. Although reports of talking pigs are rare, neuroscience journals are full of other, more pedestrian, observations.

Admittedly, few people presented with a talking pig would say, "Well, that is just one instance of a talking pig. I won't believe in talking pigs until I see more." On the other hand, most scientists prefer that you replicate your observations if possible. **Replication** means observing the same phenomena under the same conditions multiple times. For example, if I observed that granule cells in the cerebral cortex could be labeled with an antiserum for the inhibitory neurotransmitter GABA in the brain of a mouse, I would next attempt to determine if similar labeling is observed in the cerebral cortex of other mice. Replicating the observation assures me that this might be a general phenomenon for this type of mouse and not some peculiarity of the brain of the first mouse I examined.

Whenever possible, you should quantify your observations (see Box 4.1). Quantification can allow more precision than possible with verbal descriptions. Images can be quantified using analysis software. (For many purposes, NIH Image software is sufficient, and this is currently available as a free download from the Scion Image website: see http://rsb.info.nih.gov/nih-image/about.html.)

BOX 4.1	**MORE, PLEASE!**
	Scales of Measurement

Variables can be measured using four types of scales of measurement.

The **nominal scale** is a categorical scale, with the categories not in any obvious ranked position relative to each other. For example, categorizing synapses into two categories, as having synaptic vesicles that are either largely flattened or largely round, is an instance of using a nominal scale. Categorizing neurons as labeled for GABA immunoreactivity or for serotonin immunoreactivity is another example of a nominal scale of measurement. Classifying subjects as male or female, categorizing memory tasks as measuring either implicit or explicit memory, and comparing patients with either Alzheimer's or Parkinson's disease would be further examples.

The **ordinal scale** is a ranked ordering of instances. For example, ranking the effects of mutations at various points on a molecule by the severity of phenotypic effects makes use of an ordinal scale. Measuring the severity of head injury as mild, medium, severe, and very severe would be another example of an ordinal scale. In both examples, the measures are categorical, but we can put the categories into some meaningful order.

The **interval scale** is a measurement with equal intervals between the points on the scale, so that the differences between values are meaningful, but with no meaningful zero (the origin of the measurement scale is arbitrary). Measuring temperature using a Centigrade or Fahrenheit thermometer is an example of using an interval scale. There are equal intervals between 10–11° and 20–21°C, but 0°C does not mean you have "zero temperature." Thus, you cannot say that today is twice as warm as yesterday, because today it is 20°C and yesterday it was 10°C. The judgment "twice as" applies just to these numbers, not to the variable being measured (temperature). Measuring gene expression as relative to the expression of a control gene would be another example of an interval scale; a "zero" value here indicates similar expression as the control gene, but does not indicate "zero gene expression."

The **ratio scale** also has equal intervals between the points on the scale, but in addition, this scale has a meaningful zero, and the ratios between the measurements are meaningful. An example of a ratio scale measurement is measuring time. This has a meaningful zero, in that zero seconds really means "zero time." Another example is measuring the amount of a substance in a unit such as milligrams—for instance, "15 mg nerve growth factor." Note that ratio scales are used for time, even in cases where it is unlikely that the researcher will measure a time of zero. For instance, even though it is impossible for an action potential to travel from the soma to the synapse in zero seconds, using time to measure this event is still using a ratio scale.

Why is it important to consider scales of measurement? They can have a big impact on your research project. I will discuss scales of measurement in later chapters when we consider other methods for summarizing data or drawing conclusions from experiments using statistical tests. Table 4.1 sums up the mathematical operations possible for each scale of measurement. This table highlights the importance of using the ratio scale whenever possible, because this is the only scale that allows all common mathematical operations. At times, technology limits us from using a ratio scale, and then we must make do with an ordinal or interval scale.

In general, choose the ratio scale of measurement when possible. It gives you more options in terms of the mathematical operations you can perform and, as you will see later, the most options in terms of the statistical tools you can employ. The ratio scale is the most versatile scale of measurement.

Table 4.1 Mathematical Operations Applicable to Data Depend on Scale of Measurement

Scale of Measurement	Possible Mathematical Operations
Nominal	None
Ordinal	Rank order
Interval	Add; subtract
Ratio	Add; subtract; multiply; divide

measured periodically
time vs event sampling
when an event occurs

Naturalistic observations occur in the natural environment, outside the laboratory. When measuring spontaneous behavior, use an approach that allows replication and quantification. One approach is **time sampling,** where you observe an animal's behavior for, say, 1 minute every 15 minutes. **Event sampling** counts the number of times a particular behavior or event occurs during the observation period.

Structured observations can happen in the natural environment, but the researcher has intervened in some way to shape the situation. Sometimes structured observations are used when the behavior of interest is infrequent, and the researcher must set up a situation that will increase the frequency of the event. For example, if you were interested in why dogs "scent-roll" (i.e., roll their bodies in stinky stuff), you might want to set out some particularly attractive substances to elicit this behavior from the animals at a time and location convenient to your observations.

Generally, a neuroscientist will want to collect information about the physiological state of the animal under observation. In some cases, it is possible to capture the animal and briefly collect a blood sample to analyze. In other cases, you can measure hormones or metabolites from the animal's scat (feces) or other droppings. For example, in a study of captive timber wolves, researchers assayed cortisol levels in wolf urine collected from snow. Cortisol levels were unusually high in the lowest-ranking female and in the second-ranking male. The authors interpreted these data as reflective of the social stress these two individual animals were experiencing, from aggressive encounters with other wolves in the pack (McLeod, Moger, Ryon, Gadbois, & Fentress, 1996). A study of wolves living in the wild suggested a different conclusion; in this study, analyses of cortisol levels in feces left in prominent locations (presumably by dominant members of the wolf pack) was higher than feces collected from other locations (Barja, Silvan, & Illera, 2008). The authors suggest that subordinate members of a captive wolf pack might feel more stressed because they cannot move away from the dominant members, a tactic used in the wild to avoid attack.

New technology allows miniaturized devices that can be attached to an animal in the wild allowing novel insights from naturalistic observations. For example, it had been reported that the sloth spent about 15.85 hours a day asleep. These measures had been taken from animals in captivity. When researchers attached miniature devices to measure brain activity associated with sleep to sloths living in the Panama rainforest, they found that sloths in this setting slept only 9.6 hours a day (Rattenborg et al., 2008; see Figure 4.1).

Figure 4.1 | Recordings of Brain Waves From a Three-Toed Sloth Living in the Rainforest in Panama.

The sloth has a recorder attached to its head, and brain waves (EEG) as well as muscle activity (EMG) are recorded. Examples of the recordings are shown on the right. In (b) the arrow marks the transition from sleep to wakefulness.

SOURCE: Rattenborg, Voirin, Vyssotski, Kays, Spoelstra, Kuemmeth, et al., 2008. © Royal Society Publishing.

CASE STUDIES

A **case study** is an in-depth description of one particular individual. In many instances in neuroscience, that individual is a person with partial brain damage. Perhaps the most famous case in the field of neuroscience is that of H. M., reported by Scoville and Milner (1957). This patient had a portion of the cerebral cortex (the medial temporal area) removed bilaterally as a surgical treatment to relieve his severe epileptic attacks. The unanticipated effect of this surgery was dramatic: H. M. apparently could form no new long-term memories. Although his perceptual, motor, and intellectual capabilities were otherwise intact, H. M. could not recall anything that had happened to him since the surgery (see Box 4.2 on page 61). Interestingly, he was able to retain information over short delays, if there were no interruptions. Thus, it appeared he had intact short-term memory, or working memory. Moreover, he could remember events from his childhood, thus showing his deficit was not being unable to access stored memories but an inability to form new long-term memories. After study, researchers even discovered that H. M. could learn new motor skills, such as the mirror-drawing task shown in Figure 4.2.

Figure 4.2 A Record of the Performance of Patient H. M. on the Mirror Drawing Task

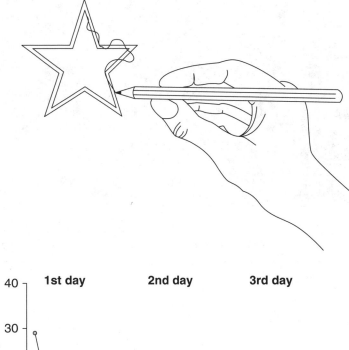

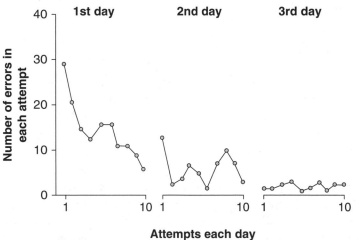

In this task, the patient must try to draw a simple object, such as the star shown here, while looking at the object in a mirror. The task is initially very difficult, but with practice, it becomes easier. As is apparent from the record, H. M. was able to improve in his performance on this task, even though each day he had no memory of ever having carried out the task before.

SOURCE: Parkin, 1987, Fig. 6.6. Reprinted by permission of the Taylor & Francis Group.

His performance on this task clearly improved over repeated trials, although he never remembered having done the task before.

Why is this case of H. M. so important in the history of neuroscience? The clear dissociation of memory systems apparent in H. M., coupled with the knowledge of the location of brain damage, encouraged researchers to pursue questions about representation of memory in the brain. The current field of cognitive neuroscience grew from such observations.

Whereas each individual is a separate case, it can also be useful to analyze multiple cases with similar performance deficits or similar areas of brain damage. This is the method of **multiple case studies.** Another design that is a common variant of the case study is the **case control design.** In this design the investigator first selects a group of cases with the characteristic of interest, and then they create a control group that resembles the cases in as many relevant ways as possible. For example, a study to determine if mood and personality changes are a commonly occurring side effect of a new treatment for Parkinson's disease, deep brain stimulation of the subthalamic nucleus used a group of 25 patients who had this treatment 3 years prior to the start of the study (Castilli et al., 2008). The control group were patients with Parkinson's disease who were on the waiting list for this treatment and thus met all the criteria for being judged suitable for this treatment. This group of patients was also selected to be similar to the case group in variables such as age, sex, duration, and severity of the disease. Results indicated that the treatment did not lead to a higher level of depression or mood changes, and in fact may have caused a reduction in obsessive-compulsive symptoms that can be associated with Parkinson's disease.

BOX 4.2	**MORE, PLEASE!**
	Double Dissociation

Cognitive neuroscientists are especially interested in the demonstration of **double dissociation.** The presentation of cases with damage to one area, call it Area A, who demonstrate the ability to carry out Process 1 but not Process 2, and other patients, with damage to Area B, who cannot complete Process 1 but can easily complete Process 2, demonstrates a double dissociation (see Figure 4.3). For example, people with posterior lesions to the brain show deficits in remembering specific words, but they can recall and apply the rules of grammar. People with anterior lesions have the opposite problem: They can remember words but cannot apply rules of grammar. Thus, the first group is able to add "-ed" to a word to indicate past tense but is unable to remember a specific irregular form of a past-tense word (for example, "go" turns into "went"), and the second group is just the opposite. Assuming these two processes are independent, such a demonstration suggests that independent neural circuits might underlie these two processes. The hypothesis that the brain may be organized into modules in which separate functions are processed by anatomically and physiologically separate neural units is supported by findings of double dissociations, but these findings do not necessarily imply that modules exist (Plaut, 1995). In considerations of possible neural networks that might explain double dissociations, computer simulations can demonstrate plausible alternatives to the module hypothesis (Cowell et al., 2009).

Figure 4.3 | A Double Dissociation

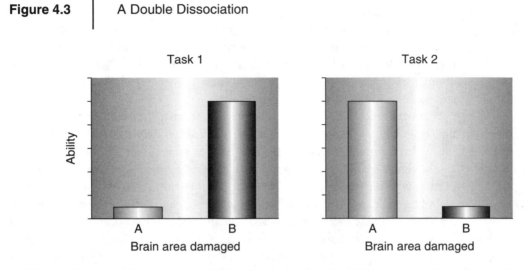

Participants with damage to one area—call it Area A—demonstrate the ability to carry out Task 2 but not Task 1. Other participants, with damage to Area B, cannot complete Task 2 but can easily complete Task 1. This presentation demonstrates a double dissociation.

THE EXPERIMENT

Science begins with observational studies and case studies; these lay the foundation for further research. Neuroscience is now progressing beyond observations of behavioral consequences of brain damage to more tightly controlled experiments. What is unique about the design of an experiment? An experiment must involve an independent variable and a dependent variable. The **independent (or predictor) variable** is the manipulated variable, the variable the experimenter changes across the experimental groups. The **dependent (or outcome) variable** is the measured variable, the tool by which the experimenter will assess the effects of the independent variable. The investigator's question is, "Does the independent variable affect the dependent variable?" The difference between an observational study and an experiment is the active manipulation of a variable in an experiment. For example, to test the idea that the neuropeptide Y receptor agonist might have anxiolytic effects, we could design an experiment using a standard test of anxiety, such as the elevated plus maze, comparing the behavior of 20 hamsters that received the drug with 20 untreated hamsters. In this case, the independent variable is the drug treatment, and the dependent variable is performance in the elevated plus maze (see Figure 4.4).

Figure 4.4   An Elevated Plus Maze

The maze consists of two platforms, one with high walls and one with no walls. The test animal, usually a rodent, is placed in the center. The animal is allowed to explore the maze for a standard amount of time—for example, 5 minutes. A more anxious animal will spend more time in the arms with walls and will rarely venture out into the open arms. Common dependent variables measured are the amount of time spent in the open arms and the number of entries into the open versus the closed arms.

SOURCE: Photo © Mary Harrington.

INDEPENDENT-SAMPLES DESIGN

Experiments can get much more complicated than this example and can, in fact, have many independent variables and multiple dependent variables. However, let us not start with a complicated design. To begin, let us examine the **independent-samples design.** In an experiment with the independent-samples design, the experimenter varies one independent variable across two groups. In the simplest case, one group experiences one level of the independent variable (this is the *treatment group*), and the other group experiences the other level of the independent variable, which in this example would be the control condition (this is the *control group*). For example, suppose your hypothesis was that the recently discovered hormone ghrelin plays a role in regulating food intake. How might you test this

[handwritten margin notes:] one ID and 2 groups both getting it or the other is group is control

hypothesis? One way is to inject one group of rats with ghrelin dissolved in a solvent and perform vehicle injections on a second group of rats. (*Vehicle injections* involve the injection of the solvent used to dissolve the ghrelin, as a control for all the variables associated with picking up a rat and giving it an injection. Chapter 5 will discuss these variables in further detail.) You could then examine the animals and measure how much each rat eats. In this example, the independent variable is the injection, either ghrelin or vehicle injection. The dependent variable is food intake measured over time. If you had not included a control group, you would not be sure the ghrelin injection induced the changes in food intake. Perhaps the stress of being picked up, handled, and given an injection could change food intake. Inclusion of the control group, treated exactly the same as the animals in the treatment groups except for the ghrelin, allows any difference between the groups to be attributed to ghrelin administration.

If you carry out an experiment with just one subject in each group, you might find differences between the subjects, but how do you know if those reflect chance variability? A key feature of experimental design is to carry out the identical procedure multiple times, using enough subjects to reduce the effects of chance variation in the results.

CONTROLLING OTHER VARIABLES

Critical to this design is the control of other variables—that is, keeping other factors identical between the groups. The experiment using ghrelin injections is not a good one if the rats in the two groups are of different ages, because the rate of growth might change with age. You can probably think of many other variables you should control such as sex, strain, or housing conditions. This is an essential feature of experimental design: The only variable that differs across the two groups should be the independent variable. All other variables should be **controlled variables**, explicitly eliminated or made identical for the two groups.

A **confounding variable** is particularly important to avoid. A confounding variable is a variable that changes with the independent variable. We use vehicle injections to provide a control group that experiences all of the factors that accompany the ghrelin injection, such as being picked up and receiving an injection to control for all those possible confounding variables. There remains a possibility of other confounding variables. Suppose you fed the rats with vehicle injections of chocolate-chip cookies and the ghrelin-injection rats dry rat chow. If the vehicle-injected rats ended up heavier than the ghrelin-treated rats, you could not conclude that this difference was a result of the ghrelin. It might instead be attributable to the different diets. This is an obvious example of a confounding variable, and you are not likely to make such a mistake in your experimental design; but confounding variables can be more subtle. Consider the first example, the hamsters being tested in the elevated plus maze. What if you tested all the drug-treated animals first, followed by all the control untreated hamsters? A confounding variable in this case is the time of testing because hamsters may perform differently at varying times of day. A better design is to test hamsters in an alternating order, so that the time of testing does not vary along with the independent variable, drug treatment. Note that a confounding variable is not simply an uncontrolled variable. Because a confounding variable varies with the independent variable, it can account for the differences across the experimental groups in the measured dependent variable. A confounded variable severely weakens your experimental design.

RANDOM ASSIGNMENT

Experimenters have to expect that they may not be able to control every single extraneous variable. In fact, they can never be sure they have *thought* of every variable that should be controlled. **Random assignment** is a powerful tool that scientists use to address this problem. By randomly assigning the subjects to the conditions, any possible variables associated with the subjects are in theory equally distributed across the conditions. For example, we might randomly assign rats to the conditions of ghrelin or vehicle injection. Some rats are probably destined to gain more weight in the future just by their genetic background; these rats might be assigned to either the treatment or the control groups when we use random assignment of subjects to groups. In addition, if we use large enough sample sizes, the effect of genetic variance will be minimized even below the low levels expected due to the use of highly inbred rat strains.

Randomization is used for more than assignment of subjects to conditions. The order of treatment might be randomized across subjects in the example with hamsters in the elevated plus maze. The amount of noise in the testing room might vary during the time of testing, the ease with which we handle the hamsters might change, the hamsters might have levels of anxiety that change with time of day; all of these variables might alter our results. Random assignment to groups with different treatment orders will help to ensure that these extraneous environmental variables and subject variables do not affect the results from one group more than the other group (see Box 4.3). Random assignment is truly a powerful tool, because it can control for an extraneous variable the experimenter has not even thought of.

BOX 4.3	TOOLS OF THE TRADE
	Random Elements

How do you randomize? You cannot do this by thinking of "random" numbers in your head—you are not likely able to generate true random orders. Try it! Challenge a friend to either (1) flip a coin 100 times, writing down if it came up either heads or tails, or (2) make up a "random" series of heads or tails without actually flipping a coin. Leave the room as your friend does this. When you return, look at the sequence generated and count the number of times either three heads or three tails are present. If there are more than three occurrences of three similar outcomes in a row, chances are your friend actually flipped the coin. If there are fewer than three occurrences of three in a row, chances are your friend tried to make up the random sequence.

So how can you generate a truly random order? You can use a computer; for example, Excel has a function called "RANDBETWEEN" in which you specify the range of numbers and it generates random numbers within that range. If all else fails, you can pick numbers out of a hat. Just be sure that after picking a number from the hat, you replace it, so that with each draw you have an equally random chance of drawing out any number.

INFERENTIAL STATISTICS

You will often want to describe the pattern of results for more than a single sample. In many cases, you will want to determine if two samples differ. For example, you may be asking, "Do the rats treated with ghrelin eat more than the rats treated with control injections?" or "Do the hamsters treated with the neuropeptide Y receptor agonist show less anxiety than the hamsters treated with vehicle injections?" Statistically speaking, you are asking, "Do these two samples come from different populations?"

A **population** is the entire collection of cases of interest. A **sample** is a smaller subset drawn from that population. In most cases, you have not tested the entire population, but have tested only a sample from that population. You will base conclusions about the population on statistics derived from the sample.

If you want to draw inferences from your samples to the entire underlying populations, you will need to use **inferential statistics,** statistics that are based on the laws of probability and that allow us to judge if samples are from different populations or if there are "statistically significant" differences.

Drawing a Sample From a Population

To select a sample from a population, you should first define the population you would like to sample, for example, all the rats in your lab colony. Then you determine how you will select your sample. There are multiple ways to do this; below I describe several possibilities.

Random Sampling

If possible, select a **random sample** by randomly choosing cases taken from the entire population, with each case selected independently from the next. This will give you the most freedom from problems of interpretation, as you will see later. In random sampling, each member of the population has an equal chance of being selected for the sample.

Stratified Random Sampling

like subgroup sampling

There may be instances when you would like to be sure that your sample contains fair representation of different groups within your population. You can use **stratified random sampling** to select cases randomly from within subpopulations (or strata) of your entire population (see Figure 4.5). For example, if you wanted a sample of retinal ganglion cells, you might decide to select a number of randomly chosen retinal ganglion cells from each of the two major classes of retinal ganglion cells, alpha and beta cells, either proportionate to the number of these cell types in the total population or oversampling rarer cell types of particular interest. The two subsamples of alpha and beta cells are then combined to form the total sample.

Figure 4.5 | Stratified Random Sampling

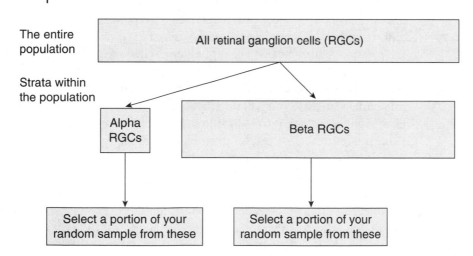

Stratified random sampling is a method for taking a random sample in which subsamples are represented according to the proportion they are represented in the population.

In the mammalian retina, there are many more beta retinal ganglion cells (RGCs) than alpha cells. Estimates of the population indicate there can be 14 beta cells for every alpha cell. The stratified random sample would represent these two cell types in the proportion found over the entire retina. Oversampling from the alpha RGCs will ensure sufficient numbers in each sample to say something useful about each group.

Being careful about how a sample is chosen from the population will help ensure that the results from your experiment are applicable to the larger population to which you want to generalize the results.

Testing the Null Hypothesis

One of the truly weird concepts in statistical inference is that of testing the null hypothesis. The **null hypothesis** (H_0) is the hypothesis that there is no difference between any of the groups in the experiment. You may think, "But my hypothesis was that the groups would differ!" Call this your experimental hypothesis. Inferential statistics are set up not to test your experimental hypothesis but to test the null hypothesis.

Because the null hypothesis is the assumption that the groups do not differ, accepting the null hypothesis means concluding that the groups do not differ. Thus, rejecting the null hypothesis is concluding that the groups do, in fact, differ. If you reject the null hypothesis and conclude the groups differ when the null hypothesis is true and they do not actually differ, then you have made an error. This is called a **Type I error.** For example, if, in fact, there is no effect of my neuropeptide Y receptor antagonist on anxiety, but I conduct a small experiment and conclude from my results that this antagonist does alter anxiety, I have made a Type I error.

There is always some risk of making a Type I error when using inferential statistics. By convention, researchers usually accept up to a 5% chance that you will reject the null hypothesis when it is actually true. This is usually expressed as "$p < .05$," which means "the probability of making a Type I error is less than .05 (that is, 5%)." The cutoff value of a probability of a Type I error that you will accept is called **alpha** (α). When you use computer software to calculate inferential statistics, you will usually be given the exact probability of a Type I error (for example, $p = 0.033$). If that probability value is less than the cutoff value or alpha that you set, for example, .05, then you may infer that your test indicates you can reject the null hypothesis.

A **statistically significant** difference between groups is a difference between samples that gives a test statistic value that meets or exceeds the critical value of your inferential statistic determined by alpha. Rejecting the null hypothesis means you infer that there is a *statistically significant* difference between your groups, and you indicate the level of risk of a Type I error that you accepted in making this conclusion. If you would like to be more careful not to make a Type I error, you can set your alpha level to something more rigorous, for example, $\alpha = .001$. In this case you would only reject the null hypothesis if $p < .001$. Note that the p value is based on the data and is the probability of the sample statistic occurring if the population statistic were really at the point specified by the null hypothesis. The alpha level, on the other hand, is not based on the data, but is determined in advance of the analysis.

One conceptually challenging aspect of this testing is that your statistics are not proving your experimental hypothesis. They are allowing you, with some measure of caution, to reject the null hypothesis. You are controlling the probability of a Type I error, but you could make another type of error. Accepting the null hypothesis when, in fact, it is false is called a **Type II error.** The probability of making a Type II error is called **beta** (β). For example, if I ran my experiment and inferred from the results that the neuropeptide Y antagonist had no reliable effect on the anxiety of hamsters, when there is such an effect of this drug, then I have made a Type II error. The **power** of a test is defined as ($1-\beta$). Your goal is to minimize β, or to make ($1-\beta$) as large as possible, so you have the greatest chance of detecting an effect if there is one. In general, β is set to 0.2 or 0.1, giving power values of 0.80 (80%) or 0.90 (90%). The larger your sample size and the better your sample represents the underlying population, the fewer your chances of making a Type II error. For example, you can imagine that if the antagonist has a minor effect on anxiety, then perhaps with a small sample of hamsters, I might not be able to measure a reliable effect. Increasing the sample size can help to reduce the chances of making a Type II error.

For a given sample size, if I set my cutoff probability value or alpha to be very low, to reduce my chances of making a Type I error, I will increase my chances of making a Type II error. I need to decide what is most important. In an exploratory study on neuropeptide Y and anxiety, testing a small sample to determine if there is an effect that I would be interested in studying further, I might set alpha to .05, accepting increased chances of making a Type I error, the chance of concluding there is an effect when, in fact, there is not. In a clinical trial on neuropeptide Y and anxiety, testing a small sample of people to determine if this neuropeptide Y antagonist should be introduced for wide clinical use, I might set alpha to .001, being unwilling to base further decisions on a result that has a high probability of Type I error. Table 4.2 summarizes possible outcomes.

Table 4.2 Summary of Cases With Type I and Type II Error

	Null Hypothesis Is True	*Null Hypothesis Is False*
Decide to reject null hypothesis	Type I error	Correct decision
Decide to accept null hypothesis	Correct decision	Type II error

THE POWER OF THE EXPERIMENT: INFERRING CAUSE AND EFFECT

If you have carefully controlled all other variables and are manipulating only the independent variable, then any difference between your two groups in the dependent variable is either due to the independent variable or to the effects of chance (see Figure 4.6). If your inferential statistics support the conclusion that the difference between the groups is unlikely to be due to chance variation, then you can conclude that your independent variable probably caused the difference in the dependent variable.

Figure 4.6 | Outline of a True Experiment

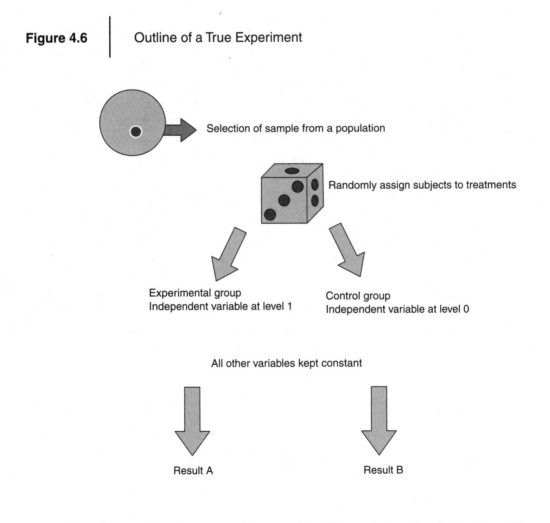

Conclusion: The independent variable caused the difference between "result A" and "result B"

This is the power of an experiment: It can allow us to cautiously make conclusions about cause and effect. We can move beyond simple description and careful observation, and we are able to determine causation. As an example, consider research on the role of the gene *per1* in circadian rhythms. Experiments showed that *per1* mRNA was transcribed in the neurons of the suprachiasmatic nucleus in animals exposed to light during the dark phase of their light-dark cycle. Animals not exposed to light during the dark phase did not show this mRNA in these neurons. These experiments demonstrated that light during the night caused *per1* mRNA transcription in suprachiasmatic nucleus neurons. We know from other studies that light at night resets circadian rhythms, part of the mechanism that allows external cycles to synchronize these rhythms. Does increased transcription of the *per1* gene cause resetting (phase shifts) of circadian rhythms? Light at night might be associated with many variables. How can we determine which are the variables necessary for the phase resetting action of light? A research team devised an experiment to do just that (Akiyama et al., 1999). This experiment involved blocking *per1* mRNA using antisense RNA (complementary RNA that binds to and inactivates the target mRNA). This study showed that light no longer reset circadian rhythms when *per1* mRNA was blocked in the suprachiasmatic nuclei (see Figure 4.7). From this

Figure 4.7   Actograms of Animals Housed in Continuous Darkness and Administered a Brief Light Pulse on the Day Indicated by the Arrow

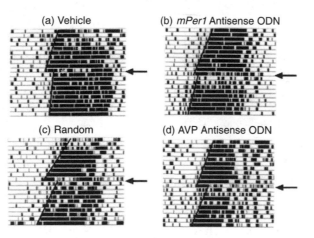

(a) Vehicle   (b) *mPer1* Antisense ODN

(c) Random   (d) AVP Antisense ODN

The daily activity of each animal appears as black marks plotted relative to the time of day, with each successive day in the experiment plotted below the previous day. The record in (a) shows the shift in phase of activity onset following a light pulse with a vehicle injection. In (b), this phase shift is reduced when the light pulse is accompanied by injection of antisense oligonucleotide directed against the mRNA for mPer1. Several controls are presented as well. In (c), the animal was injected with an oligonucleotide with a random sequence, and it is apparent that the light pulse can still shift the time of activity onset. In (d), the animal was treated with antisense directed against a different mRNA, that for vasopressin, a treatment that did not alter the phase shift to light.

SOURCE: Akiyama et al., 1999, Fig. A. Reprinted by permission of the Society for Neuroscience.

experiment, we can conclude that increased transcription of *per1* mRNA is *necessary* for light-induced resetting of the circadian clock of the mouse. We know it is necessary because blocking the increase in *per1* blocked the resetting action of light. If we could devise a way to hold all other variables constant and simultaneously increase just the *per1* mRNA, then we would be able to determine if increasing *per1* mRNA is *sufficient* for light-induced resetting of the mouse circadian clock.

In reality, we cannot always make strong conclusions about cause and effect. This is because no experiment is completely error-proof. Perhaps an important variable was not controlled. In your published report, you should include information on exactly what variables were controlled and which were not, because it may be possible in a later analysis of multiple published reports to determine a particular methodological detail that is important to control. Perhaps a fluke event caused the difference between groups, and we would get different results if we did the experiment again. Scientists are always relieved when they hear that other scientists can replicate the results of their studies.

It remains possible that the technique we used to manipulate the independent variable or to measure the dependent variable was flawed. Increased confidence comes from **convergent evidence,** results from experiments using widely divergent techniques that converge onto the same conclusion. For example, recall the observations of those "chilled out" hamsters given a drug that increased neuropeptide Y signaling? A study using mice in which the gene for neuropeptide Y was inactivated reports that these mice behaved in behavioral tests in a pattern suggesting increased anxiety. A recent paper gives even more convincing convergent evidence to link neuropeptide Y with anxiety. This paper examines people with a certain style of promoter region of the neuropeptide Y gene (the region that controls level of expression of the gene) that is associated with less neuropeptide Y in the brain as measured postmortem (Zhou et al., 2008). These people with lower levels of neuropeptide Y were on average more prone to have anxiety disorders and showed increased fMRI activation in the amygdala after seeing a disturbing face. Each study has some drawbacks but when many studies using different techniques support a link between neuropeptide Y and anxiety, the research community becomes more convinced.

Another approach is to conduct a **meta-analysis,** collating and statistically analyzing results from multiple studies on the same topic. For example, one meta-analysis of 64 studies, including 2,418 patients with major depressive disorder and 1,974 healthy individuals showed reductions in volume of frontal regions of the brain, as well as prefrontal areas, the hippocampus, the putamen, and the caudate nucleus (Koolschijn et al., 2009). Even though these changes were not apparent in every one of the 64 studies, a meta-analysis can give a quantitative analysis pointing to effects that are common to many studies. A primary concern in drawing conclusions from any experiment is whether extraneous variables were properly controlled. The next chapter describes methods for controlling variables in experiments.

✓ CHECK YOUR UNDERSTANDING

1. Identify the scale of measurement used:

   a. Amount of radioactively labeled protein in counts per minute

   b. Membrane potential measured in mV

   c. Phosphorylation state of the channel: phosphorylated or not phosphorylated

   d. Cortical area as identified by Brodmann (1909; see Figure 4.8)

   e. Effectiveness of stimuli in activating a neuron, measured by relative rank

   f. Sleep stage, as determined by EEG and EMG recordings: either stage I, II, III, IV, or REM

   g. Number of neurites measured following application of growth factor

2. Can you identify an independent variable and a dependent variable? Below are some examples to help you evaluate your understanding. Remember, the independent variable is the manipulated variable; the dependent variable is the observed or measured variable. Another trick is to try to summarize the experiment in a phrase of this structure: "The effect of ___ on ___." The experimenter is looking for the effect of the *independent* variable on the *dependent* variable.

   a. A student was interested in the role of the hippocampus in spatial memory tasks. She decided to compare performance on a radial arm maze by rats with hippocampal damage to performance by rats given sham surgery.

   b. A specific blocker of sodium channels was applied to a nerve cell. All action potentials ceased. A nerve cell with no blocker applied continued to exhibit action potentials.

   c. Participants learned a procedural memory task involving recognition of the orientation of an object appearing in peripheral vision. Following the training session, participants went to sleep in the lab. Researchers woke up some participants every time they entered slow wave sleep (SWS) and woke up other participants every time they entered rapid eye movement (REM) sleep. When tested the next morning, only the participants allowed REM sleep showed any signs of improvement on the memory task.

   d. The pattern of electrical stimulation was varied, and researchers measured the resultant dopamine release.

Figure 4.8 | Cortical Areas as Defined by Brodmann (1909): (a) Lateral View; (b) Midsaggital View

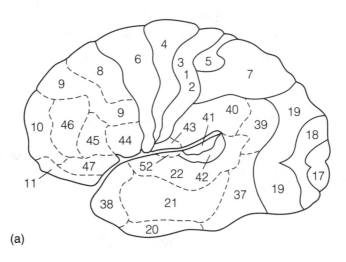

(a)

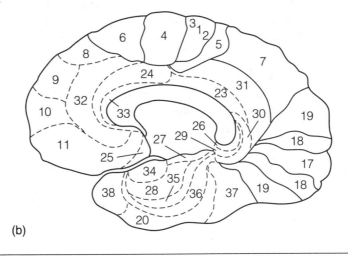

(b)

SOURCE: Kolb & Wishaw, 1996, Fig. 3.3, p. 55. Reprinted by permission of W. H. Freeman.

3. Now check that you can detect important flaws in experiments. Each experiment below has a major flaw in the experimental design. What is it?

a. To determine the behavioral effects of this drug, a researcher gives a newly developed specific serotonin reuptake inhibitor to a group of 100 rats. The rats are tested on three behavioral tests: the elevated plus maze, the radial arm maze, and the rotarod.

b. A student tests performance on a memory task before and after sleep. She trains her participants at 10 a.m., and then tests them at both 10 p.m. and 10 a.m. the following day. Participants performed better at the final 10 a.m. test session so she concludes that sleep improves performance on this task.

c. One rat in a study of cocaine addiction showed exceptionally high levels of motivation for cocaine as measured by lever-pressing behavior and showed very high levels of dopamine in the nucleus accumbens, a brain area linked with addictive behaviors. The researcher concluded that dopamine acting in the nucleus accumbens causes high motivation for cocaine.

d. An experiment demonstrated that a specific portion of the GABA receptor was crucial for anesthetic action. In this study, control mice (older mice from the colony of mice maintained at the research center) were compared with transgenic mice missing the critical portion of the GABA receptor. The transgenic mice had to be tested at 7 days of age, because they did not thrive due to the genetic alteration. Mice were randomly assigned to groups and the depth of anesthesia was determined for each of three common anesthetic agents.

4. What is the general principle for determining if something is necessary and sufficient? Use the guide below:

a. If x is necessary for y, then when I remove x, ___.

b. If x is sufficient for y, then when I add x, and hold all other variables constant, ___.

THINK ABOUT IT 🧠

1. Sometimes it simply takes a critical mass of data before investigators in an area will accept new findings. For example, consider the case of H. M., discussed earlier. Brenda Milner demonstrated in 1962 that H. M. could learn new motor skills, despite the persistent and global amnesia for learning about "words, digits, paragraphs, faces, names, maze routes, spatial layouts, geometric shapes, nonsense patterns, nonsense syllables, clicks, tunes, tones, public and personal events, and more" (Cohen, 1984, p. 83). Suzanne Corkin, working with Brenda Milner, conducted studies showing preserved "repetition priming" in H. M., where prior exposure to words or objects enhanced later recognition of those words or objects (Milner, Corkin, & Teuber, 1968). We now consider these findings as indicative of preserved habit learning, similar to motor skill learning. The idea of separate memory systems, however, was not

prevalent at the time, and investigators did not incorporate these results into their models of human memory immediately. Does this indicate experimenters in this field were biased? Why or why not? Why do you think experienced scientists are conservative about changing their theories based on the results of one or two observations?

2. Look back at the example in this chapter about the role of the *per1* gene in circadian clock resetting by light. The experiment using *per1* antisense demonstrated that increased transcription of the *per1* gene was *necessary* for light-induced resetting. What experiment would you do to determine if *per1* transcription was *sufficient* for resetting circadian rhythms?

3. Most studies on the treatment of chronic insomnia test effects of either pharmacological or behavioral treatments, but not both. In a meta-analysis (Smith et al., 2002), 21 different studies were compared. This analysis indicated both treatment approaches were similarly effective on most measures of sleep quality. In their discussion, the authors note that participants in all these studies were not randomly assigned to treatments but instead had chosen either pharmacological or behavioral treatments. How might this influence your interpretation of the results? The authors suggest this could increase the ability to generalize their findings to the clinical setting (when patients self-select treatment approaches). Do you agree? Why or why not?

4. Statistical concepts review:

   a. Define "sample" and "population."

   b. What is the "null hypothesis"?

   c. Explain why your significance level (alpha) is the probability of making a Type I error.

SUGGESTIONS FOR FURTHER READING

Angrosina, M. V. (2007). *Naturalistic observation.* Walnut Creek, CA: Left Coast Press.

Barlow D. H., Nock, M., & Hersen, M. (2009). *Single case experimental designs: Strategies for studying behavior for change.* Boston: Pearson/Allyn & Bacon.

Barry, S. R. (2009). *Fixing my gaze: A scientist's journey into seeing in three dimensions.* New York: Basic Books.

Gonzalez, R. (2009). *Data analysis for experimental design.* New York: Guilford Press.

Rosenbaum, P. R. (2002). *Observational studies.* New York: Springer.

Woodbury-Harris, K. M., & Coull, B. M. (2009). *Clinical trials in the neurosciences.* New York: Karger.

Controlling Extraneous Variables

CHAPTER
5

A primary tenet of the experimental method is to manipulate only one variable, keeping all other variables constant or controlled. For example, we might design an experiment to test the role of the "Nogo" receptor in axonal regeneration. We will compare axon regeneration following spinal cord injury in animals treated with a blocker of the Nogo receptor with results from animals not treated with the receptor blocker. If the groups differ, we conclude that the Nogo receptor plays a role in axon regeneration.

WHAT VARIABLES NEED TO BE CONTROLLED?

Must every variable be controlled? You will need to make a careful judgment as you design your experiment. The beauty of the experiment is that you can conclude that your independent variable caused the difference in the dependent variable *as long as no other variables differed across the groups.* When you design an experiment, you will realize it can be very difficult to ensure that absolutely no other variable changed across the groups. If animals were tested on different days of the week, that is an uncontrolled variable. What about the identity of the person testing the animals? You can begin to see that the experimenter must worry about controlling as many variables as possible, but that some variables are probably more important than others, depending on your particular experiment. It is helpful to study papers reporting other experiments on the same topic. Variables important to control in the study of circadian rhythms (for example, the lighting of the animal's housing room) are different from variables important to control in the study of development of motor learning (for example, prior motor experience).

CONTROLLING SUBJECT VARIABLES

Subject variables are variables associated with each subject or participant in your experiment, such as the age, prior experience, or body weight of the subject. As discussed in Chapter 4, random assignment is a powerful tool for controlling variables. If you randomly assign subjects to groups, you will distribute the multitude of subject variables you did not explicitly control across those groups. With a large enough sample size, you can be assured that there is no reason to suspect the groups differ on those characteristics. Of course, in most research situations with laboratory animals, you can select subjects of a particular gender and age, with a particular range of prior experience, perhaps from a specially inbred population. Be aware that even genetically identical mice can show individual differences. A fetus positioned next to two males in utero receives different hormone exposure than one next to two females, and this influences later behavior (for a review, see Ryan & Vandenbergh, 2002). Many other pre- and post-natal factors can lead to individual differences (Lathe, 2004) or can make one group of mice behave in a different manner from another. When your experiment depends on human participants, you will be even more concerned about controlling subject variables. One approach is to explicitly control for as many variables as you can and then use random assignment to take care of the rest.

Within-Subjects Design

In some instances, the experimenter might want to control for variables associated with the subject by conducting an experiment using the **within-subjects design.** In the within-subjects design, each subject of the experiment experiences all the experimental conditions. For example, if the design is simple, with one independent variable and one control condition, then in a within-subjects design, each subject experiences both the independent variable and the control condition.

Let us say you are interested in the effect of a new anesthetic on the sensitivity of GABA receptors to the neurotransmitter GABA. This is of interest because the GABA receptor seems to play a crucial role in the loss of consciousness associated with the effect of anesthesia. You might approach this question by measuring a response such as the whole cell current evoked by GABA application, reflecting the passage of ions through the GABA receptor. You could construct a dose-response curve for GABA application either with or without anesthetic. You can measure this response from *Xenopus* oocytes (frog eggs) that have been injected with mRNA encoding for GABA receptor subunits. Researchers use this approach in part because these oocytes are large and sturdy, providing an easily manipulated cell for expression of the GABA receptors of interest. Their membranes are also not studded with a multitude of other receptors, keeping the experimental situation simple. Because each oocyte might differ slightly in terms of the expression of GABA receptors, a within-subjects design is wise. You could measure a dose-response curve for GABA action for each oocyte in the presence and in the absence of anesthetic.

Experimenters often employ the within-subjects design in studies measuring levels of brain activity using a technique such as **fMRI (functional magnetic resonance imaging)**. The between-subjects variability in fMRI is so great that an experimenter gains a major advantage if a within-subjects design can be used (Huettel, Song, & McCarthy, 2008).

Matched-Samples Design

In a **matched-samples design,** you control for a variable associated with the experimental units by measuring that variable and then matching subjects in the experimental and control group for that variable. For example, in studying the effects of practice on the brain areas activated during a mental imagery task, you might assign participants to groups based on their initial ability to complete the mental imagery task. People vary widely in native ability for mental imagery tasks, and thus this is an important variable to control. You could randomly assign participants to groups and hope that mental imagery ability was equally distributed across the groups, but in reality this works best only for large samples; in some cases it is impossible to randomize. If you have a small sample, and can measure this important variable in a pretest, then it is best to use a matched-samples design. To match the samples, first administer a pretest to measure mental imagery ability. Then order the people from first to last according to their score on the pretest. If your experiment consists of two groups, an experimental and a control group, you can take the first two top-scorers on the pretest and randomly assign one to the experimental group and one to the control group. Proceeding down the list, two people at a time, you could fill your two groups with people matched on mental imagery ability. Now you could conduct your study with two groups, knowing that the experimental and control groups were matched in terms of mental imagery ability (see Figure 5.1).

Figure 5.1 Schematic Showing the Matched-Samples Design

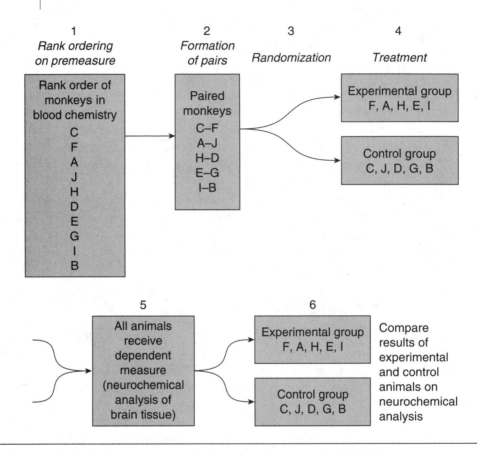

SOURCE: From Ray, *Methods Toward a Science of Behavior and Experience,* 7E. © 2003 Wadsworth, a part of Cengage Learning, Inc. Reproduced by permission. www.cengage.com/permissions

Attrition

Attrition is the loss of subjects before or during your experiment. You can randomly assign who begins a study, but you have little control over who completes it. Selective attrition in one experimental group can raise concerns about confounding variables. Might the subjects who dropped out differ in some way from those who remained? When you design your study, you should be concerned if one condition is somehow less attractive to participants and might encourage a higher dropout rate than the other conditions do. For example, if you design a study on the effects of sleep deprivation on learning, participants assigned to the condition of having only 2 hours of sleep during the night might drop out at a higher rate than those assigned to the condition of having 8 hours of sleep. You might be left with participants in the 2-hour sleep group who normally do not need much sleep. Thus, although you may have started with random assignment to groups, due to selective attrition, you ended up with groups that differ on more than just the independent variable. The presence of the confounding variables weakens your conclusions from this study.

Assessing an Intervention for Reading Disability

A recent study provides examples of some of the design characteristics just discussed. In this study (Shaywitz et al., 2004), researchers wanted to assess if one particular intervention program, a *phonologically based intervention program*, would help develop neural circuits known to be associated with skilled reading, the left hemisphere posterior (occipitotemporal) circuits. They measured brain activation using fMRI.

The researchers might have chosen to conduct the experiment entirely within subjects, measuring fMRI activity before and after the phonologically based reading program intervention. Such a design, however, would not control for normal developmental changes that might occur over time. Given that the interventions lasted 8 months, this was an important concern. Thus, they also included a control group of children who were of a similar age, but did not have a reading disability.

A second concern was that any differences between the groups might be due to the additional hours of practice reading that the children in the phonologically based reading program experienced. The authors included a third control group, children who were reading disabled and were enrolled in typical reading-related interventions in the school, such as remedial reading or time in the resource room. In this way, they could determine if group differences were due to the phonologically based reading intervention program of special interest to the researchers or if changes in brain activity were also observed with more typically administered programs.

The experiment's design thus included three groups of subjects: control group children, children with reading disabilities enrolled in typical school intervention programs, and children with reading disabilities enrolled in the phonologically based intervention program. The fMRI activity was assessed at the beginning of the study, immediately after intervention, and 1 year following intervention. The authors stressed that prior studies had demonstrated that fMRI assessment 1 year after intervention was critical, allowing researchers to determine if the intervention's effects were lasting.

Unfortunately, attrition was a major problem in collecting data 1 year later. Although 25 of the original 37 children in the phonologically based intervention program group returned for the final fMRI, only 4 of the 40 children in the other two groups returned for this follow-up evaluation. The authors speculated that parents who were enthusiastic about their children's progress in developing reading skills were more motivated to return the child for the final fMRI. They suggested that future studies might compare groups of children receiving two different types of intensive interventions for reading disabilities, instead of using a control group of children receiving only standard interventions.

And what were the results? The phonologically based intervention did increase activity in left hemisphere brain regions of interest, and these increases in activity were evident both immediately after intervention and also at the 1-year follow-up. Will future teachers take brain scans to determine how well their students are doing? Based on this study, some already are.

WHEN A SUBJECT VARIABLE IS YOUR INDEPENDENT VARIABLE: QUASI-EXPERIMENTS

When a subject characteristic is your independent variable, you can often design a study that is otherwise like a true experiment. You can control other variables carefully and measure your dependent variable in an unbiased and objective manner. Of course, you are usually unable to randomly assign subjects to groups, so you are missing a key quality of a true experiment, making this a **quasi-experiment**. For example, the investigator may be interested in the differences between the brains of people with multiple sclerosis and the brains of healthy controls. Obviously, this researcher cannot begin the experiment by randomly assigning participants to either the multiple sclerosis or control condition. This is an example of a research question that only a quasi-experiment can address. You can apply methods to control for other subject variables that might be relevant, such as the matched-samples design. For example, in a study comparing patients with multiple sclerosis to healthy controls, you could match participants on age, gender, other health variables, and so on.

The inability to randomly assign participants to groups poses important problems for interpreting results. Even if you have all other important variables carefully controlled, your results could be due to multiple confounding variables. Your two groups may differ not just in the diagnosis of multiple sclerosis. They also may differ in lifestyle factors, drug history, and ability to care for their own general health. Anything correlated with the experience of multiple sclerosis in our current society will be different between your two groups. If you find differences between the groups in your dependent measures, such as different levels of brain activity in specific regions, how can you determine if multiple sclerosis causes this difference or if a variable associated with multiple sclerosis causes it?

Transgenic or Knockout Mice

An increasingly common technique is to use transgenic, *knockout* or *knockin*, mice to investigate an independent variable. A **transgenic** mouse has a segment of artificially constructed DNA (a *transgene*) incorporated into its genome that may cause that mouse to produce the protein coded for by the transgene. A **knockin** mouse has a gene inserted at a targeted site in the genome, allowing over-expression

[handwritten margin note: Not an experiment more like an investigation into a theory]

[handwritten margin note: artificial DNA added in]

of the protein product of that gene. A **knockout** mouse has a particular gene inactivated or disrupted, so the protein product of that gene is no longer produced or is produced in a truncated form and thus is no longer functional (see Figure 5.2). Control mice for such an experiment are called **wildtype** mice, and they are best chosen from littermates of the mutant mice. Genotyping is used to determine which mice have the genetic alteration and which are genetically normal.

If you are comparing mice with a mutation in, say, the sodium channel gene, with control mice, is this a true experiment or a quasi-experiment? Generally, experimenters deliberately produced mice with the specific gene mutation, thereby giving the appearance of this being a manipulated variable. However, the independent variable is a subject variable and thus this is a quasi-experiment. Many of the studies currently published in leading neuroscience journals are quasi-experiments, comparing such genetically altered mice to controls.

What are some of the problems in making interpretations? Differences between mutated and control groups might be attributed to the mutated gene, or they might

Figure 5.2 | A Conditional Knockout

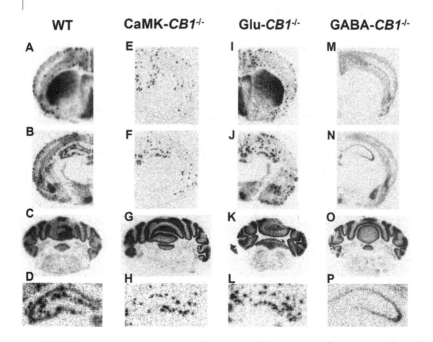

Brain sections showing location of mRNA for cannabinoid 1 receptors (CB1; shown in black) for wildtype mice (WT) and for three different types of conditional knockout mice. The "CaMK-CB1-/-" mice lack CB1 in all principal neurons but maintain CB1 in GABA-containing cells (scattered dots in E, F, and H). The "glu-CB1-/-" mice lack CB1 in cortical cells that contain the neurotransmitter glutamate. The "GABA-CB1-/-" mice lack CB1 in cells using the neurotransmitter GABA.

SOURCE: Monory et al., 2006.

be due to the myriad compensatory changes induced in a system developing and functioning without that gene. A change in one gene can cause a cascade of changes in a developing system, so by the time you study the adult you are looking at the net effect of many variables, some directly attributable to your transgene and others being more indirect consequences (see Box 5.1). You can apply some of the design principles we have discussed, such as using a within-subject or a matched-sample design, to strengthen your experiment. One important control group specific to this approach is that of littermates without the transgene. Littermate controls can help determine if the transgene alters offspring by effects on the mother, effects experienced either prior to birth or before weaning.

These difficulties are what spur researchers to develop ways to produce "conditional" gene knockouts: ways to control the activation of a gene by various conditions. You might use a spatial or a temporal conditional knockout. A **spatial conditional knockout** would have the gene inactivated only in certain brain regions, whereas a **temporal conditional knockout** would have the gene inactivated only at certain times in development. The inactivated gene can be controlled by a substance fed to the animal in some cases or by a regulatory region that restricts expression only to certain cell types (for more details see Gaveriaux-Ruff & Kieffer, 2007). With a conditional knockout, a better controlled experiment is possible. One group of your conditional knockout mice can be treated so as to disrupt function of your gene of interest at a specific time or in a specific brain region, while a second group of the conditional knockout mice could serve as controls. For example, researchers were interested in identifying where in the brain marijuana acted to produce its effects (Monory et al., 2007). Marijuana acts largely through the CB1 receptor and, while this is most densely located on GABA-containing cells in the cerebral cortex, it is also found on cells in many other brain areas. Using various strains of mice with the CB1 receptor gene inactivated in different cell populations, they were able to find that different effects of marijuana (e.g., effects on movement, pain response, or body temperature) were mediated by different brain regions. Surprisingly, the cortical GABAergic neurons with high levels of CB1 receptors did not seem important in mediating these responses.

Researchers are aware of these common interpretational difficulties and generally consider studies of transgenic mice as one portion of a wider series of studies furnishing convergent evidence for a hypothesis. For example, transgenic mice with disruption of the neuropeptide Y gene show alterations in common measures of anxiety in mice (see Figure 5.3), and researchers consider this evidence in the context of other studies, for example, using drugs to alter neuropeptide Y levels to determine if we can support a strong link between anxiety and this peptide. Each technique has some drawbacks, but when a new technique provides further support for a hypothesized link between neuropeptide Y and anxiety, researchers may focus less on each specific technique's drawbacks.

Figure 5.3 | Loss of Neuropeptide Y Increases Anxiety

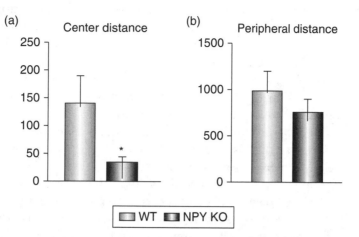

Transgenic mice with disruption of the neuropeptide Y gene show increased anxiety-related behaviors in a common test of anxiety. In the open field test, neuropeptide Y knockout mice show decreased entries into the central area (a) but no change in locomotor activity in the peripheral areas of the open field (b).

SOURCE: Bannon et al., 2000. Reprinted by permission of Elsevier.

MORE, PLEASE!

A Cautionary Tale

Gap junctions are close connections between neurons that allow electrical transmission. Scientists once thought that gap junctions were very important in the ability of cells in a particular brain area, the "inferior olive," to fire in synchrony and in oscillatory patterns. This firing pattern may underlie the ability of these cells to generate temporal patterns of movement through their connections with the cerebellum.

Surprisingly, when researchers studied mice with a major gap junction gene mutated, the inferior olive cells were still able to oscillate (DeZeeuw et al., 2003). Does this result indicate that gap junctions are not necessary for this oscillatory firing pattern? Perhaps not. The explanation for the finding may be that the cells from the mutant mice use a completely different mechanism from the one used in control mice. Researchers showed that through changes in structure (thicker dendrites) and changes in ion conductances, the neurons in the mutant mice were able to produce rhythmic activity. This study may simply demonstrate a different mechanism for producing oscillatory firing, but it does not determine if control mice use gap junctions to synchronize the neurons.

In addition, this study provides a caution regarding the interpretation of the many studies in neuroscience where animals with a single gene mutation are studied. The absence of that gene may change the nervous system in novel and unforeseen ways.

PLACEBO CONTROLS

The use of a placebo control is common in studies using drug administration in humans. **Placebos** (from the Latin "to please") were originally inert pills that physicians gave to patients with a malady for which there was no other treatment. Surprisingly, there is a measurable improvement from a placebo treatment in many cases. To what should we attribute this improvement? There are probably many causes. Sometimes a person's health improves simply with the passage of time, an event referred to as an unexplained remission. On the other hand, some studies have included groups with no placebo and compared these to groups given a placebo; if there is greater improvement in the placebo-treated group, the difference in improvement cannot be attributed to unexplained remission. Sometimes the attention from a physician and the sense of being treated will buoy a person up and, through a still poorly understood process, lead to improvement in health. Placebos are more effective the more dramatic they are; larger pills are more effective than smaller ones, surgical interventions more effective than less invasive approaches. Expectation is an important factor as well; if both the patient and the doctor express an expectation that the treatment will be effective, the placebo effect is larger. There is an interesting literature on the neurobiological effects of placebos (for example, see Price, Finniss, & Benedetti, 2008). For example, patients with Parkinson's disease are often treated with medication that increases dopamine release or implanted electrodes in the subthalamic nucleus. Studies show that placebo treatments can have beneficial effects on motor symptoms. These beneficial placebo effects are actually accompanied by increased dopamine release or changes in firing patterns of subthalamic nucleus neurons.

In some cases, it is difficult to control for the **placebo effect**. Studies of seasonal affective disorder (i.e., the "winter blues," a depressed mood that regularly occurs on a seasonal basis) have suggested that some people with this disorder show lifted moods if they expose themselves to bright lights for several hours a day. Circadian rhythms researchers found this unsurprising because the decrease in the number of hours of daylight experienced by organisms living far from the equator triggers seasonal responses. In fact, circadian researchers predicted that treatment with several hours of light in the morning would be more effective than the same light treatment given midday. Did the results support this prediction that morning light would be most effective? Several studies found some support for this, but the effect was not overwhelming. What might be happening? One possibility is that people were experiencing a placebo effect. Disrupting your daily routine to sit in front of a light box for several hours may lift your mood by the mere sense of being under treatment. How could researchers control for this effect? Asking people to sit in front of dim lights is one possibility, but this might be less effective as a placebo as well as less effective as a light stimulus. One study used sham "negative ion generators" as a **placebo control group** for bright light therapy (Eastman, Young, Fogg, Liu, &

Meaden, 1998), and this study indicated that bright light has an antidepressant effect greater than the placebo effect.

There are ethical concerns when conducting a study using placebos. Participants should be told before they give consent to participate in the study that they may receive a placebo instead of an active treatment. In many instances, it is not ethical to use a placebo. If there is an established treatment for the disorder, then the control group should receive that conventional treatment. You then compare the effect of your new treatment, given to the experimental group, to the effect of the conventional treatment given to the control group. If you recruit more potential participants than you are able to treat at one time, you can use the participants placed on the waiting list as a control group, later providing these participants with a treatment.

SINGLE- AND DOUBLE-BLIND STUDIES

One way to control for placebo effects is to conduct a **single-blind procedure.** In a single-blind study, participants do not know if they are in the experimental or the control group. A single-blind study design helps to control for the participants' expectations about effects of the treatments you are testing. You should carefully consider the ethical justification for such a design because participants are not fully informed about exactly what treatment they will receive before consenting to the experiment. It can be difficult to conduct a single-blind study if the treatment produces an effect that is obvious to the participant. For example, recall the "cranial electrical stimulation" discussed in Chapter 1. It would be difficult to keep the participant blind in this instance because the electrical stimulation produces a tingling sensation in the earlobes.

In a **double-blind procedure,** neither the participants nor the experimenters administering the treatments know who is in the experimental group and who is in the control group. Of course, in animal research, the animals do not have awareness or expectancies about their assignment to experimental or control groups, so we do not use the terms *single-blind* and *double-blind*. When an animal study is conducted so that the experimenter is not aware of which subjects are in which experimental group, we simply call it a *blind* study. Why conduct a blind study? This design controls for **experimenter effects,** subtle effects the experimenter can have on the outcome of the experiment. Generally, experimenter effects are biased toward the hypothesis. This bias is in most cases unconscious and in many cases quite subtle. For example, if you were conducting behavioral tests of mice that you hypothesized were going to act more aggressive than the mice in the control group, you might handle the mice differently as you placed them into the test arena, being more hesitant in your handling of mice you expected to be more aggressive. These mice might then act differently during the test, in part because of the difference in handling. Another possibility would be that you would interpret an ambiguous behavior differently depending on whether you expected that mouse to be aggressive or not. To protect yourself against the question of potential experimenter effects, conduct your experiment blind to the treatments whenever possible.

Often researchers conduct a **blind analysis,** in which they code their samples so that as they analyze the data they are unaware of prior treatments. For example, in analyzing brain sections from people with autism to compare with brain sections from controls, you could cover the original labels on the slides with labels that are coded. During data collection, as you measure cell size or count cell numbers, you would be blind to the identity of the brain sample, keeping track of your measurements using the codes on the slides. Only after you finished collecting data would you look under the labels and determine which slide came from which group of participants.

Striving for objective measures whenever possible will also protect you from experimenter effects. Using an image analysis software package to determine cell diameter is better than attempting to measure the diameter yourself, but both would be better than judging if a cell is "small," "medium," or "large." Using multiple observers and checking for good inter-rater reliability is another good approach. Often experimenters will include a **positive control** and a **negative control** to check that the procedure is working reliably. A positive control is a sample that should definitely demonstrate a positive reaction, and a negative control is a sample that should show a negative reaction. For example, in an experiment measuring cell death in neural development, fragmented DNA would be one reasonable dependent variable to measure, because this is associated with cell death. A positive control would be a brain section to which the experimenter applied an enzyme that will fragment the DNA (DNase). This specially treated brain section should give a positive signal in the assay. A negative control might be a brain section that did not receive one critical reagent but was otherwise treated identically to the other sections. This section would not be expected to show staining in the assay.

Vehicle Controls and Sham Surgery

In animal research, one control group for a study involving drug administration is often a **vehicle-control group.** The *vehicle* is the solution in which the drug is dissolved, such as saline or artificial cerebrospinal fluid. Animals in the vehicle-control group are treated exactly as the animals getting the drug except that no drug is dissolved in the vehicle. Thus, if the drug is administered with an intraperitoneal injection, the vehicle-control group animals receive the vehicle through an intraperitoneal injection. Comparing results from the vehicle-control group with a separate group of untreated animals allows you to detect any effects of the injection procedure on the dependent variable (see also Box 5.2).

If your experimental group is receiving surgical interventions, you will want to include a control group receiving **sham surgery.** This group is anesthetized for surgery, placed in any special apparatus necessary for surgery, and is treated exactly as the experimental group except for the step that is thought to alter the critical variable.

BOX 5.2	**TOOLS OF THE TRADE**
	A Few Special Concerns for Pharmacological Studies

Several special concerns arise in the design of drug studies. It is critical to include a dose-response curve to characterize effects, since these can provide information of the specificity and mechanism of action of the compound being tested. A big mistake students often make is in the spacing of the doses administered. Generally, drug doses are varied by log units (see Figure 5.4). An inadequate range of doses tested will not allow a full description of the dose-response relationship, which is the fundamental relationship to describe in initial studies.

The example in Figure 5.4 also highlights a common method for pooling results from cases that have different baseline level responses. Here the researchers have *normalized* the responses to the maximum current demonstrated by that particular oocyte in response to GABA. To do this, they took each measured current and divided it by the maximum current for that particular oocyte.

Figure 5.4 | Dose Is Often Varied by Log Units

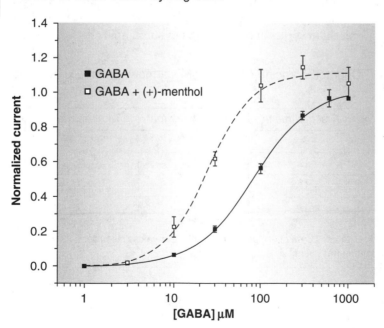

A dose-response curve for oocytes treated with either GABA or with GABA and menthol, demonstrating the sensitivity of GABA receptors to modulation by menthol. Note the spacing of drug concentrations used by log units, a common design within pharmacological studies. Note also that the evoked current responses were normalized to the maximum response for each oocyte tested to allow comparison across the sample.

SOURCE: Hall et al., 2004. Reprinted by permission of Elsevier.

CONTROLLING ORDER EFFECTS: COUNTERBALANCING

In the experiment described in *Within-Subjects Design* section, where you were measuring a dose-response curve for GABA action for each oocyte with and without anesthetic, one potential worry is that you might observe an **order effect** if the order of the experimental conditions influences the results. This is always a concern for within-subject designs. For example, if you always tested the oocytes with the anesthetic condition first, perhaps previous exposure to anesthetic would influence the GABA response in the control condition. On the other hand, if you always tested the oocytes with the control condition first, then previous exposure to GABA might influence the GABA response in the anesthetic condition.

What can you do to control for an order effect? Randomizing the order of the conditions is one good approach. Another approach is to **counterbalance** the order of the conditions, to design the study so that equal numbers of subjects experience the various possible orders of the conditions (see Figure 5.5). In our oocyte experiment, this is relatively easy; we could test half the oocytes with the control condition first and the anesthetic condition second; the other half of the oocytes would experience the anesthetic condition first and the control condition second. The main advantage of using a counterbalanced order instead of a randomized order is that after using a counterbalanced order, the experimenter can measure the order effect and can determine if the order of conditions had a substantial effect on the response measured.

Figure 5.5 | Counterbalancing for Order of Treatments in an Experiment

Subject	First treatment	Second treatment	Third treatment	Fourth treatment
1	A	B	C	D
2	D	C	A	B
3	C	D	B	A
4	B	A	C	D

The four treatments, A, B, C, and D, are given to subjects so that every possible order is used and each of the four subjects receives a different order of treatment.

TIME-SERIES DESIGN

A **time-series design** is a within-subjects design that involves measures of the dependent variable taken at different times, with the experimental or control treatment applied between the measures. This is particularly suited to single-subject designs.

The simplest time-series design is the ABA design, which has three stages. First, the dependent variable is measured under control conditions to establish a baseline. Then, the experimental condition is applied and the dependent variable is measured under the experimental conditions. Finally, there is a return to the control condition and the dependent variable is measured again. This third condition is important to include because a change in the dependent variable over time might indicate an effect of the independent variable or might be simply from a change due to time. The third condition should show a return of the dependent variable back to baseline levels. Thus, this design involves control ("A"), experimental ("B"), and control ("A") conditions (see Figure 5.6).

Figure 5.6 | Time-Series Design

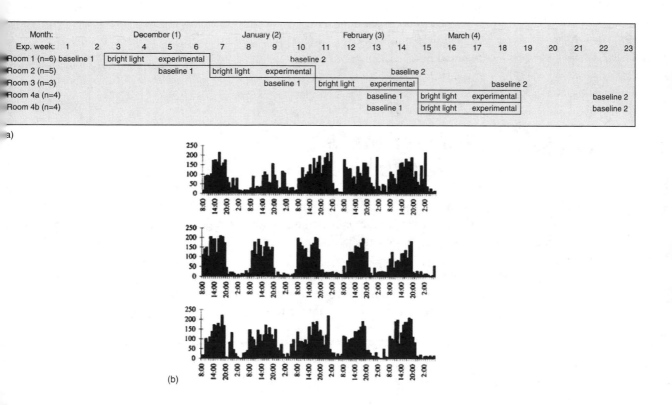

(a)

(b)

This study examined the effect of bright light on the rest-activity rhythm of Alzheimer patients. (a) Protocol of the study: Patients were studied during a baseline period and then exposed to bright light in the dayroom for 4 weeks, followed by a return to original conditions for a second baseline measure. The timing of the experimental treatment was staggered to allow measurement of a possible seasonal effect. (b) Example of data from one patient in the study: Activity was measured from a wrist-worn monitor. Five days of baseline activity before treatment (top panel) demonstrates the disorganization in daily rhythms associated with dementia. During bright light treatment, rest-activity rhythms become less variable with no change in amplitude (middle panel). After treatment is withdrawn, the patient reverts back to original pattern (lower panel).

SOURCE: Van Someren, Kessler, Mirmiran, & Swaab, 1997.

More complex time-series designs are possible. For example, you could have an ABABA design, to determine if the effect of the independent variable replicates over two applications. A time-series design with more than one independent variable might be an ABCA design or an ABACA design.

All of these designs suffer from interpretational problems because the dependent variable may change over time independently of the experimental conditions. Think of time as a major uncontrolled variable in these studies. Necessarily, the measures taken under control and experimental conditions vary by more than the independent variable; they also vary in the time they were collected. Any other factor that has changed during that time might alter your dependent measures and thus might account for any differences you observe. For example, in studies using fMRI activity as a dependent variable, "scanner drift," or noise intrinsic to the MRI machine that slowly changes over time, can present problems in interpreting data (see also Box 5.3).

BOX 5.3

TOOLS OF THE TRADE

The Design of fMRI Experiments

Special considerations apply to the design of experiments using fMRI to assess brain activity. The textbook *Functional Magnetic Resonance Imaging* (Huettel, Song, & McCarthy, 2008) describes them well, and a student starting to work with fMRI experiments should consult it for more detailed information.

A common research design is the **blocked design**, where the experimental conditions occur in an alternating order, with each level of the independent variable presented for an extended time, in blocks (see Figure 5.7). This design is preferred when the experimenter is interested in changes in brain state.

In some instances, an **event-related design** is preferable, where brain activity is measured following short-duration presentations of stimuli in discrete events or trials (see Figure 5.8). This design would be appropriate when an experimenter is interested in changes in the brain that are caused by properties of presented stimuli.

Always in interpreting fMRI study results, keep in mind that you may be able to conclude that a change in brain activity is associated with your task, perhaps that your task caused the change in brain activity, but you can never conclude from studies using this technique that the brain activity caused the behavioral performance.

Figure 5.7 | Example of a Blocked Design in an fMRI Experiment

(a)

"Carrot" "Mailbox" "Knife" "Tiger" "Sweater" "Teapot" "Auto" "Doorbell" "Spider" "Parsley"

"Plant" "Handbag" "Pebble" "Chess" "Book" "Phone" "Anger" "Watch" "Window" "Night"

(b)

Task A | Task B | Task A | Task B | Task A | Task B | Task A | Task B

(c)

Task A | Rest | Task B | Rest | Task A | Rest | Task B | Rest

The participant reads 10 words with background music in one block (Task A). This contrasts with Task B, when the participant reads ten words with no background music. The experimenter doesn't analyze the response to individual words, but assumes that the cognitive processes of interest occur throughout the block. The experimenter can design the study as shown in (b) alternating Task A and Task B blocks, or the experimenter can insert a rest condition between each block, as shown in (c).

SOURCE: Huettel et al., 2008. Reprinted by permission of Sinauer Associates, Inc.

Figure 5.8 | Example of an Event-Related fMRI Experiment Design

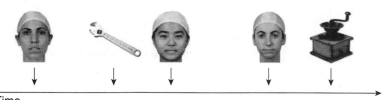

Time

The participant simply watches a screen where occasionally a face or an object appears. The figure shows a time axis and indicates the relative position in time when each image is presented. The experimenter analyzes the brain activity immediately following the faces and compares this to fMRI activity following objects.

SOURCE: Huettel et al., 2008. Reprinted by permission of Sinauer Associates, Inc.

✓ CHECK YOUR UNDERSTANDING

1. Independent variable and dependent variable. For each experiment below, define the independent variable and the dependent variable.

    a. To determine if the pattern of brain activation differs when recalling true versus false memories, researchers used PET scans to observe brain activity when participants recalled words from a list previously presented, as well as words very similar to the words on the original list, ones the participants thought were on the list but actually were not. The hippocampus was active in both instances, but the left temporal parietal area was active only in the cases of true memories.

    b. A study measured responses from patients with mild brain injury from a recent traumatic event with a control group matched on several relevant variables. It measured selective and sustained attention, verbal and nonverbal fluency, and verbal memory (Mathias, Beall, & Bigler, 2004).

    c. The role of the molecule "Hedgehog" in brain development was investigated using zebrafish. In the first experiment, Hedgehog signaling pathways were pharmacologically blocked, and researchers observed that development of the pituitary was disrupted. In the second experiment, researchers reported that zebrafish with genetic mutations in the components of the Hedgehog signaling pathway showed alterations in the structure of the pituitary (Sbrogna, Barresi, & Karlstrom, 2003).

2. This experiment has a major flaw. What is it? *Does luteinizing hormone releasing hormone (LHRH) increase the number of calcium channels in neurons? To test this, a researcher applied LHRH to cell cultures and measured the density of calcium channels. While there was a progressive loss in cells, an expected result for this type of cell culture, the surviving cells showed increased numbers of calcium channels. A control group of cell cultures without LHRH did not show the cell loss or increased numbers of calcium channels. The researcher concluded that results supported the hypothesis that LHRH increased the number of calcium channels.*

    a. No control group

    b. A major confounded variable

    c. Selective attrition

    d. Experimenter bias

2. In an experiment using antibodies to label serotonin-containing neurons, the brain sections processed with no antibodies applied to them are:

   a. Positive control

   b. Primary control

   c. Negative control

   d. Inverse control

3. From a well-controlled fMRI study showing that when participants judged a moral conflict there was increased activity in the Anterior Cingulate Cortex (ACC) you can conclude that:

   a. Brain activity in the ACC caused the moral choice.

   b. Considering moral conflicts caused a change in activity in the ACC.

   c. People judging moral conflicts are less likely to have increased activity in the ACC.

   d. The ACC is a brain area controlling moral conflict resolution.

4. Show how to counterbalance the order of treatments A, B, C, and D.

Subject	First treatment	Second treatment	Third treatment	Fourth treatment
1				
2				
3				
4				

THINK ABOUT IT

Each of the experiments described below has a major flaw. Can you determine what it is?

1. A researcher wanted to demonstrate that the use of Ritalin in childhood predisposed women to substance abuse in adolescence. She asked all her friends how many years they had taken Ritalin as children and how often they took drugs in college. She had to discard several data points because they were probably not accurate; she was pretty sure some friends had not told her the truth. Her results supported her hypothesis.

2. A student was under time pressure to get his thesis completed. Unfortunately, the drug he needed for his experiment was on back order and would not be available for another month. He used the month to collect all his control data, so that when the drug arrived, all he had to do was to collect the data from the drug-treated group to complete his experiment.

3. To demonstrate the role of integrins (cell adhesion receptors) in changes in the nervous system associated with learning and memory, a research team measured several changes in the hippocampus that were well established as measures related to learning and memory. They compared results from control experiments using mice from a common inbred strain to results from knockout mice missing a specific integrin.

4. When Josie counted labeled cells in Area X, there were, as she had expected, very few labeled cells, or at least the cells were not so densely labeled that she thought they were appreciably above background levels. When she moved to count cells in Area Z, much to her delight, her hypothesis was confirmed: these cells looked much more densely labeled.

SUGGESTIONS FOR FURTHER READING

Bandettini, P. A. (2009). What's new in neuroimaging methods? *Annals of the New York Academy of Science, 1156*, 260–293.

Gavériaux-Ruff, C., & Kieffer, B. L. (2007). Conditional gene targeting in the mouse nervous system: Insights into brain function and diseases. *Pharmacology Therapy, 113*, 619–634.

McCutcheon, J. E., & Marinelli, M. (2009). Age matters. *European Journal of Neuroscience, 29*, 997–1014.

Pangalos, M. N., Schechter, L. E., & Hurko, O. (2007). Drug development for CNS disorders: Strategies for balancing risk and reducing attrition. *Nature Reviews Drug Discovery, 6*, 521–532.

Pollo, A, & Benedetti, F. (2009). The placebo response: Neurobiological and clinical issues of neurobiological relevance. *Progress in Brain Research, 175*, 283–294.

More Than One Predictor Variable

Factorial Designs

So far, we have considered only experiments where one variable was manipulated. In many cases, more than one independent variable is manipulated, leading to factorial designs or more complex designs. You need an excellent background in statistics before using complex experimental designs, because the design of the experiment must be compatible with the constraints of the statistical tests you intend to employ for analysis. In this chapter, you will get a basic introduction to these complex designs, leaving the details necessary for a professional level of competence to a course in advanced research design.

WHY INCLUDE MORE THAN ONE INDEPENDENT OR PREDICTOR VARIABLE?

One reason to include more than one independent variable in an experiment is to examine interactions between independent variables. A **factorial design** is a research design that includes more than one independent variable. The term *factorial* indicates that all possible combinations of all levels of the independent variables are examined. This allows the investigator to assess whether the association between the intervention/condition and the outcome is different for subgroups.

For instance, in one study, the volume of the hippocampus on the left and right sides of the brain was measured in three groups of people. Participants were patients with schizophrenia, people who had relatives with schizophrenia, or healthy controls. The focus was on the hippocampus, because previous studies had indicated that this brain region was smaller in patients with schizophrenia. The hippocampus is important in learning and memory, and it is particularly important in the types of learning and memory that are most impaired in patients with schizophrenia. The researchers were interested in determining risk factors for schizophrenia and therefore hypothesized that a decrease in hippocampal volume might also occur in relatives of patients with schizophrenia. They did see differences among these groups of participants, but only for the left hippocampus. Thus, including both left and right hippocampus in the experiment was very important because the results differ depending on which side of the brain is analyzed. The relatives of patients with schizophrenia showed reduced left hippocampal volume, similar to the patients with schizophrenia, indicating that this may be an effect of a genetic contribution to the cause of schizophrenia (Seidman et al., 2002).

Another example is the study by Lu et al. (2005), in which the researchers sought to determine the neural pathways underlying an addict's craving for cocaine during withdrawal. They studied rats that had been trained to press a lever to get intravenous cocaine infusions. Another lever was always present, and pressing this lever had no effect. After 10 days of the rats self-administering cocaine, the experimenters started the withdrawal phase, in which they no longer gave the rat access to cocaine. Rats were then brought back to the chamber with two levers after 30 days of withdrawal. They demonstrated their craving for cocaine by pressing more often on the lever that had previously delivered cocaine than the lever that was not previously associated with cocaine. Earlier research showed increased levels of phosphorylated extracellular signal-regulated kinase (pERK) in the central amygdala in rats given this test for cocaine craving. The amygdala is a brain region involved in emotion and some forms of learning, and pERK is an important cellular signaling molecule. To test if pERK in the central amygdala is a necessary signal for drug-induced craving, the researchers administered a drug that blocks pERK. The drug was directly infused into the central amygdala in some rats, and in other rats the same drug was infused into the nearby basolateral amygdala. Figure 6.1 shows the experimental design. Cocaine craving was detected at high levels in rats given the drug in the basolateral amygdala and in control rats given vehicle infusions into either area of the amygdala. The rats given infusions of the drug that blocks pERK into the central amygdala responded much less to the lever previously associated with cocaine. Perhaps this research will point toward a treatment to help people resist drug cravings during drug withdrawal.

Figure 6.1 | Schematic Showing the Design of the Experiment

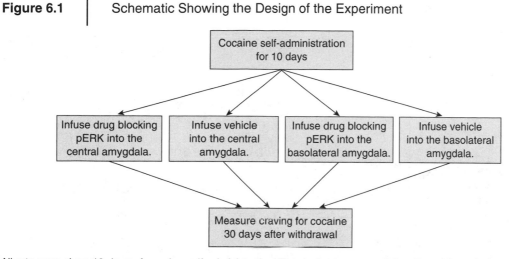

All rats were given 10 days of cocaine self-administration. Then animals were split into four groups. One group of rats received infusions of a drug that blocks phosphorylation of extracellular signal-regulated kinase (ERK) into the central amygdala, and another group of rats received control infusions of the vehicle into the same area. A third group of rats received infusions of the drug into a nearby area, the basolateral amygdala, whereas a fourth group received control vehicle infusions into the same area. Craving for cocaine 30 days after withdrawal was measured in all rats by testing lever pressing in the chamber where cocaine had previously been administered.

SOURCE: Lu et al., 2005.

DESCRIBING FACTORIAL DESIGNS

The simplest factorial design is the 2×2 factorial design, with two independent variables, each with two levels. The number of **levels** of an independent variable is the number of different values of the variable. For example, if you wanted to study age and nicotine as the two independent variables, each independent variable would have two levels in a 2×2 factorial design, such as one group getting no nicotine and the other group getting a moderate dose of nicotine, with two ages, young and old, tested in each condition. A similar study with more levels of the independent variable could include groups with no nicotine, a low dose of nicotine, a moderate dose, and a high dose. In that case, the independent variable "nicotine" has four levels. If you also studied young and old ages, then you would be carrying out a 4×2 factorial experiment. A 4×2 factorial design has two independent variables, one with two levels and the other with four levels. A $5 \times 3 \times 2$ factorial design contains three independent variables, the independent variables having, respectively, five, three, and two levels. Although this would be complex to set up and interpret, it allows the potential to understand complex higher order relationships. To summarize, the terminology for labeling factorial designs uses one numeral for each independent variable, and the numeral indicates the number of levels for that independent variable (see Figure 6.2).

Figure 6.2 | Schematic Representation of 2 × 2, 3 × 3, and 2 × 3 × 2 Factorial Designs

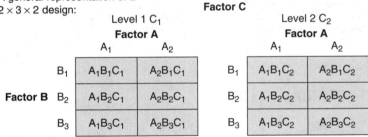

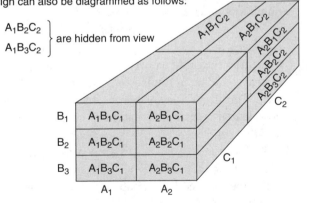

Note that the total number of treatment conditions in each design can be obtained by multiplying the number of levels of each factor.

Because a factorial design includes all possible combinations of all levels of the independent variables, a 2×2 factorial design includes four groups. The number of groups increases rapidly as the design increases in complexity. A 3×4 factorial design has 12 groups. A 3×2 factorial design has 24 groups. Let's say you needed a minimum of 5 subjects in each group to have a reasonable estimate of the variation in responses. That means you need 20 subjects for a 2×2 factorial, 60 subjects for a 3×4 factorial, and a whopping 120 subjects for a $3 \times 4 \times 2$ factorial design.

In a factorial design, you might be able to control for important subject variables by conducting a *within-subjects design,* in which each subject experiences each combination of the independent variables. Thus, in the within-subjects 2×2 factorial design, each subject experiences each of the four possible combinations.

A **mixed design** is another possible variant. In a mixed design, one or more independent variables are varied within subjects, while one or more other independent variables are between subjects. To specify the design of a study with a mixed design, you should describe the specific variables. For example, you might say: "This study was a 2×4 mixed factorial, with the variable of surgery (brain surgery or sham surgery) varied between subjects and the variable of drug dose (0.1, 1, 10, or 100 mg/kg) varied within subjects."

DESCRIBING RESULTS FROM FACTORIAL DESIGNS: MAIN EFFECTS AND INTERACTIONS

You can analyze the results from a factorial experiment to see if each independent variable alone had an effect on your dependent variable. The effect of one independent variable, ignoring the variation in the other independent variable, is called the **main effect** of that independent variable.

Of course, a major advantage of conducting a factorial experiment is to measure interactions between the independent variables. If the effect of one independent variable depends on the level of another independent variable, then you have an **interaction.** For example, in the experiment shown in Figure 6.1, the effects of the drug versus vehicle infusion (one independent variable) depended on the brain target (the other independent variable). Drug infusion reduced cocaine craving only when it was infused into the central amygdala and not when it was infused into the basolateral amygdala.

You can use statistical techniques to determine if main effects or interactions are significant in a statistical sense (for example, see the analysis of variance, discussed in Appendix A). For a simplified discussion of this admittedly complex topic, let us consider possible results of a 2×2 factorial experiment, with the results summarized by the mean for each group. For these simplified examples, you can assume that any difference in the means reflects a meaningful difference between the groups and that each mean represents the average score of a sample of subjects. I show each possible outcome summarized in Figure 6.3 in three forms: a table of the means, a line graph, and a bar histogram.

In this hypothetical 2 × 2 factorial, let us call one independent variable "A" and the other independent variable "B." Each independent variable has two levels, labeled "1" and "2." The table in Figure 6.3 shows the results in one scenario. The mean for each group is identical. There is no main effect of either independent variable and no interaction.

Figure 6.3 | Possible Outcome of a 2 x 2 Factorial Design

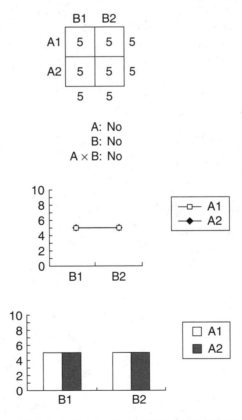

One possible outcome of a 2 × 2 factorial design: no main effect of either independent variable and no interaction between the independent variables. The two independent variables are labeled A and B, and each has two levels. All four samples had the same mean, as shown in the table, the line graph, and the histogram.

Figure 6.4 shows examples of two other possible outcomes. On the left is the outcome of a main effect for independent Variable B but no main effect of A and no interaction between A and B. There is a main effect for Variable B because the dependent variable shows greater values at Level 2 of Variable B as compared to Level 1. Because we look for main effects of individual independent variables by ignoring the levels of the other independent variable, it is often helpful to add to our summary tables the means for each independent variable while ignoring the other independent variable. This is done in Figure 6.4 (note where the means are added for each row or column). Thus, the means for

Figure 6.4   Two Potential Outcomes of a 2 × 2 Factorial Design

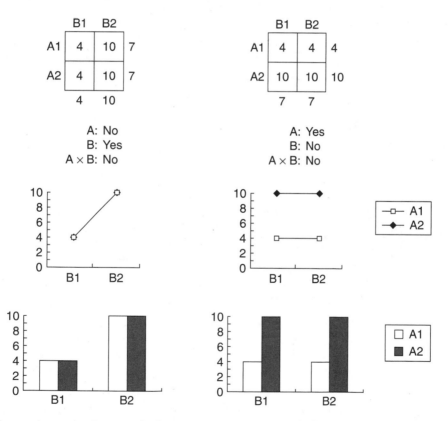

In this and subsequent examples, the row and column means are given adjacent to the table to allow comparisons for the main effect of each independent variable. In the example shown on the left, there is no main effect of independent Variable A, as indicated by the overall means for groups A1 and A2 being identical (7). There is a main effect for independent Variable B, indicated by the overall mean for the B1 sample (4) being less than the overall mean for the B2 sample (10). There is no interaction between A and B. On the right, there is a main effect of Variable A but no main effect of Variable B and no interaction between A and B.

both levels of Variable A are 7 in this example, indicating no main effect of Variable A. On the right in Figure 6.4 is the outcome of a main effect for independent Variable A but no main effect of B and no interaction between A and B.

Figure 6.5 shows results when both independent variables have main effects, but there is no interaction or when both independent variables have main effects and there is an interaction. You will note that the two lines on the graph on the right are not parallel. This indicates an interaction. Of course, in the real world, we can expect some variability. We rely on statistical tests to determine if there is a statistically reliable interaction between the variables, but in these simplified cases, the presence of lines that are not parallel indicates an interaction between the independent variables.

Figure 6.5 | Other Possible Outcomes of a 2 × 2 Factorial Design

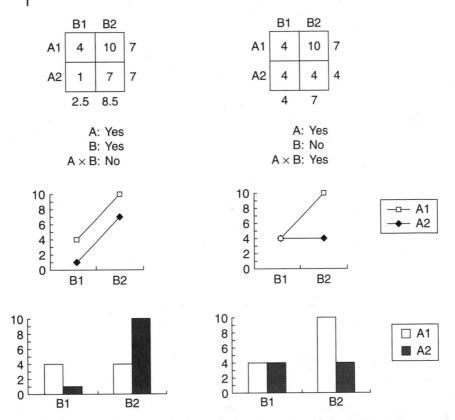

On the left, each independent variable produced a main effect, but there is no interaction between the two independent variables. On the right, there is similarly a main effect for each independent variable, and there is an interaction between the two independent variables. The effect of Variable A on the dependent variable depends on the level of the other independent variable, Variable B. When B is at level one, A has no effect on the dependent variable; however, when B is at level two, A has a large effect on the dependent variable. This is an interaction.

What does an interaction mean? You determine this by carefully examining the results. As a rule, when there is an interaction, you must discuss the effect of one independent variable taking into account the level of the other independent variable. In the example in Figure 6.5, variable B alters the dependent variable only when variable A is at level 1. When variable A is at level 2, there is no effect of variable B on the dependent variable. Note that I stated earlier that this case demonstrated an outcome where there is a main effect for variable B as well as for variable A. The statement that there is a main effect of variable B is based on the summary of the data only when we do not consider variable A. In fact, the more accurate statement of the results is the complex one, that variable B alters the dependent variable only when variable A is at level 1.

Figure 6.6 shows two examples of results when there is a main effect of only one independent variable and there is an interaction between the two independent

Figure 6.6   Possible Outcomes of a 2 × 2 Factorial Design

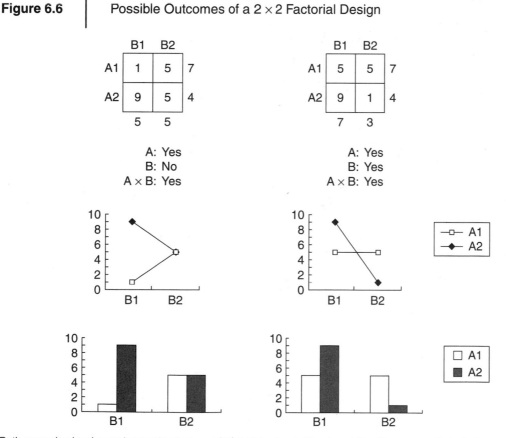

Both examples involve an interaction between independent variables A and B, with an example including a main effect for A shown on the left and a main effect for B shown on the right.

variables. Note that on the graph on the right, the two lines cross. The effect of the independent Variable A is opposite when the other independent variable changes level. What is the main effect of A? Clearly, the main effect of A cannot be described without stipulating the level of B. Note that in each of these examples, there is a main effect for only one of the independent variables. The other variable has no main effect, but that variable does influence the results; its effect on the dependent variable depends on the level of the other independent variable.

Figure 6.7 demonstrates the results when there is no main effect for either independent variable, but there is an interaction between the two independent variables. As you study this graph, note that the effects of each independent variable depend very much on the level of the other independent variable. However, if you had done your experiment using just one independent variable alone, you

| **Figure 6.7** | Interaction but No Main Effects |

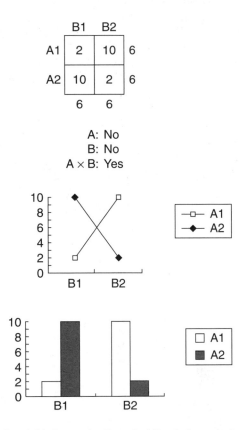

Example of a 2 × 2 factorial design that yielded no main effects for either independent variable, but an interaction between the two independent variables.

might not have measured any difference between the groups. To measure the effect of the independent variable on the dependent variable, you must consider the level of the other independent variable.

EXAMPLES OF 2 × 2 FACTORIAL EXPERIMENTS

Example 1

Do agricultural chemicals have lasting effects on brain and behavior? A study by Skinner and colleagues (2008) looked at the effects of exposure to an agricultural chemical, vinclozolin, over 3 generations. They had two groups of pregnant rats, one group exposed to vinclozolin and one not exposed. They then studied the offspring of the offspring of these original rats, what they call the "F3" generation (you might think of these as the grandchildren of the original rats). They measured different changes in levels of gene expression in the hippocampus and the amygdala, as well as different effects on anxiety and activity, in the male and female rats of the F3 generation. Interestingly, the females that descended from vinclozolin-exposed mothers showed more anxiety than females from control-group mothers; the opposite effect was seen for males. This is a 2 × 2 factorial design, with two independent variables, chemical exposure (exposed or not) and gender of the F3 offspring (male or female). There is an interaction; the effect of the mother's chemical exposure depends upon the level of the other independent variable, gender of the F3 offspring.

Example 2

Menthol, an active ingredient of peppermint, can have effects on neurons, possibly acting on receptors that also respond to cold temperatures. To determine if menthol might alter sensory input to the nervous system, researchers studied the communication between "dorsal root ganglion" neurons that normally provide sensory input and the "dorsal horn" spinal cord neurons that are the first recipients of this input (Tsuzuki, Xing, Ling, & Gu, 2004). They studied these neurons in cell culture, measuring miniature excitatory postsynaptic currents (mEPSCs) in dorsal horn neurons. The dorsal horn neurons were studied either when cultured alone ("monoculture") or when cultured in the same dish as the dorsal root ganglion neurons ("coculture"). When menthol was applied to the coculture, there was an increase in mEPSCs. This effect was not observed in the monocultures. Cold stimulation caused a similar increase in mEPSCs in cocultures but also caused a decrease in mEPSCs in monocultures (see Figure 6.8).

This is a 2 × 2 factorial design, with two independent variables, type of culture (monoculture versus coculture) and type of stimulation (menthol or cold stimulation). There is an interaction between the two independent variables; we cannot describe the effect of type of stimulation without taking into account the type of culture.

Figure 6.8 | Effects of Menthol on Neurons

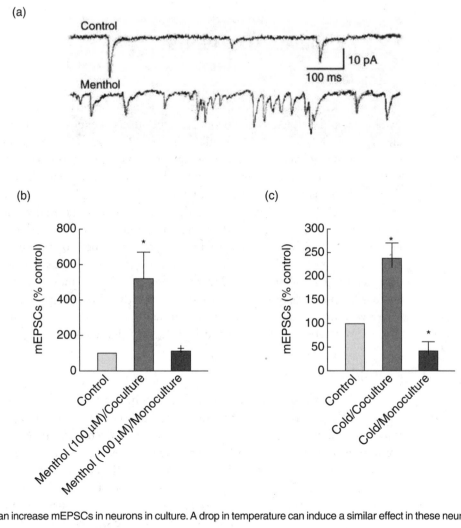

Menthol can increase mEPSCs in neurons in culture. A drop in temperature can induce a similar effect in these neuron cultures.

SOURCE: Tsuzuki, Xing, Ling, & Gu, 2004, Fig. 1. Reprinted by permission of the Society for Neuroscience.

OTHER DESIGNS WITH MORE THAN ONE INDEPENDENT VARIABLE

You will not use a factorial design every time you include more than one independent variable. Recall that the term *factorial* means that every possible combination of every level of each independent variable is included. This is not always the best design. You should first determine the research question you would like to answer and then select the design that makes the most sense.

For example, consider the experiment conducted by Tillerson et al. (2001). I will first describe this experiment in a simplified manner and then describe the additional conditions that make this experimental design complex. This research group was intrigued by reports (Taub, Uswatte, & Pidikiti, 1999) that stroke patients show improved function in an affected limb if they are forced to use the weakened limb for a time after the stroke. They wondered if a similar therapy might help patients suffering from Parkinson's disease, a neurodegenerative disorder that involves progressive motor weakness. They decided to test this hypothesis using rats with damage to the dopaminergic cells that degenerate during Parkinson's disease. To induce this damage, they injected some rats with 6-hydroxydopamine, a neurotoxin that selectively destroys dopaminergic neurons. They placed these injections on one side of the brain only, so that the rat has one side of its body experiencing motor weakness, while the other side of the body is unimpaired. One group of rats received a plaster cast that immobilized the good forelimb, the one on the side unaffected by the neurotoxin, for the week following surgery. This treatment forced the rat to use the limb weakened by the dopaminergic neurotoxin treatment. A second group of rats received the injection of neurotoxin but no cast. A third and a fourth group of rats received all the anesthesia and procedures for surgical injection of the neurotoxin, but were not administered any neurotoxin; these are the sham surgery controls. One group of sham surgery rats received casts on one limb for the week following surgery, and the other group received no cast. Thus, in this experiment, there are two independent variables: type of surgery (neurotoxin injection or sham surgery) and limb treatment (cast or no cast).

To measure limb use after these treatments, the researchers videotaped rats exploring a transparent cylinder and scored the number of times the rat used either limb while rearing up and down and exploring the walls of the cylinder. They found that rats with the injection of neurotoxin and no cast were asymmetric in their forelimb use 2 months after surgery. This indicates that the loss of the dopaminergic cells on one side of the brain in these rats caused a lasting motor weakness on one side of the body. The rats with sham surgery showed no deficits after surgery; they used both forelimbs with equal frequency. What was the effect of the cast? Rats with a cast on one limb for a week after sham surgery showed no lasting effects from the cast treatment on their limb use; they used both forelimbs with equal frequency when tested 2 months later. Amazingly, rats treated with the neurotoxin but wearing a cast for the week following surgery also showed no motor weakness when tested 2 months later. Thus, results from this 2×2 factorial design indicate that forcing the use of a limb weakened by damage to dopaminergic neurons can prevent lasting motor effects of that damage. Figure 6.9 gives a schematic representation of these results.

Figure 6.9 | Schematic Representation of the Results From the Tillerson Experiment

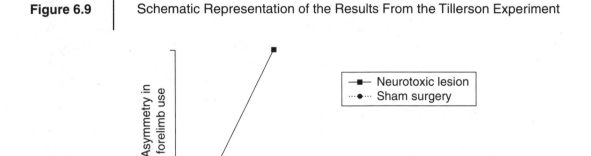

Effects of neurotoxic lesions on asymmetry in use of the forelimbs were abolished by treatment with a cast on one limb to encourage use of the weakened forelimb during the week after surgery.

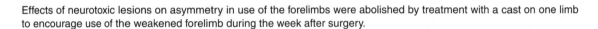

SOURCE: Tillerson et al., 2001. Reprinted by permission of the Society for Neuroscience.

Up until now, this looks like a 2×2 factorial design, right? However, the preceding description of this experiment is extremely simplified. The researchers actually included more experimental groups: rats that received casts to immobilize the unimpaired limb during the second week after surgery, for example. They also included more dependent variables than the one discussed. For example, they tested limb use at multiple times following surgery, and they measured levels of dopamine and dopamine metabolites in the brain (see Figure 6.10).

The analysis and interpretation of complex designs such as this one can be challenging, but there are good reasons to include multiple groups and multiple times. In this case, the researchers kept the number of animals used to investigate this question to a minimum by conducting an experiment with a complex design. The same rats could be used to gather information at different times, and the final measures of neurochemistry could be collected from the same animals that were used for behavioral testing. The researchers could measure the effect of varied timing of cast treatment against the same control groups, again reducing the need for animal subjects. Another advantage is that they could examine correlations between the dependent measures. For example, they found that the degree of dopamine depletion in the brain was correlated with motor weakness in the forelimb ($r = 0.75$; see Chapter 7). This is strong support for their hypothesis that forcing use of a weakened limb actually protects against neuronal damage. This study points to exciting new possibilities for the treatment of Parkinson's and other neurodegenerative disorders with intensive physical therapy.

Figure 6.10 | Further Results From the Tillerson Experiment

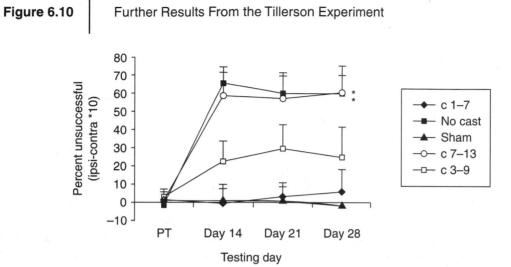

Animals were tested prior to the experiment ("pt" or pretest), and days 14, 21, and 28 following surgery. One group received sham surgery ("sham"). The limb was either not in a cast ("no cast") or in cast for days 1–7 ("c 1–7"), days 7–13 ("c 7–13"), or days 3–9 ("c 3–9"). The test was conducted by bringing a rat toward a countertop and gently brushing its whiskers on the edge of the countertop. An intact rat will place both forelimbs on the countertop. A rat was scored as "unsuccessful" if only one limb was placed on the countertop.

SOURCE: Tillerson et al., 2001. Reprinted by permission of the Society for Neuroscience.

✓ CHECK YOUR UNDERSTANDING

Do you ever find yourself sitting on the couch, lazily watching an exercise show on TV? Let us face it; that is never going to get you physically fit. In the same way, you will never grasp factorial designs just by passively sitting there. Get out a pencil and paper and complete the exercises below.

1. What is a factorial design?

2. How many independent variables are there in a 2×10 factorial design?

3. How many groups are there in a 4×3 factorial design?

4. In a 4×6 factorial experiment, there are two independent variables. One independent variable has ____ levels and the other one has ____ levels. Thus, there are ____ groups in this experiment.

5. A 4×3 factorial experiment has ____ independent variables. If there are 10 subjects per group and the experiment is totally between subjects, you will need ____ subjects in total.

6. Draw a plot that illustrates results from a 2 x 2 factorial experiment with two main effects and a significant interaction.

THINK ABOUT IT

For each of the following descriptions of experiments, summarize the results in a table. Determine if there appears to be a main effect of each independent variable and if there is an interaction.

1. Does early developmental exposure to aspirin alter adult male sexual behavior? Pregnant rats were given drinking water treated with a children's chewable aspirin for 7 days prior to giving birth and 7 days following birth (Amateau & McCarthy, 2004). Sexual behavior of male offspring was observed when they were adults. Two trials were used for observing behavior. On the first trial, males exposed to aspirin took 450 seconds before mounting the female, whereas control male rats mounted the female after 100 seconds. On the second trial, males exposed to aspirin took 275 seconds before mounting the female, whereas control males mounted the female after 150 seconds.

2. Researchers studying Alzheimer's disease are interested in the function of the amyloid peptide. In research directed toward understanding the response of neurons to extracellular amyloid peptide, primary cultures of human neurons were exposed to either amyloid-1–40, amyloid-1–42, a reverse control peptide amyloid-40–1, or cultures were left untreated (Zhang et al., 2003). To determine if factors in the serum within the culture medium might alter the cellular response, half the cultures were maintained without serum and half received serum. Levels of a neural growth factor receptor were measured. Results from all groups were similar except for two conditions that showed increased receptor levels: (1) cells exposed to no serum and amyloid-1–40 and (2) cells exposed to no serum and amyloid-1–42.

3. Replot the data in Figures 6.4 through 6.7 as line graphs with Variable A shown as the two categories on the x axis and Variable B as the two lines demarcated by different symbols.

SUGGESTIONS FOR FURTHER READING

Gonzalez, R. (2009). *Data analysis for experimental design.* New York: Guilford Press.

Correlational Designs

CHAPTER

7

DESIGNING A CORRELATIONAL STUDY

A **correlational design** can allow you to measure the relationship between two or more variables. In this design, you might measure two or more variables on a continuous scale for each experimental unit. We will focus on a simple linear correlation, when the expected relationship between the two variables is a linear one. There are other correlational designs, such as the point biserial correlation in which one variable is measured on a binary scale instead of a continuous scale, and designs with multiple correlations. An advanced statistics textbook, such as the one cited at the end of this chapter, would be a good source for information on such designs.

You can carry out a correlational study fairly easily. Pick two variables you can measure from the same subject or case. For example, if the neurons in a stained slide were your cases, you could measure the length of the major dendrite emanating from a neuron and the width of the soma or cell body. Collect the observations, two numbers for each neuron, and you have the data for a correlational study.

Correlation of variables is useful when it is difficult to manipulate variables. For example, consider the study on brain areas and memory published by Rodrigue and Raz (2004). These researchers were interested in determining if specific neuroanatomical changes could be associated with the commonly reported decline in memory seen with aging. This question lends itself very well to a correlational design. The researchers measured the change in volume in certain brain areas between two brain scans taken 5 years apart and calculated an "annualized percent shrinkage" for each participant. They also had participants complete a series of tests designed to measure their ability to remember newly learned items after a short time delay and combined the memory test scores to get a "delayed memory composite score" for each participant.

SCATTERPLOTS

As the first step of analysis in a correlational design, examine a **scatterplot,** with each of the two variables of interest shown on the *x* and *y* axes and each individual case shown as a point (see Figure 7.1). You can put either variable on the *x* or *y* axis, although if you suspect one variable might be the explanatory factor in the relationship, it is customary to put that variable on the *x* axis. Examining the scatterplot, you determine if the relationship between the two variables appears to be linear. If the scatterplot suggests a nonlinear relationship, there is no sense proceeding with a specifically linear correlational analysis. In fact, two variables may be strongly related in curvilinear manner, but a correlational analysis looking for a linear relationship could wrongly suggest the two variables are not related at all. This makes the first step, examining the scatterplot for the shape of the relationship, particularly

Figure 7.1 | Scatterplot Showing Relationship Between Annualized Shrinkage of the Entorhinal Cortex and Memory Test Scores

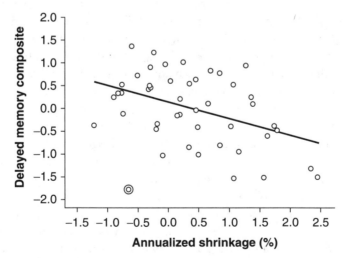

Each white point indicates the value of the two variables for one participant. The line indicates the linear relationship between the two variables; as shrinkage of the entorhinal cortex increased, memory scores decreased. The circled point was considered an outlier.

SOURCE: Rodrigue & Raz, 2004, Fig. 3A. Reprinted by permission of the Society for Neuroscience.

important. A scatterplot can help you determine if two variables have a linear relationship (see Figure 7.1) or a nonlinear relationship (see examples in Figure 7.2). There are special techniques for measuring the strength of a nonlinear relationship between two variables, which are not covered here.

Figure 7.2 | Scatterplots Showing Curvilinear Relationships of Two Variables

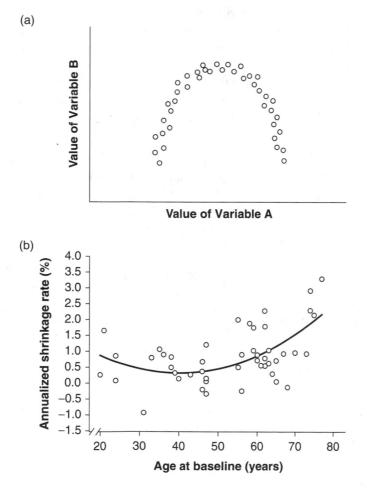

(a) This scatterplot demonstrates two variables that are strongly related in a curvilinear relationship. The Pearson product correlation coefficient (see text) would be zero, indicating no relationship, because this coefficient measures the strength of a linear relationship only. Other techniques would be needed to analyze results such as these. (b) This scatterplot shows two variables that are related but are better fit by a quadratic curve rather than a line. The annualized shrinkage of the hippocampus is shown as a function of the participant's age. These two variables appear to be related, but advanced analysis techniques indicated that a quadratic curve (drawn on the scatterplot) describes the relationship better than a straight line does.

SOURCE: Rodrigue & Raz, 2004, Fig. 1C. Reprinted by permission of the Society for Neuroscience.

THE PEARSON PRODUCT CORRELATION COEFFICIENT

The strength and the direction of the linear relationship between the two variables is summarized in the **Pearson product correlation coefficient,** "*r*." The value of *r* lies between −1 and 1. An *r* value greater than 1 or less than −1 is impossible. How do you interpret various *r* values? As Figure 7.3 shows you, *r* = 0 indicates no linear relationship between the two variables. An *r* = −1 value indicates a perfect negative linear relationship. An *r* = −1 indicates a perfect positive relationship. The *r* value generally lies somewhere between these extremes. An *r* = .77 indicates a moderately strong positive linear correlation, as opposed to an *r* = .50, which indicates a weaker positive linear relationship.

You need to use either interval or ratio scales (see Chapter 4) to measure your variables in a correlational study if you want to summarize your results using the Pearson product correlation coefficient.

Figure 7.3 | Scatterplots Illustrating a Range of Possible Outcomes for a Correlational Design

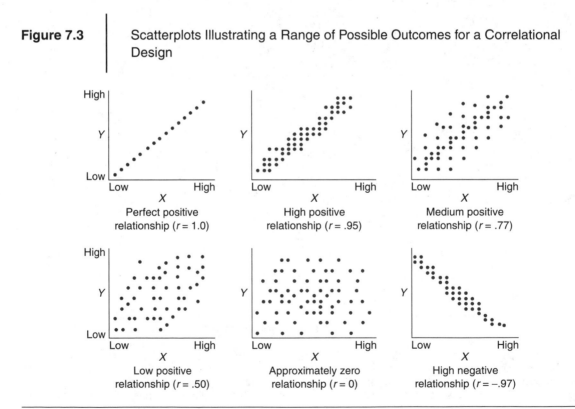

SOURCE: From Ray, *Methods Toward a Science of Behavior and Experience,* 7E. © 2003 Wadsworth, a part of Cengage Learning, Inc. Reproduced by permission. www.cengage.com/permissions

The Pearson product correlation coefficient is not resistant to the effects of **outliers,** points well out of the range of the other points. For example, study the scatterplots in Figure 7.4. In Figure 7.4 (a), most points fall into a pattern suggesting a moderate positive linear relationship. However, the two points falling outside the overall pattern of the majority of points influence the value of the correlation coefficient r so that we end up with an r value suggesting a stronger positive relationship than is warranted by the majority of the data points. In Figure 7.4 (b), although the general scatter of points suggests a moderate positive linear relationship, two outliers fall outside the general cluster, and these outliers would artificially reduce the magnitude of the measured relationship between the two variables. Be aware of the potential effects of outliers and, when you examine your scatterplot, note the presence of outliers. How can you determine if an outlier is influencing your results? Calculate the r value without that point and see if the resultant r value differs dramatically from the r value found with all points included. Rodrigue and Raz (2004) did just this with the data in Figure 7.1, and they found that deletion of one outlier point improved their r value from the original $r = .40$ to $r = .48$. They report both values because they have no reason to completely delete the outlier point from the data set. The original value, $r = .40$, is the most correct to cite. Note, however, that the relationship might be even stronger than this reported value indicates, given the influence of this outlier.

Figure 7.4 | Location of Outliers Can Influence the Correlation Coefficient

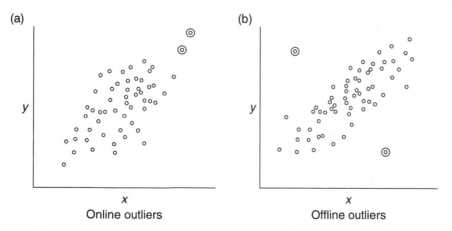

(a)

y

x
Online outliers

(b)

y

x
Offline outliers

In (a), the two circled outliers will increase the strength of the measured correlation. In (b), the two outliers will decrease the strength of the correlation.

Although this discussion focuses on the Pearson product correlation coefficient, a measure restricted to variables on a ratio or an interval scale, you should be aware of another statistic. If you have measured a variable using the ordinal scale of measurement, you can calculate the strength of the correlation using the **Spearman rank correlation coefficient** (for more information, see Heiman, 2001). This correlation coefficient is also more resistant to the effects of outliers, so in some instances you might use it if you were concerned about the effects of outliers.

CAUTIONS IN INTERPRETING RESULTS FROM CORRELATIONAL STUDIES

Remember that correlational studies are not true experiments. When you find that two variables are strongly correlated, you cannot make strong conclusions about what causes that relationship. In particular, you must remember that *correlation does not imply causation.* A strong correlation between two variables is an important *clue,* and it is a finding that deserves careful interpretation. Whether one variable acts to cause the associated changes in the other variable is impossible to answer from correlational studies. One explanation for a strong correlation between two variables is that a **third variable** influences the relationship. A third variable is a variable that is related to each of the other two variables and, by this association, makes the two variables you did measure look correlated. Yet the unmeasured third variable is actually the causal factor. For example, as Figure 7.1 shows, the delayed memory score was correlated with the changes in volume in the entorhinal cortex for participants in this study. Does this mean that these two variables directly affect each other? Does loss of entorhinal cortex cause poor memory performance? Might a third variable explain this relationship? In this case, a plausible third variable is the age of the participant; perhaps older participants have both poorer memory and reduced entorhinal cortex volume. In fact, the authors investigated this variable and found that while memory scores did decline with age (see Figure 7.5), there was no correlation between age and shrinkage of the entorhinal cortex (see Figure 7.6). To totally explain the original correlation between entorhinal cortex shrinkage and delayed memory score as being due to age, the third variable, age would have to be correlated with *both* original variables—entorhinal cortex shrinkage and delayed memory score.

The correlation you measure is, of course, indicating the relationship between the two variables only *within the range you measured.* Always be cautious when applying your findings outside of that range. The shape, direction, and magnitude of the relationship may change dramatically as you alter the range of values of the measured variables (see Figure 7.7 on page 120). In some instances, you might explain a failure to find that two variables are correlated by the problem of **restricted range**, not examining data from a wide enough range.

Figure 7.5 | Investigating a Third Variable

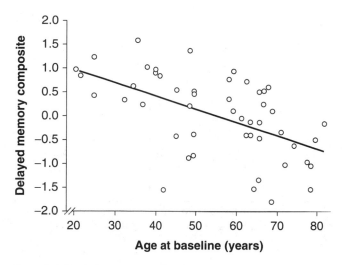

This figure demonstrates the correlation between age and memory.

SOURCE: Rodrigue & Raz, 2004. Reprinted by permission of the Society for Neuroscience.

Figure 7.6 | Investigating a Third Variable

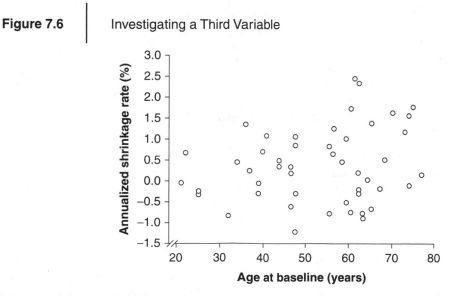

This scatterplot demonstrates the lack of statistically significant linear relationship between the age of the participant and the annualized shrinkage of the entorhinal cortex.

SOURCE: Rodrigue & Raz, 2004. Reprinted by permission of the Society for Neuroscience.

Figure 7.7 | Scatterplots Showing Restricted Range and Correlation

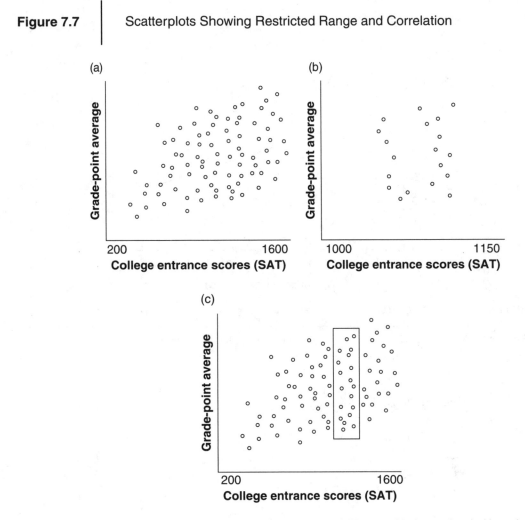

When sampled over a wide range (from 200 to 1,600), scores on the SAT are positively correlated with grade-point average, as (a) shows. When a highly restricted range of SAT scores (from 1,000 to 1,150) are sampled (b), there is no correlation with grade-point average. The scatterplot in (c) shows the placement of the sample with too restricted a range within the larger sample that adequately samples the range of possible SAT scores.

SOURCE: Leary, 2001, Figs. 6.4 & 6.6. Copyright © 2001 by Pearson Education. Reprinted by permission of Allyn & Bacon.

In a study related to how brain state changes with behavioral state, researchers focused on the neuropeptide orexin that has been shown to help regulate sleep-wake states. Lack of orexin produces the sleep disorder narcolepsy. To measure activation of the neurons, these neuroscientists used measures of "Fos," a protein marker for certain types of cell activation (Hoffman & Lyo, 2002). When they measured Fos protein within neurons containing the neuropeptide orexin, the percentage of orexin neurons containing Fos was positively correlated with the amount of wakefulness and negatively correlated with the amount of rapid eye movement sleep (see Figure 7.8). Note from these scatterplots that if the researchers had studied animals with 0% to 5% REM or 80% to 100% wakefulness, then they would have concluded that these behavioral state variables are not related to the percentage of orexin neurons containing Fos. They were able to discover this relationship only because they sampled a wide enough range of behavioral states.

You cannot treat correlation coefficients like ordinary numbers. For instance, you cannot calculate several correlation coefficients and then take the average of them. A correlation of 0.6 does not represent a relationship that is twice as strong as a correlation of 0.3. You can compare Pearson correlation coefficients by using the square of the coefficient (r^2) In a general sense, r^2 is the proportion of variance in one set of measures that is accounted for by variation in the other measure. Thus, a correlation of 0.6 means that 36% of the variation in one measure is accounted for by variation in the other measure. You can also determine the probability of that particular r value occurring by chance, given your specific sample size, and thus determine the statistical significance of the r value.

Figure 7.8 Relationship Between Percent of Neurons Containing Orexin That Are Also Labeled for "Fos" Protein and Prior Wakefulness

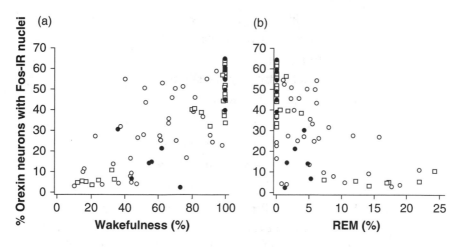

(a) There is a positive correlation between percentage of orexin neurons containing Fos-IR (immunoreactive) nuclei and percentage of wakefulness in the time immediately before examining the brain ($r = 0.78$). (b) There is a negative correlation with the percentage of rapid eye movement (REM) sleep in the same time ($r = 0.63$). To ensure an extensive range of behavioral states, the researchers sampled brains from animals in three experiments. In Experiment 1 (●), brain tissue came from animals sampled at different times of day. In Experiment 2 (●), the stimulant metamphetamine was given to the animals to increase wakefulness. In Experiment 3 (□), researchers sleep deprived animals for 2 hours before taking measurements.

SOURCE: Estabrooke et al., 2001, Fig. 7. Reprinted by permission of the Society for Neuroscience.

In summary, three major problems plague interpretation of correlational studies. Correlation does not imply causation, a caution that applies to all correlational studies. If a strong correlation has been measured, the researcher must worry about a potential third variable explaining the result. If no correlation or a weak correlation appears, the researcher should worry about the potential for a problem with restricted range. Despite all these cautions, a strong correlation means *something*. If two variables are strongly correlated, there is often a relationship worth investigating. At times I fear that the mantra "Correlation does not imply causation" can lead young scientists to dismiss the information contained within a correlational study. There is certainly interesting information to be gained from such studies, and in some cases they are the best approach to the research question of interest.

✓ CHECK YOUR UNDERSTANDING

1. When analyzing results from a correlational study you should first plot the results in a scatterplot. Here you are looking for:
   a. Outliers
   b. A linear relationship
   c. A curvilinear relationship
   d. All of the above

2. An "r" value of 1.5 indicates:
   a. A strong positive correlation
   b. A strong negative correlation
   c. A mistake in your calculations
   d. A curvilinear relationship

3. The independent variable in a correlational study is:
   a. The variable that follows in time
   b. The variable that best predicts the results
   c. There is no independent variable
   d. The variable you expect causes the results

4. The scale of measurement that you should use in a correlational study using the Pearson correlation coefficient is/are:
   a. Ordinal scale
   b. Either ratio or interval scales
   c. Either nominal or ratio scales
   d. Only ratio scale

5. A correlation coefficient is strongly affected by outliers. Thus it is considered to be a:

a. Resistant measure

b. Reliable measure

c. Unreliable measure

d. Not a resistant measure

6. The best explanation for why you might be a strong correlation between the number of churches and the number of bars in different towns is:

a. Correlation does not imply causation

b. Restricted range

c. Third variable

d. Using the wrong scale of measurement

THINK ABOUT IT

1. Design critique: The volume of gray matter in certain cortical areas can be calculated from magnetic resonance imaging (MRI). Posthuma et al. (2002) report that the volume of gray matter is correlated with general intelligence (abbreviated "g," measured by a standardized test, the WAIS-IIIR). Monozygotic twins (identical twins) had a correlation of 0.26 between gray matter and g, and dizygotic twins had no correlation between gray matter volume and g (the correlation for dizygotic twins was not statistically significantly different from zero). The authors conclude that genetic factors, rather than environmental factors, cause the correlation between general intelligence and brain volume. Do you agree with this conclusion based on the results of their study? Why or why not?

2. Draw a scatterplot of the following data. The correlation coefficient for these data is $r = 0.90$. What would you conclude in your results section from this analysis?

Subject	Body weight (grams)	Serotonin in Area X (mol/mg tissue)
1	100	.03
2	110	.05
3	105	.06
4	130	.09
5	160	.25
6	90	.03
7	100	.04
8	125	.05
9	105	.01

3. There is a particular pleasure we sometimes feel when witnessing another's misfortune. This strange pleasure is called "schadenfreude" and is especially intense when an envied person falls upon a bit of poor fortune. Researchers looking for brain correlates of schadenfreude found an area of the ventral striatum activated in experiments when participants reported experiencing schadenfreude in response to made-up scenarios presented to them during fMRI scans (Takahashi et al., 2009). Striatal activation was correlated with activity in another brain region, the dorsal anterior cingulate cortex, an area that showed activity related to feelings of envy they measured from their participants (see Figure 7.9). What cautions would you advise in drawing conclusions from this correlational study?

Figure 7.9 Scatterplot Showing Relationship Between Activity in an Area Associated With Envy (the Dorsal Anterior Cingulate Cortex) and Activity Associated With Schadenfreude (the Ventral Striatum)

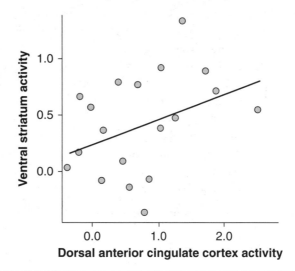

SOURCE: Modified from Takahashi et al., 2009.

SUGGESTIONS FOR FURTHER READING

Griffiths, D. (2009). *Head first statistics: A brain friendly guide*. Sebastopol, CA: O'Reilly Media.

ON THE WEB

Gazzaniga, M. S. (2008). *Essay: Arts and cognition: Findings hint at relationships* (The 2008 Progress report on brain research). Available from the Dana Foundation website: http://www.dana.org/news/publications/detail.aspx?id=10768

Becoming an Independent Investigator

CHAPTER

8

You now have a background on the basics of experimental design and can begin your training as a professional scientist by actually conducting experiments. I will try to cover some topics in this chapter that may be of common interest to students with a wide range of backgrounds starting a research career in neuroscience. I am inspired by the relevance of much of the general advice in Santiago Ramón y Cajal's book *Advice for a Young Investigator*, first published in 1897. Despite being more than 100 years old, this book has advice that is still relevant today. I will intersperse quotes from that book within this chapter.

TRAIN AS A SCIENTIST

Throughout this book I have encouraged you to find a mentor and, using what resources are currently available to you, begin research by conducting experiments. This hands-on training is essential for your development as a neuroscientist. You would not learn a craft by listening to a lecture about it; the best way to learn experimental skills is by conducting experiments and interpreting your results. You will also find the results of your own investigations enlivening and inspiring. On the other hand, I encourage you to continue taking classes to broaden your training. In particular, having a solid background in each major scientific discipline

NOTE: Excerpts in Chapter 8 from Cajal, S. (1999). *Advice for a young investigator*. Cambridge, MA: MIT Press. (Original work published 1897.)

(physics, chemistry, biology, and psychology) is good preparation for a career as an interdisciplinary scientist. Taking as much math as possible as well as acquiring skills in computer science will give you necessary quantitative tools for thinking about your data and summarizing your findings. If you are curious and tenaciously follow a question in your research, you will soon be straying into new territory; a broad scientific background will allow you to read widely and discuss your ideas with scientists trained in other fields.

Think of yourself as a scientist, not just a neuroscientist. For example, you may want to follow your current interest in the social neuroscience of empathy by conducting fMRI studies. Clearly, you will want specialized training in social psychology, the physics of electricity and magnetism, and computer-based analysis of large data sets. Your training should also include courses with a broader sweep, so that you can adapt over the years, as your interest in empathy leads you in new directions. For example, you may find that interactions between the digestive system and the brain underlie some "gut reactions," and a course in physiology will allow you to delve into primary literature relating to that. On the other hand, you may find the relationship between empathy and health of interest, and will want some background in immunology to better understand studies on links between training such as compassion meditation and immune system markers (see Pace et al., 2009). You cannot safely assume that your interests will always stay within a clearly demarcated field, even if your field of choice is one as broad as neuroscience. It may be better for you to think of yourself as a scientist, rather than as a neuroscientist, or as a cognitive neuroscientist. Seeing yourself as a young scientist, perhaps with a current interest in a subfield such as cognitive neuroscience or molecular neuroscience, may keep you open to training your mind for a lifetime of investigations into uncharted territories.

> If a supreme intelligence knew all the mysterious explanations linking all phenomena in the universe, there would be *one single science* instead of many different sciences. The frontiers that appear to separate fields of learning, the formal scaffolding of our classification scheme, the artificial division of things to please our intellects—which can only view reality in stages and by facets—would disappear completely in the eyes of such an individual. (Ramón y Cajal, 1999, p. 55)

SELECTING A RESEARCH PROBLEM

Often a beginning student will worry that the research problem his or her mentor has suggested as a good first project is too small and likely insignificant.

Ramón y Cajal (1999) is quite reassuring on this topic, pointing out many examples of observations that were once thought of minor importance and only later became obviously highly significant:

> In summary, there are no small problems. Problems that appear small are large problems that are not understood. Instead of tiny details unworthy of the intellectual, we have men whose tiny intellects cannot rise to penetrate the infinitesimal. Nature is a harmonious mechanism where all parts, including those appearing to play a secondary role, cooperate in the functional whole. In contemplating this mechanism, shallow men arbitrarily divide its parts into essential and secondary, whereas the insightful thinker is content with classifying them as understood and poorly understood, ignoring for the moment their size and immediately useful properties. No one can predict their importance in the future. (p. 17)

It is also important to consider that many discoveries that have had great benefit for human health and welfare were achieved through basic science and the ultimate applications of the discoveries were often not clear for many years.

> For the present, let us cultivate science for its own sake, without considering its applications. They will always come, whether in years or perhaps even in centuries. It matters very little whether scientific truth is used by our sons or by our grandsons. The course of progress obviously would have suffered if Galvani, Volta, Faraday, and Hertz who discovered the fundamental properties of electricity, had discounted their findings because there were no industrial applications for them at the time. (Ramón y Cajal, 1999, p. 19)

A beginning student might have an impression that a scientific discovery is a huge accomplishment, something way out of his or her reach as a student and perhaps forever. I hope you are now more aware that science is progressive and discoveries are often small incremental steps (see Box 8.1).

> Discovery is often a matter of simply fitting a piece of data to a law, or wrapping it in a broader theoretical framework, or, finally, classifying it. Thus, it may be concluded that to discover is to name something correctly, something that had been christened incorrectly or conditionally before. (Ramón y Cajal, 1999, p. 54)

BOX 8.1	**MORE, PLEASE!**
	Steps in Implementing Your Project

Follow these steps to get a good start to a research project:

1. Start with a clear research question of interest to both you and your research mentor.

2. Read reviews and journal articles and understand what has previously been done on this question.

3. Specify your research hypothesis. Write a detailed protocol for your experiments, review the plan with your mentor, and keep that plan in your lab book so you can follow it closely. Before you start your project, secure approval from the IRB or IACUC as necessary.

4. Conduct your experiments, keeping detailed notes in your lab notebook.

5. Analyze the results as soon as possible. Discuss the findings with your mentor. Sometimes it is possible to alter the experimental protocol based on feedback from the early results, something you should only do with the approval of your mentor and the appropriate regulatory committees.

6. Take every opportunity to discuss your results with other scientists. Give a lunch-bag talk at your institution or present your work at a scientific meeting.

KEEPING A LAB NOTEBOOK

As you begin your research on a topic, you should keep all your notes in one place. This is often in a bound notebook. You should ask your mentor for guidance in how you should maintain this notebook, because different labs have different procedures. Your lab notebook is the property of the lab you are working in, so if you would like to keep copies of the notes for yourself, you should use a type of notebook that includes a carbon sheet and extra pages to provide a copy you can take with you. Always date your entries, and staple or tape in stray papers so they will not be misplaced. Do not write notes on the experiment somewhere else, intending to neatly copy them into your book at a later point; it is better if your book is slightly messy but accurate, and copying over notes can bring in errors. A lab notebook should be understandable to the scientist who is directing the experiments, so write clearly, in a common language, and keep to abbreviations you know the head of the lab will understand. This should be a place where your mentor can survey your progress and help you determine future directions. I will tell you to write down absolutely every detail, even ones you think you will remember, but it is my experience that students only learn to do this through the experience of being asked about a key detail of their experiment and finding they are unable to retrieve that, either from their memory or their lab notebook.

You will likely also have computer files that contain data from your experiments. Treat these with similar principles. Keep the raw data protected and perform analyses on a copy, so you can always go back to the raw data. The files should be organized so that your supervisor can find information. There should be explanatory notes that help guide others as to the content of the files, and explanations if data were altered or discarded. The files should be backed up and a copy should remain in the lab in a secure location.

MASTERING YOUR TECHNIQUE

As you begin your investigations, you will apply a particular technique. You should take the approach of learning a craft, aiming to get as good as you possibly can be in mastering this technique. You can read protocol books and methodological papers both to understand how to conduct your experiment and to understand the history and full background of that technique. You can correspond with other experts using that technique, and perhaps visit a lab acknowledged to be an expert in that technique, where you will likely receive tips that never made it into the published protocol books. However, there is no substitute for working long hours with a focus of simply becoming the best possible in this technical approach. Your ability to make novel discoveries will depend on your mastery of the technique you are applying. Ramón y Cajal (1999) recommends that you aim to achieve mastery of the most difficult techniques:

> The latest research techniques can be given preference, but first priority must go to the most difficult because they are the least exploited. Time wasted on experiments that don't work does not matter. If the method has very high resolution, the desired results will have real importance, and will repay our eagerness and zeal quite handsomely. Moreover, difficult techniques provide us the inestimable advantage of proceeding almost alone, finding very few imitators and competitors along the way. (p. 65)

The entire process is sure to take a lot longer than your first estimate. Even with years of experience, I should double my estimates for how long it will take me to master a new technique. When using a technique that is new to you, it is critical to carefully design your experiment with both positive and negative controls. Constantly question your results and strive to perfect your approach with patience and hard work. You do not need the brains of a genius at this stage of investigation; patience and ambition are much more important. Ramón y Cajal (1999) suggests that a scholar of science has two key emotions: "a devotion to truth and a passion for reputation" (p. 40). Because you will be judged on the quality of your results, it does not matter to your reputation if this takes you a long time. Even if other students are more quick-witted or faster when completing exams, in science you can succeed with long hours of concentrated toil. Someone who has found that schoolwork comes very easily to them may not have cultivated the potential to engage in long hours of focused concentration. " . . . as a very common compensation *slow* brains have great endurance for prolonged concentration. They open wide, deep furrows in problems, whereas facile brains often tire quickly after scarcely clearing the land" (p. 24).

COMMUNICATING YOUR RESULTS

Conducting experiments and keeping the results to yourself serves no purpose. Science is a social activity, and a key obligation is to communicate your findings in a timely and clear manner. Your initial presentations will probably be informal talks at lab meetings, when you can summarize experimental procedures and results and expect to get quick feedback on your thoughts. You will very likely then present a poster at a scientific meeting, and will be able to quickly explain your findings to interested people who come by your poster. You might be asked to give a talk at a scientific meeting, often fitting all of your findings into a 10 minute time slot. Finally, you will want to write up your results in a paper for publication in a peer-reviewed journal article.

There are many resources available to you to help hone your communication skills. See the suggestions listed at the end of this chapter for some sources that I have found most useful. Use Appendix B for guidance as you learn to write an effective paper for publication. Remember to be considerate and thorough in acknowledging the sources for your ideas and the prior research that provided a scaffold for your contribution. Take pleasure in your own findings, but maintain the humility that every insightful scientist shares.

> Even when the work of a genius is subjected to critical analysis and no errors are found, it is important to realize that everything he has discovered in a particular field is almost nothing in comparison with what remains to be discovered. (Ramón y Cajal, 1999, p. 10)

REVIEW OF ALL RESEARCH DESIGNS

We have now examined a wide variety of research study designs. The exercises that follow draw upon all these designs. Before you attempt them, it might be helpful to review the designs we have considered.

In a **descriptive study,** a phenomenon is observed in a careful and replicable manner.

A **case study** is the in-depth description of a single subject. If you include in your study more than one individual with the same disorder, this would be a **multiple case study.** If you also include control subjects for each case, this is a **case control design.**

In a **correlational design,** two variables are measured from each subject. Researchers examine the relationship between the two variables to determine if the value of one variable changes systematically with the other.

An **experiment** examines the effect of at least one independent variable on a dependent variable. All other variables are controlled. A **two-group experiment** measures the effect of one independent variable, with two levels, on a dependent variable. A **multiple-group experiment** measures the effect of one independent variable, with more than two levels, on a dependent variable. A **quasi-experiment** has many characteristics of a true experiment, but lacks a critical aspect, most often being random assignment of subjects to groups.

A **factorial design** measures the effect of more than one independent variable on a dependent variable. Factorial design experiments are described by the number of independent variables and the number of levels of each independent variable. For example, a 3 x 4 factorial has two independent variables, one with three levels and the other with four levels.

Each independent variable may be varied either within subjects or between subjects. In a **within-subjects design,** each subject experiences each level of that independent variable. In an **independent-samples design,** also called a **between-subjects design,** each subject experiences only one level of each independent variable.

A **time-series design** measures the dependent variable over time, with the level of the independent variable changed in a sequential manner.

✓ CHECK YOUR UNDERSTANDING

A. For each research study briefly described here, indicate the independent variable(s), the dependent variable(s), and the research design. Specify the research design as completely as possible.

1. A study of Vietnam veterans demonstrated that the severity of symptoms of posttraumatic stress syndrome was inversely related to the volume of the hippocampus (Gilbertson et al., 2002).

2. Phosphorylation of the microtubule-associated protein tau was shown to be increased in the hippocampus of hibernating ground squirrels (Arendt et al., 2003). Ground squirrels were killed either 2 days after the onset of torpor (low body temperature associated with hibernation) or 7 days after the onset of torpor. Brains from these animals were compared to those from ground squirrels killed either 1 hour or 8 hours after arousal from torpor. Brain tissue from a control group of animals that had not been hibernating was included.

3. To develop better treatments for people with spinal cord injuries, researchers conducted a study using rats given a moderate contusion injury of the ninth thoracic spinal cord segment (Takami et al., 2002). All rats in this study received the same injury. Rats were randomly assigned to treatment groups 1 week following the injury. Treatment consisted of an infusion of Schwann cells, olfactory ensheathing glia, a mixture of Schwann cells and olfactory ensheathing glia, or culture medium. Once a week, an observer blind to the treatment group assessed how well the rats used their hind limbs. Twelve weeks after surgery, the rats were humanely killed and spinal cord tissue was examined for nerve regrowth.

4. If some sex differences in the brain arise from mechanisms using cell death, would these sex differences be reduced in the brains of transgenic mice over-expressing a protein that can reduce cell death? Brains from male and female mice over-expressing Bcl-2 were compared to wildtype control mice (Zup et al., 2003). Transgenic mice showed reduced sex differences in hypothalamic and spinal cord areas important for regulation of sexual behavior.

5. Poremba and associates (2003) measured the rates of glucose use in the primate auditory cortex using an awake, passively listening rhesus monkey. The researchers compared the glucose use in one hemisphere of the brain with that in the other hemisphere, which was isolated from all auditory input. They found a very large area of cortex responding to auditory input when mapped in this way.

6. A method for culturing embryonic inner ear cells was developed (Bianchi, Person, & Penney, 2002). Researchers found that cells in culture formed groups, and in some groups, hair cells could be detected. The hair cells showed further development over time in culture, with increases in hair-cell-specific proteins and in the number of characteristic stereocilia.

7. Studies directed toward treatment of amyotrophic lateral sclerosis (ALS) often use mice with a mutation in the gene for superoxide dismutase-1, because these mice display the symptoms of this disease and the progressive degeneration of spinal cord motor neurons underlying this disorder. A study using these mutant mice compared motor neuron degeneration in mice injected with a virus carrying the growth factor "insulin growth factor-1." Results were compared with mutant mice treated with a virus carrying another growth factor and mutant mice injected with a virus containing no growth factor (Kaspar, Llado, Sherkat, Rothstein, & Gage, 2003).

8. Openings of single ion channels in cultured cortical neurons were measured following application of N-methyl-D-aspartate (NMDA) to activate the glutamate receptors (Kleckner & Pallotta, 1995). Channel openings occurred in bursts. Although the first channel opening in each burst had a shorter duration than the rest, all subsequent channel openings showed a similar duration of open time.

9. Do leptin injections cause animals to eat less because they make them feel nauseous? Rodents cannot vomit, so it is difficult to determine if they feel nauseous. One way to answer this question is to pair leptin injections with a distinctive taste. If animals later avoid that taste, they probably were conditioned to dislike the taste because it was paired with that sick feeling. To determine if the animals could show such "taste avoidance conditioning," a control group had the new taste paired with injections of lithium chloride, a substance known to induce such conditioning (Buckley & Schneider, 2001).

10. Previous research suggested that some patients with particular types of temporal lobe damage show a deficit in naming animals, fruits, and vegetables, but have no problem in naming furniture, tools, and articles of clothing. Researchers suggested that this type of damage disrupts the patient's ability to name living things, sparing the ability to name nonliving things. Study of one such patient indicated that the naming deficit was also observed when the patient was asked to name musical instruments (Dixon, Piskopos, & Schweizer, 2000). The authors propose that the deficit is better described as specific to "psychological distance" rather than to the living-nonliving dichotomy.

B. List the important variables in the study described in the abstracts below and indicate if they are independent, dependent, or controlled variable. Then give your best description of the experimental design of the study.

Abstract 1

Social isolation prevents exercise-induced proliferation of hippocampal progenitor cells in female rats.

Social isolation negatively affects the behavior and health of laboratory rats. Recently, it has been found that social isolation retards exercise-induced neurogenesis in the hippocampal dentate gyrus (DG) of male rats. Since male and female rats react differently to housing changes and exercise opportunities, we investigated whether social isolation would also suppress the exercise-dependent increase in proliferation of dentate gyrus progenitor cells in females. Accordingly, female rats were housed either alone (isolated) or in groups (social) with (exercise) or without (sedentary) the opportunity to run in an exercise wheel. Proliferating progenitor cells were labeled with bromodeoxyuridine (BrdU). As expected, exercise increased the number of BrdU+ cells in socially housed animals. However, isolation prevented this running-induced increase. Our results expand upon previous findings by showing that the female brain is also susceptible to the suppressive effect of social isolation on exercise-induced neurogenesis (Leasure & Decker, 2009).

Abstract 2

Epigenetic regulation of the glucocorticoid receptor in human brain associates with childhood abuse.

Maternal care influences hypothalamic-pituitary-adrenal (HPA) function in the rat through epigenetic programming of glucocorticoid receptor expression. In humans, childhood abuse alters HPA stress responses and increases the risk of suicide. We examined epigenetic differences in a neuron-specific glucocorticoid receptor (*NR3C1*) promoter between postmortem hippocampus obtained from suicide victims with a history of childhood abuse and those from either suicide victims with no childhood abuse or controls. We found decreased levels of glucocorticoid receptor mRNA, as well as mRNA transcripts bearing the glucocorticoid receptor 1_F splice variant and increased cytosine methylation of an *NR3C1* promoter. . . . These findings translate previous results from rat to humans and suggest a common effect of parental care on the epigenetic regulation of hippocampal glucocorticoid receptor expression (McGowan et al., 2009).

C. The questions below all relate to a study on Alzheimer's disease using mice with a transgene that makes them a good model of Alzheimer's disease.

1. Researchers compared transgenic Alzheimer's disease mice with control wildtype mice (Kuchibhotla, Lattarulo, Hyman, & Bacskai (2009). They measured astrocyte activity in the brains of living mice, visualizing

amyloid plaques (a pathology associated with Alzheimer's disease), and intracellular calcium levels in neurons and astrocytes. The study is best described as:

a. An observational study

b. A multiple case study

c. An independent-samples design

d. All of the above

2. Based on the description above, the independent variable(s) in this study is (are): _____

3. Based on the description in Question 3, the dependent variable(s) in this study is (are): _____

4. The Alzheimer's disease mice in this experiment are referred to as "APP/PS1." Figure 8.1 below shows that there was a higher percentage of active astrocytes in the Alzheimer's disease mice when compared to the wildtype mice brains. In a subsequent experiment, the authors compared the Alzheimer's disease mice, who had signs of Alzheimer's disease present (as shown by the amyloid plaques) with young mice of the same strain, before they developed AD.

Figure 8.1 | Results From the Experiment

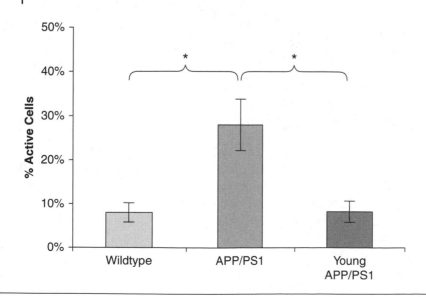

SOURCE: Kuchibhotla, Lattarulo, Hyman, & Bacskai, 2009.

The best conclusion from this figure would be:

    a. There is no reliable difference among the three groups.

    b. Inferential statistics allow conclusions that all three groups differ from each other.

    c. Inferential statistics indicate that wildtype and APP/PS1 differ, and Young APP/PS1 differ from wildtype.

    d. The descriptive statistics (mean and standard error of the mean) allow the conclusion that that there are significantly more active cells in the APP/PS1 mice.

    e. None of the above

5. In comparing the older Alzheimer's disease mice that have developed plaques with the younger Alzheimer's disease mice that have not yet developed plaques, the authors would like to consider the presence or absence of plaques as the independent variable. In this case age is a:

    a. Confounding variable

    b. Uncontrolled variable

    c. Controlled variable

    d. Dependent variable

6. The increased astrocyte activity was organized into waves of increased intracellular calcium that spread from cell to cell across the cerebral cortex. The cell that started each wave (the "initiator cell") was often located near an amyloid plaque, with measurements indicating they were an average of 25 microns away from the plaque. The scale of measurement used here was:

    a. Nominal

    b. Ratio

    c. Ordinal

    d. Interval

7. Does altered neuronal activity cause the changes in astrocytic activity? To test this, you could apply tetrodotoxin to block neuronal activity and measure astrocyte activity in wildtype versus Alzheimer's disease mice brains. The flaw in this experiment is:

    a. No control group; the necessary control group is _____

    b. A confounding variable, which is _____

    c. An important uncontrolled variable, which is _____

    d. There is no flaw apparent

8. I would like to apply this study to develop a new treatment for Alzheimer's disease. I have a drug that I now think could be very helpful in memory problems given its effect on astrocyte activity. But I want to be cautious in drawing conclusions. Given that I want to reduce the risk of raising false hopes and declaring the drug is helpful when in fact it is not, I should:

   a. Reduce my risk of a Type I error by increasing alpha

   b. Change alpha to .001 to reduce my risk of a Type II error

   c. Reduce the risk of a Type I error by changing alpha to .001

   d. Use $p < .05$

THINK ABOUT IT

Each of the following papers is short and would be appropriate to help you apply concepts learned in this book. For each paper, answer the 12 questions in Table 3.2.

1. Vaiva, G., Ducrocq, F., Jezequel, K., Averland, B., Lestavel, P., Brunet, A., et al. (2003). Immediate treatment with propranolol decreases post-traumatic stress disorder two months after trauma. *Biological Psychiatry, 54,* 947–949.

2. Thilo, K. V., Santoro, L., Walsh, V., & Blakemore, C. (2004). The site of saccadic suppression. *Nature Neuroscience, 7,* 13–143.

3. Posthuma, D., De Geus, E. J., Baare, W. F., Hulshoff Pol, H. E., Kahn, R. S., & Boomsma, D. I. (2002). The association between brain volume and intelligence is of genetic origin. *Nature Neuroscience, 5,* 83–84.

4. Abizaid, A., Mezei, G., Sotonyi, P., & Horvath, T. L. (2004). Sex differences in adult suprachiasmatic nucleus neurons emerging late prenatally in rats. *European Journal of Neuroscience, 19,* 2488–2496.

5. Bilkei-Gorzo, A., Racz, I., Michel, K., & Zimmer, A. (2002). Diminished anxiety- and depression-related behaviors in mice with selective deletion of the Tac1 gene. *Journal of Neuroscience, 22,* 10046–10052.

6. Genn, R. F., Tucci, S., Edwards, J. E., & File, S. E. (2003). Dietary restriction and nicotine can reduce anxiety in female rats. *Neuropsychopharmacology, 28,* 1257–1263.

7. Tobin, V. A., Hurst, G., Norrie, L., Dal Rio, F. P., Bull, P. M., & Ludwig, M. (2004). Thapsigargin-induced mobilization of dendritic dense-cored vesicles in rat supraoptic neurons. *European Journal of Neuroscience, 19,* 2909–2912.

8. Grashow, R., Brookings. T., & Marder. E. (2009). Reliable neuromodulation from circuits with variable underlying structure. *Proceedings of the National Academy of Science, 106,* 11742–11746.

SUGGESTIONS FOR FURTHER READING

Ramón y Cajal, S. (1999). *Advice for a young investigator* (N. Swanson & L. W. Swanson, Trans.). Cambridge MA: MIT Press.

Schwartz, M. A. (2008). The importance of stupidity in scientific research. *Journal of Cell Science, 121,* 1771.

Schwartzkroin, P. A. (2009). *So you want to be a scientist?* New York: Oxford University Press.

Tufte, E. R. (2006). *The cognitive style of PowerPoint.* Cheshire, CT: Graphics Press.

ON THE WEB

Guidelines for preparing and presenting scientific posters:

Swarthmore College. (n.d.). *Advice on designing scientific posters.* Available from: http://www.swarthmore.edu/NatSci/cpurrin1//posteradvice.htm

Society for Neuroscience. (n.d.). *Presentation tips* [Fact sheet]. Available from: http://www.sfn.org/am2009/index.aspx?pagename=resources_presentation

General advice to young scientists:

Cullen Lab [Neuroimaging of Action and Perception]. (n.d.). *Advice to young scientists.* Available from: http://psychology.uwo.ca/culhamlab/Academic Advice.html

Advice for success in graduate school:

University of Western Ontario. (n.d.) *Survival skills for graduate students.* Available from: http://www.physpharm.fmd.uwo.ca/undergrad/survivalwebv3/frame.htm

Working With Your Data

You have collected data to test a hypothesis, and now you want to analyze your results. Should you immediately input your numbers into a statistical software package and look for "statistically significant" results? If you make this your first step in analysis, you will miss a major opportunity. You can learn a lot from your numbers about the phenomenon you are studying, but only if you first spend some time getting to know them. My advice: Begin by examining the distribution of your data, then study and compare the descriptive statistics for each group. Only after careful study of your data set will you be prepared to select the appropriate statistical test. The results of that statistical test may be what are most often reported in final published reports, but the initial close examination of the data can yield unexpected bonuses. You may discover important information from further examining data points that fall outside the overall pattern. Do not ignore the discrepancies; such points often lead scientists to new and fruitful avenues of research.

EXAMINING THE DISTRIBUTION

The initial graph for displaying your data is a graph of the **distribution**. The distribution of a quantitative variable shows the pattern of variation. Was there an extraordinary amount of variation in your sample? Is there a pattern, such as all values bunching up in one area or the other? You can easily answer these questions by a glance at a graph of the distribution. The most common type of display of the distribution is a **frequency histogram,** which divides the range of values of the variable into intervals of equal size. These intervals are placed on the x axis, and the frequency or number of occurrences is plotted using the y axis. For example, consider the data in Figure A.1. This is hypothetical data, the type we might have collected had we conducted an experiment to determine if an NPY agonist reduced anxiety-related behaviors in an elevated plus maze.

Figure A.1 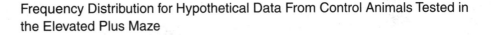 Frequency Distribution for Hypothetical Data From Control Animals Tested in the Elevated Plus Maze

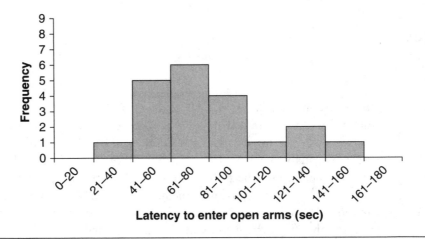

Your first step in data analysis is to examine the distribution. You can describe a distribution by its **shape, central tendency,** and **spread.** To begin, look at the overall shape. A distribution with one major peak is called **unimodal.** If the distribution has two major peaks, then it is **bimodal.** A distribution is **symmetric** if the shape of the distribution on either side of the midpoint is similar. If it is asymmetric, then it might be described as **skewed.** A distribution is negatively skewed if the bulk of the values fall to the right of the midrange point (larger values). The tail of the distribution appears to the left of the peak. I would label the distribution in Figure A.1 as unimodal and roughly symmetric. The distribution of data in Figure A.2, on the other hand, might be better described as skewed.

Figure A.2 | Hypothetical Data From Drug-Treated Animals Tested in the Elevated Plus Maze

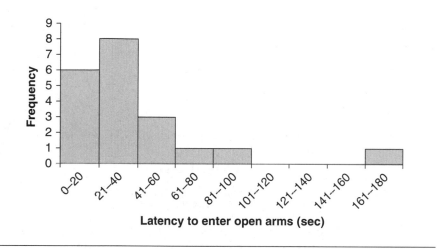

Looking at the overall pattern of your distribution might help you notice a few points that fall outside the overall pattern. These points might be outliers, individual data points that deviate strikingly from the overall distribution. For example, one point in the distribution of data in Figure A.2 falls outside of the general cluster of points. This data point might be considered an outlier; you will need to later determine if they qualify as outliers using quantitative criteria, one example of which will be introduced later in this appendix.

If you want to compare distributions of data sets with different total numbers of observations, you might use percents, often in this situation referred to as **relative frequencies**. All your frequency histograms should have the same y axis, from 0% to 100%, allowing easy comparisons across samples.

A frequency histogram resembles a bar graph, but these are very different creatures. The frequency histogram provides information about one variable only; the bar graph summarizes information on multiple variables. The x axis in a bar graph may consist of distinct categories, with no quantitative relationship. The x axis of a frequency histogram represents equal intervals of the total range of one variable (see Figure A.1). To distinguish these two very different types of graphs, leave a space between the bars of a bar graph, but leave no space between the bars of a frequency histogram.

STATISTICS

You may be interested in drawing conclusions about the entire population of interest, such as all human cortical neurons, but you will have data collected from a smaller sample drawn from that population. Statistics are calculated measures from a sample, often used to estimate parameters of the population.

Descriptive Statistics

To describe the distribution of data in your sample, recall that you should describe the shape, center, and spread. I have discussed ways to describe the shape. What about the center and spread? Descriptions of the center of a distribution are called **measures of central tendency,** whereas descriptions of the spread are called **measures of variability.** I will discuss these in turn.

Measures of Central Tendency

A simple way to describe the center of the distribution is to give the midpoint, more properly called the **median.** You find the median by ordering all the observations from smallest to largest. If you have an odd number of observations, the one in the middle of the ordered list is the median. If you have an even number of observations, then two observations will fall in the middle; find the average of these two observations and that average is the median.

Another measure of central tendency is the **mode,** the most commonly occurring number. What if you have a bimodal distribution, with two major peaks? The median will not fairly represent the center of the distribution. In this case, you may prefer to report the two modes.

By far the most common representation of the center of a distribution is neither the median nor the mode but the **mean**—the measure of central tendency that many common statistical tests use. The mean, or average, of a set of observations is the sum of all the observations divided by the number of observations. You should be mindful that the mean is a good measure of central tendency for a symmetric distribution or a distribution that is not skewed. If the distribution is not symmetric, another measure might better achieve your goal of representing the center of the distribution of data points. Why? Consider the measures of central tendency for the data in Figures A.1 and A.2 (see Table A.1). The outliers influence the mean such that it is larger than the median or the mode. The mean is more strongly influenced by a change in the value of one or two observations than is the median. The median is a much more appropriate measure in these examples. When the shape of a distribution is strongly skewed, the median is the optimal measure of central tendency (see Figure A.3).

Table A.1 | Measures of Central Tendency for Two Distributions With Different Shapes

Measure of Central Tendency	Data in Figure A.1	Data in Figure A.2
Mean	77.7	38.2
Median	71	23.5
Mode	66	21

Figure A.3 | Mean, Median, and Mode of Normal and Skewed Distributions

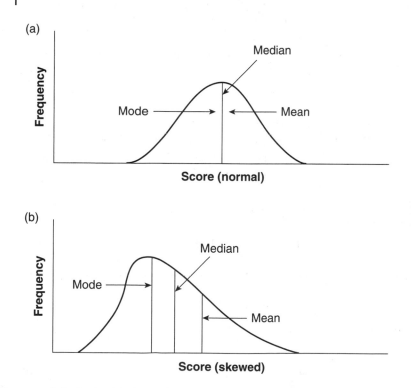

For a sample with a normal distribution (a), the mean, median, and mode are all good estimates of central tendency. For a sample with a skewed distribution (b), the median or mode are better estimates of the central tendency than is the mean.

SOURCE: From Ray, *Methods Toward a Science of Behavior and Experience,* 7E. © 2003 Wadsworth, a part of Cengage Learning, Inc. Reproduced by permission. www.cengage.com/permissions

When you examine the distribution of your data, you may be interested in more than describing the distribution's shape and selecting the most appropriate measure of central tendency. You will also be sleuthing a bit, looking for interesting details. For instance, an outlier might be a case to examine further. Why might that one animal have responded so differently to the drug treatment? Your lab book might have some hints. Perhaps the injection procedure did not go smoothly for that animal, so you may have doubts that the animal even received the drug treatment. Perhaps that animal consistently shows a different response to this drug. Examination of an outlier such as this can lead to the discovery of animals with spontaneous mutations. This is similar to how Martin Ralph discovered the circadian rhythm tau mutant hamster, an animal displaying odd behavior that an alert researcher noticed and investigated (Ralph & Menaker, 1988).

Measures of Variability

A measure of **variability** indicates the spread of the data. You should always report a measure of variability when you present a measure of central tendency. The combination of the measure of central tendency with the measure of variability furnishes a simple description of the data's distribution. Your choice of a measure of center will guide your choice of a measure of spread.

If you chose the median as your best measure for the center of the distribution, then you might turn to **quartiles** to represent the spread (see Box A.1). The first quartile is the point where 25% of the distribution falls at or below it. The median, representing the point of the 50th percentile, is the second quartile. The third quartile is the point where 75% of the distribution falls at or below it.

BOX A.1

TOOLS OF THE TRADE
Calculating the Quartiles

1. Order the observations from smallest to largest and locate the median.

2. The first quartile is the median of the observations falling below the median.

3. The third quartile is the median of the observations falling above the median.

The **interquartile range** is the distance between the first and the third quartile. This simple measure of spread tells the range of half the distribution. The interquartile range also provides an informal rule of thumb for identifying outliers. If an observation is more than 1.5 times the interquartile range above the third quartile or below the first quartile, you can flag this point as an outlier. This is an example of one possible quantitative definition of an outlier.

The **five-number summary** is the minimum, the first quartile, the median, the third quartile, and the maximum. The **box plot** uses the five-number summary to provide a graphical display of the distribution of data (see Box A.2 and Figure A.4).

BOX A.2	**TOOLS OF THE TRADE**
	The Box Plot

The central box of the box plot runs from the first quartile to the third quartile.

A line in the center of the central box indicates the median.

Observations that are suspected outliers (more than 1.5 times the interquartile range outside the central box) are plotted as individual points.

Lines extend from the central box to the largest and smallest observations that are not suspected outliers. These lines are called the **whiskers**.

Figure A.4 | Box Plots Comparing Data Shown in Figures A.1 and A.2

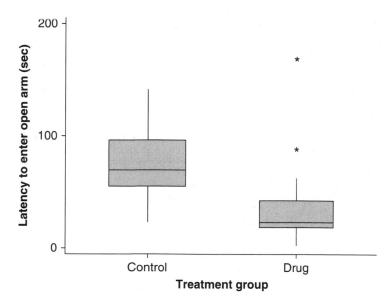

Each box indicates the range from the first quartile to the third quartile, and the line through the box indicates the median of that sample. Lines extend from the box to the largest and smallest observations that are not outliers,

If you chose the mean as your measure of central tendency, then the measure of variability that you will likely include is the **standard deviation**. The standard deviation is a measure of how much the observations vary from the mean (see Box A.3). To calculate the standard deviation, first *sum the squared deviations from the mean.* (Subtract the mean from each individual observation, square the result, and then sum all these "squared deviations from the mean.") Why are the deviations squared? If they were not all squared, some would be positive numbers, others would be negative numbers, and the sum would be zero. Squaring the deviations from the mean solves that problem and provides a measure that is larger when the *distribution* of data has greater spread around the mean.

BOX A.3	**TOOLS OF THE TRADE**
	The Standard Deviation

Subtract the mean from each observation and square the result.

Sum these squared deviations from the mean.

Divide the summed squared deviations from the mean by one less than the total number of observations $(n - 1)$.

The square root of the result gives the standard deviations.

$$s = \sqrt{\frac{\Sigma(x_i - \bar{x})^2}{n - 1}}$$

You must take the square root of the squared deviations from the mean to ensure that the standard deviation is in the same units as is the mean. Before we take the square root, the measure is called the **variance**, or s^2. The units of the variance are squared, so, for example, if the units for the mean are centimeters, then the units for the variance will be cm^2. The units for the standard deviation, however, would be the same as the mean, centimeters in this case.

We divide by $n-1$ because the last deviation can be calculated when we know the others. This occurs because all the deviations sum to zero. Thus, if you know $n-1$ deviations, the last deviation is not free to vary. The number $n-1$ is called the **degrees of freedom** of the standard deviation.

As with the mean, the standard deviation is not a resistant measure, meaning a few outliers can make the standard deviation very large. The standard deviation is a measure of variability that should be used only with the mean, never with any other measure of central tendency. It is explicitly a measure of variability around the mean. The standard deviation can provide a quantitative definition of an outlier; for example, it is common to define any points more than three standard deviations away from the mean as outliers.

The **standard error of the mean** is calculated as the standard deviation divided by the square root of n. When data are summarized by the mean and standard error of the mean, a bar graph often displays them, with the height of the bar indicating the mean. Error bars generally indicate the standard error of the mean. The top of the error bar is set to the sum of the mean and one standard error. For example, in Figure A.5, the mean for the control group was 77.7 and the standard error of the mean was 30, so the error bar extends to 107.7. Note that error bars might signify the standard deviation or some other measure, so it is essential to specify in your report what measure was used to create error bars. See Box A.4 for advice on making an effective figure.

Figure A.5   Bar Graph Comparing the Mean (+ Standard Error of the Mean) Latency to Enter the Open Arms for the Two Groups of Animals Tested on the Elevated Plus Maze (Control Versus Drug Treated)

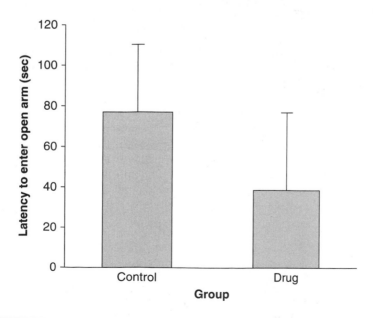

BOX A.4	**TOOLS OF THE TRADE**
	Do You Have a Good Figure?

Here I summarize a few key points from Edward Tufte's (1983) excellent book, *The Visual Display of Quantitative Information*. I recommend that you read this book; you will find it enjoyable and enlightening.

One way to assess a graphic is by the proportion of space devoted to portrayal of the data (data density). For example, Figure A.5 presents four numbers (two means and two standard errors) and two group labels, or a total of six data points. If it were printed a size of 6 square inches, it would have a data density of 1 number per square inch.

Contrast this to Figure A.6, where many more data points are presented (Haag & Borst, 2004). In this experiment, the researchers tested the response properties of neurons using a small black dot rotated at various locations in the visual field of the subject (a blowfly). For each position (defined by the azimuth and elevation of the visual field location), the researchers measured the neuron's response amplitude and preferred direction of rotation. In the summary figure, the arrow's direction gives information about the preferred direction of the neuron tested with stimuli of a particular azimuth and elevation. The arrow's length indicates the amplitude of response for each azimuth and elevation. Small circles indicate where the experimenters actually took measurements; arrows without small circles are interpolated data. The results suggest that these single neurons are detecting "optic flow fields," or the visual changes associated with self-motion. This figure has vastly greater data density than Figure A.5 does. You can improve a graphic by removing "nondata ink," or elements that do not represent the data. See the examples in Figure A.7 of the same data presented with more or less extra ink.

Figure A.6	Example of a Figure With High Data Density Response

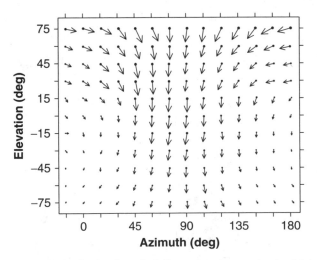

Characteristics of neurons are summarized using the orientations of each arrow to give information about the preferred direction of the neuron tested with stimuli at a particular azimuth and elevation within the visual field. Amplitude of the response at each location is summarized by the length of the each arrow.

SOURCE: Haag & Borst, 2004, Fig. 1a.

Figure A.7   Same Data Rendered in Two Figures With Varied Data Ink

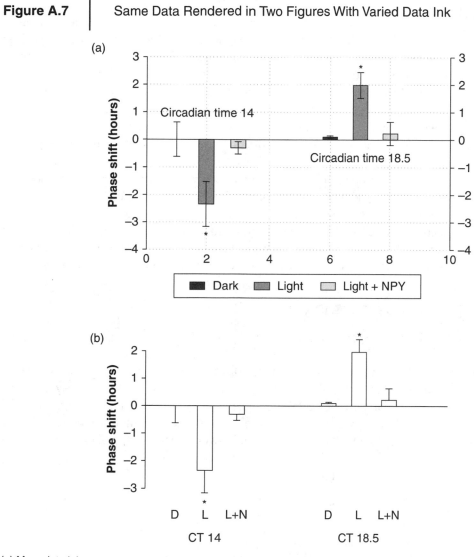

(a) More data ink or unnecessary elements clutter the figure. (b) Improved figure has less data ink.

SOURCE: Data from Yannielli & Harrington, 2000, Fig. 2.

Inferential Statistics

To make inferences from your samples to the entire population that you drew the sample from, you will need to use **inferential statistics**, which are based on the laws of probability and allow us to judge if samples are from different populations or, in other words, if there are "statistically significant" differences.

Parametric Versus Nonparametric Statistics

There are two major classes of inferential statistical tests. **Parametric inferential statistics** are based on several assumptions about the design of the study, most notably the assumption of randomly chosen, independent samples and an underlying normal distribution of the population parameters. Examples of parametric inferential statistics are the t-test and the analysis of variance (ANOVA), both described in more detail below. **Nonparametric inferential statistics** are based on fewer assumptions, generally requiring only that the samples are independent. Note that nonparametric inferential statistics do not assume that the underlying population has a normal distribution. One example of a nonparametric test is the chi-square test (see Box A.5). Other examples of nonparametric inferential statistics are the Mann-Whitney U test and the Kruskal-Wallis test. (For more information about these tests, see the resources listed at the end of this appendix.) In general, parametric tests are based on the mean and standard deviation, and nonparametric tests are based on the median or the relative ranks. In advanced courses in statistics, you will learn a series of tests that will allow you to determine which tests to apply.

BOX A.5	**TOOLS OF THE TRADE**
	The Chi-Square Test

The x^2 (chi-square) test is used in situations where you want to ask if two groups differ when your data are in the form of frequencies. If you used a nominal scale of measurement, you might use an x^2 test to analyze your results.

For example, a study of vascular growth patterns in samples from glioblastoma brain tumors indicated that patients whose tumors showed evidence of what the authors termed "bizarre angiogenesis" (very unusual patterns of blood vessels) survived less time than did patients showing normal patterns of blood vessel growth in the tumor samples (Birner et al., 2003). See the data below.

The chi-square test involves this calculation:

$$x^2 = \sum \frac{(O - E)^2}{E}$$

where "O" is the obtained frequency and "E" is the expected frequency.

The expected frequency is calculated for each cell in the table as the row total multiplied by the column total, divided by the total number of observations.

The null hypothesis is rejected if the obtained x^2 (x^2_{obt}) is greater than the critical value of x^2 (x^2_{crit}) for the set degrees of freedom. The degrees of freedom are calculated as the number of categories minus 1. In this example, $x^2(2) = 0.446$, a value that is not statistically significant.

This test has fewer assumptions than parametric tests, but there are still several key assumptions that must be met before using the x^2 test. First, the sample should be randomly selected, independent observations. To be independent, each observation should be generated by a different subject, and the score of one subject should in no way depend on the score of another subject.

This test will not perform well if the expected frequencies are very small (for example, less than 5).

Survival After Surgery	Normal Angiogenesis	"Bizarre" Angiogenesis	Total
Survived at least 12 months	15	36	51
Did not survive 12 months	14	45	59
Total	29	81	110

For both the *t*-test and the ANOVA, you must measure the dependent variable using ratio or interval scales of measurement (see Chapter 4).

The *t*-Test

The *t*-test is a parametric statistical test. It is based on assumptions of independent, randomly chosen samples and a population underlying the sample that has a normal distribution. If your sample indicates that the shape of the population distribution may be skewed, you will want to reconsider use of the *t*-test. For a single sample *t*-test, if your sample size is large (say, $n > 40$), the *t*-test may still give valid results. However, as your sample size gets smaller, the *t*-test is much more sensitive to violations of the assumption of normality. If your sample size is less than 15, you should use the *t*-test only if the data indicate the distribution is close to normal. The two-sample *t*-test can be used with smaller samples in the individual groups, as long as the sum of your two samples' sizes is greater than 10 to 15. Another assumption of the two-sample *t*-test is that the populations have similar variance ("homogeneity of variance"), an assumption that additional statistical tests can check. This is especially important if the two samples have different numbers of measures.

To summarize, the *t*-test has these assumptions:

- Independent samples
- Underlying population with a normal distribution
- Not too small of a sample size
- Homogeneity of variance

The *t*-test is a parametric inferential statistic for making inferences about either the mean of a population or a comparison of two means. This test is based on the distribution of the *t* statistic (see Figure A.8), which varies with the sample size. The associated degrees of freedom (*df*) identify each *t* distribution. The degrees of freedom arise from the standard deviation of each sample, which has $n-1$ degrees of freedom, as discussed earlier. The *t* statistic distributions are symmetric around zero and are bell-shaped. The **critical value** of *t* is the minimum value for a *t* statistic that you would accept to reject the null hypothesis at a given level of alpha (see Figure A.8). The critical value of the *t* statistic

Figure A.8 | Distribution of the *t* Statistic Showing Critical Values

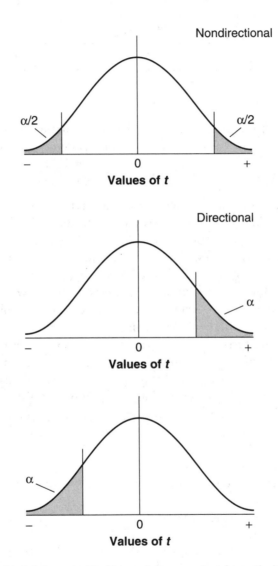

This shows the distribution of *t* statistics calculated from random samples of a particular size from a normal population (nondirectional). The difference between a one-tailed (directional) and a two-tailed test is that in a two-tailed test, the area of the distribution allowing rejection of the null hypothesis is at both the positive and negative extremes of the distribution. In a one-tailed test, the area for rejection of the null hypothesis is entirely at one extreme.

SOURCE: Keppel, 1991, Fig. 6.1. Copyright © 1991. Reprinted by permission of Pearson Education, Inc.

depends on the sample size and the level of risk you will accept for making a Type I error (e.g., alpha; see Chapter 4). To determine if the $t_{observed}$ is significant, compare it to the $t_{critical}$ in a table of critical values of t. If the observed value of t is in the region of rejection, given the level set to control the possibility of a Type I error (e.g., $p < 0.05$), then you reject the null hypothesis. This means you conclude that a difference of this magnitude is unlikely to happen by chance and that the groups show a "statistically significant" difference. If the null hypothesis cannot be rejected based on the observed t statistic, then you cannot conclude that the groups show a statistically significant difference. Note that you have not proved that the groups are from the same population; you have simply been unable to conclude that they are likely to be from different populations.

The critical value of the t statistic changes if you have a directional hypothesis or not. A **directional hypothesis** is a hypothesis that one group is larger (or, in another case, smaller) than the other group. If you want to test if the two groups differed, without making a directional hypothesis, then you should use a **two-tailed test** critical value (see Figure A.8). If you want to test a directional hypothesis, then use a **one-tailed test** critical value.

When a researcher wants to compare two samples (a between-subjects design), if each sample can be assumed to be from a distinct population, then the independent-samples' two-sample t-test may be applied. Note that "independent samples" means that the probability of a particular score occurring in one sample is not influenced by a particular score occurring in the other sample. The null hypothesis (H_0) in this case is that the two groups do not differ, formally expressed as H_0: $\mu_1 - \mu_2 = 0$, where μ_1 is the mean of the underlying population for the first sample and μ_2 is the mean of the underlying population for the second sample. Special versions of the t-test are available if samples are not independent (as, for example, in a within-subjects design).

To report the results of your t-test, you might insert one sentence such as, "The two groups differed, $t(38) = 3.56$, $p = .001$." What does this mean?

- The t indicates that you used a t-test to determine if there was a difference.
- The (38) indicates the number of degrees of freedom.
- The 3.56 is the obtained value of the t-test, the value of t calculated from your sample.
- The $p = .001$ indicates the level of probability of a Type I error or alpha. If your computer software gives you the exact probability, you should use that; otherwise, you can indicate $p < .05$. Note that the probability cannot be zero. If your computer software tells you that p = .000, it has rounded off a value that is less than .001. You should report this as "$p < .001$."

An example of the output you might get from software such as Excel appears in Figure A.9.

Figure A.9 | Results From a *t*-Test Between the Two Groups of Animals Tested on the Elevated Plus Maze

	T-Test: Two Sample Assuming Equal Variances	
	Control	*Drug*
Mean	77.7	38.2
Variance	899.3789	1,566.063
Observations	20	20
Pooled variance	1,232.721	
Hypothesized mean difference	0	
df	38	
t Stat	3.557662	
P(*T* <= *t*) one-tail	0.000512	
t Critical one-tail	1.685953	
P(*T* <= *t*) two-tail	0.001023	
t Critical one-tail	2.024394	

This analysis used Excel software. The *t*-test results would be reported in the text of a research report as: $t(38) = 3.56$, $p = 0.001$. P in Excel refers to *p*, the probability that the observed *t* statistic is less than the critical *t* value. *T* refers to the observed *t*, also called "*t* Stat."

Analysis of Variance

The **analysis of variance** or **ANOVA** is a parametric inferential statistical test for making inferences about the means of multiple populations. You might use this test if you conducted a factorial experiment. The ANOVA determines if any of the groups sampled are statistically different from any of the other groups. This test is based on comparisons of variation within the groups versus between the groups. If the variation within a group is small and the variation between groups is large, the test will be more likely to indicate a significant result.

The null hypothesis for an ANOVA is that all population means are equal. The alternative hypothesis then is that not all population means are equal.

To analyze an experiment with only one independent variable but more than two groups, you would use a **one-factor ANOVA**; to analyze an experiment with two independent variables you would use a **two-factor ANOVA**, and so on. The two-factor ANOVA is what you would use to analyze a 2×2 factorial design. There are variants of the ANOVA for mixed designs, where some factors are within subjects and others are between subjects. You will need advanced statistical software and more background than you can get from a general text such as this one if you want to analyze data from such complex designs.

The statistic that ANOVA uses is the **F-ratio**. It is the ratio of between-groups variability to within-groups variability. Similar to the procedures used for the *t*-test, after you calculate an ANOVA, you compare your obtained F-ratio to a critical F-ratio, specific for the samples' sizes and the level of Type I error or statistical significance desired (see Figure A.10). You can use computer software to determine the exact probability associated with your obtained F-ratio. If that probability is less than 0.05, you can conclude that results are statistically significant ($p < .05$).

Figure A.10   Sampling Distribution of the *F*-ratio for *F*(4, 10)

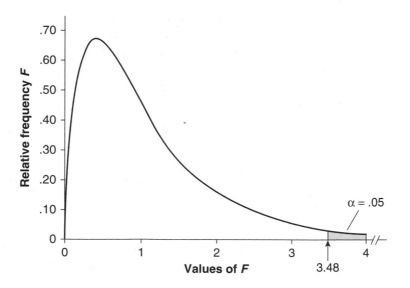

The *F*-ratio distribution is skewed, with most values occurring around the value 1.0, and negative values are absent.

SOURCE: Keppel, 1991. Copyright © 1991. Reprinted by permission of Pearson Education, Inc.

A significant *F*-ratio simply indicates that the difference of at least one group from the others is probably not due to chance but instead might be attributed to your independent variable. But which group or groups differ? You can determine that only by **post hoc tests,** statistical tests conducted following an ANOVA. It is beyond the scope of this textbook to discuss these tests in further detail, but you should be aware of the need for them.

If you conduct a 2×2 factorial design and analyze the results using a two-factor ANOVA, you will end up with three *F*-ratios: one *F*-ratio for the main effect of your first independent variable, another *F*-ratio for the main effect of your second independent variable, and a third *F*-ratio for the interaction between the two independent variables. To report your results, you generally do not include the entire ANOVA summary table in your research report. Instead, similar to reporting the results of a *t*-test, you add a statement such as, "There was a significant main effect of the first independent variable, $F(2, 12) = 5.61$, $p < .05$." Note the two terms for the degrees of freedom presented in parentheses following the "*F*." The first is the degrees of freedom between groups, and the second is the degrees of freedom within groups. Recall that the *F*-ratio is a ratio of between-groups to within-groups variability, so each component of the ratio has a degrees of freedom term. When reporting an interaction, you might say, "There was a significant interaction between the treatment group and time of testing, $F(2, 12) = 7.32$, $p < .05$." The degrees of freedom in the numerator and then the degrees of freedom in the denominator follow the *F*. Your report would continue with a description of the form of the interaction. For example, here's a possible description: "Depolarization treatment induced suppression of GABA currents when tested in the daytime, but the same treatment potentiated GABA currents when tested in nighttime."

A Few Cautions

Given the brief review here, I hope that you know how to calculate descriptive statistics on simple data sets, use software to calculate inferential statistics such as the *t*-test, report results of such tests, and interpret the meaning of at least some of the numbers in the "results" section of published reports (see Box A.6 for a brief review). You know just about enough to be dangerous or perhaps enough to be very confused.

To prepare for a career of interpreting scientific research results and analyzing results from your own experiments, you will need to know a lot more about statistics. I recommend that you take several statistics courses to gain this necessary background. You may have already had an introductory course, but you will want to gain as much background in statistics as possible. This is one of the most important tools for your scientific career. You should also keep in mind that many scientists regularly consult with statisticians, getting professional advice on the selection of statistical tests appropriate to their particular data set characteristics. Remember to consider what statistical test you will use to assess your data set before conducting your experiment. You can often incorporate design aspects to make your experiment more straightforward to analyze. For example, if you plan to use a *t*-test to compare two samples, a decision to use a sample size greater than 15 ensures you will need to be less concerned about samples with distributions that deviate from the normal, symmetric distribution.

BOX A.6	**TOOLS OF THE TRADE**
	Steps to Significance

Let's review the steps you will follow to determine if your results are statistically significant:

1. State the null hypothesis.

2. Determine the level of significance for Type 1 error associated with the null hypothesis (often $p = .05$).

3. Select the test statistic (see Figure A.11 for an overview).

4. Compute the test statistic's obtained value.

5. Determine the probability of the obtained value.

6. If the probability of the obtained value is less than the level of significance selected in Step 2, the null hypothesis should not be accepted, and the results are statistically significant.

7. If the probability of the obtained value is greater than the level of significance selected in Step 2, then the null hypothesis cannot be rejected. The results are not statistically significant.

SOURCE: Adapted from Salkind, 2002.

You should also keep in mind that "statistically significant" is not equivalent to "meaningful." A result can be statistically significant but be so small as to be meaningless in the larger context. For example, a study may find a statistically significant effect of a new antipsychotic treatment, reducing the duration of a psychotic episode by 12 hours. This effect may be so small that, within the larger context, the new drug lacks any practical or meaningful advantage and so has no clinical relevance. In the same vein, a finding that there is no statistically significant difference between groups does not mean that the independent variable might not affect the dependent variable. Perhaps a flaw in your experiment led to the result of no statistical difference. A better-designed study might find an effect of the independent variable.

Figure A.11 | A Guide to Selecting a Statistical Test for Your Initial Studies

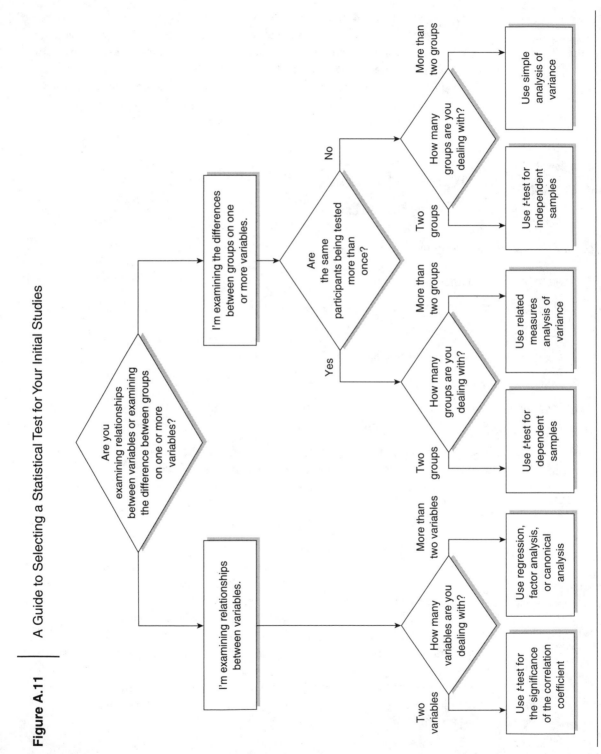

SOURCE: Adapted from Salkind, 2004, Fig. 8.1.

✓ CHECK YOUR UNDERSTANDING

1. Data that you collect are likely to show some variability. True or false: The best thing to do first is to take the average of all the observations.

2. Draw a distribution that is skewed. Then draw a bimodal distribution. Indicate the approximate location of the median, the mean, and the mode(s) in each case.

3. What is plotted on the y axis in a frequency histogram and in a bar graph?

4. What do you call a data point that falls outside the overall pattern?

5. How do you define an outlier in a typical box plot?

6. What are the five numbers in the "five-number summary"?

7. Draw a box plot and label the components.

8. What are the assumptions underlying the independent-samples' t-test?

9. What is the difference between descriptive statistics and inferential statistics?

10. I ran a t-test to determine if two groups differed with $p < 0.05$. My results: Observed value of $t = 2.05$. Degrees of freedom $= 6$. The critical value of $t = 2.45$. Write a sentence for my report's results section giving the results and conclusion.

11. The F-ratio is a ratio of ___ to ___.

12. In examining cortical neurons, I notice that most neurons have five major dendrites. Five is the

    a. Average

    b. Mean

    c. Mode

    d. Median

13. A few outliers can make the standard deviation very large. This is why we consider the standard deviation to not be a

    a. Reliable measure

    b. Resistant measure

    c. Friendly measure

    d. Variable measure

14. Descriptive statistics differ from inferential statistics in that:

    a. One is based on probability theory and the other is not.

    b. One is numerical and the other is theoretical.

    c. One is about a sample and the other is about a parameter.

    d. One has internal validity and the other has external validity.

THINK ABOUT IT

1. Two studies with identical sample sizes were conducted on the same research question. Each found that the mean of the group treated with the first level of the independent variable was 36.2, and the mean of the group treated with the second level of the independent variable was 14.3. The difference between the groups was statistically significant in the first study but not in the second study using an identical alpha level. Explain how this could happen.

2. You are conducting research to determine if a new type of plastic to be used in the manufacture of baby bottles is harmful to infant neural development. Which type of statistical error are you most concerned about minimizing: Type I error or Type II error? Contrast this situation to one where you are conducting preliminary studies to determine if it might be worthwhile to study several new compounds that might be helpful in treating Parkinson's disease.

3. Can research scientists ever prove their experimental hypotheses?

SUGGESTIONS FOR FURTHER READING

Bremer, M. (2010). *Statistics at the bench: A step-by-step handbook for biologists.* Cold Spring Harbor, NY: Cold Spring Harbor Laboratory Press.

Coolidge, F. L. (2006). *Statistics: A gentle introduction.* Thousand Oaks, CA: Sage.

Cumming, G., Fidler, F., & Vaux, D. L. (2007). Error bars in experimental biology. *Journal of Cell Biology, 177,* 7–11.

Hogan, T. P. (2011). *Bare-bones R: A brief introductory guide.* Thousand Oaks, CA: Sage.

Kirkpatrick, L. A., & Feeney, B. C. (2006). *A simple guide to SPSS for Windows for versions 12.0 and 13.0.* Belmont, CA: Wadsworth.

Lazic, S. E. (2010). The problem of pseudoreplication in neuroscientific studies: Is it affecting your analysis? *BMC Neuroscience 11*(5). doi:10.1186/1471–2202–11–5.

Salkind, N. J. (2010). *Excel statistics: A quick guide.* Thousand Oaks, CA: Sage.

ON THE WEB

StatSoft, Inc. (2010). *Electronic statistics textbook.* Tulsa, OK: StatSoft. Website: http://www.statsoft.com/textbook

Free statistical software is available at: www.statistics.com

Help in using the statistical pack Minitab is available at: http://www.minitab.com/uploadedFiles/Shared_Resources/Documents/MeetMinitab/MeetMinitabEN.pdf

Neuroscience Databases Online:

Society for Neuroscience Database Gateway: www.sfn.org/ndg

Allen Brain Atlas: http://www.brain-map.org

fMRI Data Center: http://www.fmridc.org/f/fmridc

Writing a Research Paper

Appendix B

An essential step in conducting research is communicating your results to other scientists. Scientific writing follows guidelines to help ensure complete and accurate communication. Using the description you provide, another scientist should be able to replicate your study. Given the vast number of scientific articles published each year, the writer also should be as concise as possible.

When you begin writing your manuscript, you will want to select a journal to which you would like to submit the paper for publication. The journal will have explicit guidelines regarding the paper's structure. These guidelines are generally on the journal's website and may also be printed in each issue. To help you begin practicing the basic scientific style, I have included explicit instructions here for the *Journal of Neuroscience,* published by the North American Society for Neuroscience and a leading journal in the field. Journals within the area of psychology generally recommend the American Psychological Association (APA) style. Full guidelines appear in the APA's *Publication Manual* (2009), but an overview is provided later in this appendix. Note that each journal has its own guidelines. These guidelines can be very different, as you will notice as you read journal articles. Some journals strictly limit the length of the paper and the number of figures. In some journals, such as *Science,* the figure legends and the footnotes contain much of the essential information. The journal may want the paper explicitly divided into "Introduction," "Methods," "Results," and "Discussion" sections, or its style may not allow explicit section divisions. Some journals print the article with a Methods section at the very end of the article. Some journals cite references in the text by the author's last name, whereas other journals cite by a number. You must check the style guidelines for the journal you plan to submit your paper to before you format the manuscript.

The format of a manuscript submitted for publication is not identical to the format of the published article. Journals prefer that the submitted manuscript be double spaced throughout, with sections in a particular order and specific information on specific pages. Check the submission guidelines posted on the website of the journal you are submitting your manuscript to, and follow those guidelines exactly. Sloppiness in following the guidelines will not reflect well on your general attention to detail and may give a poor impression of your scientific style.

THE PARTS OF A PAPER

Although journals vary in their requirements, there are some general guidelines for expectations. Information is presented in standardized formats; each section of the report requires specific information.

Title

When selecting a title for your paper, attempt to include as much relevant information as possible in a concise form. It is helpful if your title indicates the main result of the study. Thus, "Circadian phase shifts to light are blocked by nitric oxide inhibitors" is a better title than "The role of nitric oxide in circadian phase shifts to light." Indicating the species used for the study is often helpful. Remember that scientists will be reading your title as they search for papers relevant to their own interests.

Abstract

The abstract is a summary of the paper. Even though it appears first, most people find it easier to write the abstract after completing the rest of the manuscript. Your abstract should summarize the rationale for the study, your methodological approaches, major results, and the most important conclusions. Limit yourself to several sentences to summarize each of these aspects of the study. Write in complete sentences, and do not use subheadings.

Introduction

After studying the structure of the introduction in several published papers, you will find that most authors progress from the general to the specific. What general topic does your study address? Your first paragraph of introduction should set the stage, provide information on this basic problem, and generally include a few references to key review articles for the reader who wants more detailed background information. Within the next few paragraphs, describe the rationale for your study. Why was this study necessary? Are previous reports on this topic contradictory? Does a new technique promise to yield fresh insight into this topic? Did a chance observation in preliminary work lead to this more complete study? Keep in mind that your goal is to interest the reader. End your introduction with a statement of your hypothesis or an overview of the exact purpose of your study.

Methods

In the Methods section of the paper, you will describe the exact procedures that you followed in conducting your study. Include every relevant detail so that another scientist could replicate the study and presumably find the same results. Some details do not need to be included; when in doubt, ask yourself if those details are necessary for replication. When using specialized materials or equipment, supply the exact source, providing not just the company name but also the city and state or province (and country if outside the country publishing the journal). It is often helpful to divide the Methods section into several subsections— for example, "Animals and housing," "In situ hybridization protocol," or "Data analysis procedure."

Results

In the Results section, you will guide the reader through the findings. Proceed in an organized manner. You may initially describe the data, indicating modifications that you made to the data set prior to analysis. As you discuss the results, you may want to discuss the major findings first, with subsidiary results discussed later. If you performed several separate experiments, subheadings are generally used to separate the description of one experiment's results from the results of the other.

In establishing a result, you should provide numbers, such as descriptive statistics or summaries of inferential statistical tests, but always with a sentence clearly communicating what you expect the reader to see in the results. Thus, you might say, "The group receiving early enrichment showed more dendritic branches (34 ± 4 branches; $n = 15$) than did the group with standard housing (12 ± 2 branches; $n = 15$)." Compare that with the following sentence: "The group receiving early enrichment showed 34 ± 4 ($n = 15$) dendritic branches, and the group with standard housing showed 12 ± 2 ($n = 15$) branches." The latter version gives the same information but makes the reader infer the results.

In your Results section, refer to the figures and tables at appropriate places in the text. Label figures and tables with arabic numbers (1, 2, 3, . . .) according to the order they are cited in the text. Place each figure and table on a separate page at the very end of the manuscript.

Discussion

Begin your Discussion section with a concise summary of the major findings. Relate the findings to the hypothesis described at the end of your Introduction section. Your Discussion section should then proceed in an organized fashion. You will want to discuss how your results relate to the previously published studies on this topic. Do your results support a specific theory or suggest an underlying mechanism? Are there alternative hypotheses that could also explain your results? You might want to suggest fruitful future directions for research on this topic, in light of the results of your particular experiment. If there are discrepancies, suggest possible explanations for these. Are there cautions you would like to raise about interpreting your data? Strengths in your data you would like to highlight? As you discuss the implications of your study, be aware that nonspecialists may read your report. Provide citations to relevant review articles where appropriate. End with a conclusion that a nonspecialist could understand.

References

Your report will have two types of reference citations.

In-Text References

Provide a reference for every statement of fact, unless that fact is considered common knowledge. When an idea is not your own, you should supply a reference. The reference must appear in the text with the authors' names and dates, with full details given in the bibliography at the end of the manuscript. To start a sentence with the author's name, use the format dictated by the journal. For example, some journals require that you use just the last name and include "et al." if there are coauthors, with the date also provided—for example, "Eskes et al. (2003) reported that. . . ." Format in-text references according to the specific journal's style, generally either with footnotes or with parenthetical citations, most often with the author and date.

Bibliography

Beginning on a new page following the text of the manuscript, give a complete list of articles cited in your text. Be sure to cite only papers you actually have read. If you want to refer to a study by Estabrooke (2001), but you have only read about that article in a secondary source, then indicate this in the text: "a finding shown by Estabrooke (2001), as cited in Scammell (2003)." This is unusual in professional literature, but might be necessary in a student report, where it is not always possible to locate and read every relevant article.

Figure Legends

Immediately following the reference list, provide the figure legends (starting on a new page). These are formatted similar to the text and double-spaced. The figure legends should supply all the information the reader will need to understand the figure. Be sure you explain every abbreviation or symbol used in the figure. Begin the figure legend with a title, a short phrase describing the figure's major point. In rare cases, you might need to repeat information that also appears in the Results section of the text, but generally authors try to avoid redundancy in their manuscript. Be aware that some readers may skim your article, reading the abstract and studying the figures. The figure legend must furnish them with the necessary information to understand the figure's main point. If necessary to refer readers to the text for further details, be specific about which section of the text contains the information.

Figures and Tables

Submit each figure or table on a separate page, following all other pages of the manuscript. Design your figures using the size you would expect them to appear in a published article. This will help you choose appropriate font sizes for labels. As long as you are thinking about eventual publication, it is good practice to use color only when necessary. Many journals charge a fee for color figures. Be aware that some readers may be perusing a shoddy copy of your paper; make the symbols in the figures clearly distinguishable. Number each figure; for submission for publication, such information is generally placed on the reverse side of the paper, but for a student report, it is sufficient to put the figure number in the upper right-hand corner of the page with the figure.

Use tables only when necessary. Figures are often better for conveying your main point. A table is helpful when you must present many numbers in an organized format. Each table should be on a separate sheet and include a title. Refer to all tables in the text—for example, "As Table 2 indicates, the. . . ."

WRITING STYLE HINTS

You should consider other aspects to help your writing style conform to accepted standards for good scientific writing. The following information may help you.

Abbreviations

Use abbreviations or acronyms only if a term appears three or more times. Many scientific articles contain too many abbreviations, and this can make them confusing to read. Spell out all abbreviations at first occurrence, and then introduce the abbreviation by placing it in parentheses after the term being abbreviated. Use the metric system for all volumes, lengths, weights, and so on. Express temperatures in degrees Celsius (centigrade).

Name your experimental groups in a manner that will help the reader. "Cocaine-treated" and "Placebo control" are more helpful than "Group A" and "Group B."

Scientific Writing Style

Reading many published scientific papers is the best way I know for absorbing the style of scientific writing. However, in helping students try to master this style, I have noticed a few particular glaring errors you can easily avoid.

- When mentioning references in the text, do not include the title of the article. The title and other details appear in the reference list at the end of the article and are never included in the main text of the article.
- The word *data* is plural; be sure to use a plural form of the verb ("The data *were* . . .").
- The word *effect* is most often used as a noun ("The *effect* of the drug was . . ."), whereas the word *affect* is most often used as a verb ("My drug *affects* the response"). An important exception is when *affect* is used as a noun to mean "emotion" ("The Parkinson's disease patient often shows little *affect* in facial expressions").
- When you measure responses from people, refer to them as *participants.* Other animals can be referred to as *subjects,* or, more commonly, they are referred to by the common name of the species (for example, mice*).* If you are referring to both humans and other animals, use the term *subjects.*
- Use past tense both when describing previous research and when describing the procedures you followed to conduct the experiment. The past tense is not the same as passive voice, which you should generally avoid. "The hamster ate the sunflower seeds" is past tense; "the sunflower seeds were eaten by the hamster" is passive.
- Assume your audience consists of professional neuroscientists. You do not have to explain that you mean "statistically significant" when you use the term "significant" (and, by the way, only use the word "significant" when you mean "statistically significant"). You do not have to identify the independent variable and the dependent variable explicitly: For example, if you say that you investigated the effect of Ecstasy on neuronal degeneration, you do not need to follow up by pointing out that Ecstasy was your independent variable and neuronal degeneration was the dependent variable.

Assume a general level of familiarity with experimental design and with neuroscience techniques.
* One experiment does not prove a hypothesis. Do not use the verb *prove*; use *support* or *confirm* instead.

Scientific writing rarely includes direct quotations. I forbid my students to use direct quotes to force them to learn to put the source material in their own words and then credit the source.

JOURNAL OF NEUROSCIENCE GUIDELINES

The *Journal of Neuroscience* is the official journal of the Society for Neuroscience, which was formed in 1970 and has grown from 500 members to more than 38,000. Students are welcome to join this professional organization. Membership makes you eligible to sponsor an abstract for presentation at the annual meeting of the society. Members also receive free access to the *Journal of Neuroscience* online.

Title Page

The first page of your manuscript, the title page, has the complete title, as well as a short version of the title (no more than 60 characters and spaces). Your title page should also include the names of authors and information on the institution where the work was conducted. A sentence or two of acknowledgments appear on this page, with an indication of sources of funding as well as any people who contributed in a unique manner to the conduct of the study. Indicate the number of text pages. The pages with figures on them are counted separately. Supply also the number of words in the abstract, introduction, and discussion. List at least six key words or phrases for use in indexing. One author is designated the corresponding author, and that person's complete address, telephone and fax number, and e-mail address appear on the title page.

Several criteria determine authorship. The Society for Neuroscience has published a guide, "Responsible Conduct for Scientific Communication" (1998), which suggests three criteria for authorship. An author should have "(a) made a significant contribution to the conception and design or the analysis and interpretation of data, (b) participated in drafting the article or reviewing and/or revising for intellectual content, and (c) approved the final version of the manuscript." It is important for students working as research assistants to note that simply collecting data for a study that someone else designed, analyzed, and wrote up for publication will not qualify you for authorship on that article.

Abstract

Your completed manuscript should include an abstract, printed on a separate page immediately following the title page. The abstract is limited to 250 words.

Text

Your introduction is limited to 500 words. The introduction should begin on the page following the abstract, without a heading. You should include a Methods section of the paper, describing all methodological details. Next, provide a Results section. The last paragraph of your discussion should emphasize the most general implications of your results in a manner intelligible to a neuroscientist who is not a specialist in your field. Your discussion may not exceed 1,500 words.

References

You should be aware that the order of authors is important in that it signifies level of contribution to the paper. Refer to the reference using the exact order of authors as in the published paper. Note that when a reference has two authors, you should always include both names. When a reference has more than two authors, always cite it within the text using the last name of the first author, followed by "et al." First names are not used in the in-text citations, only last names.

The following guidelines appear on the website for the *Journal of Neuroscience* (http://www.jneurosci.org/misc/ifa_organization.shtml):

In-Text References

References should be cited in the text as follows: "The procedure used has been described elsewhere (Green, 1978)," or "Our observations are in agreement with those of Brown and Black (1979) and of White et al. (1980)," or with multiple references, in chronological order: "Earlier reports (Brown & Black, 1979, 1981; White et al., 1980; Smith, 1982, 1984). . . ."

Bibliography

In the list of references (to be typed double-spaced), papers should be given in alphabetical order according to the surname of the first author. In two-author papers with the same first author, the order is alphabetical by the second author's name. In three-or-more-author papers with the same first author, the order is chronological. The name of the author(s) should be followed by the date in parentheses, the full title of the paper as it appeared in the original together with the source of the reference, the volume number, and the first and last pages. Do not number the references. The following illustrate the format to be used:

Journal Article

- Hamill OP, Marty A, Neher E, Sakmann B, Sigworth F (1981) Improved patch-clamp techniques for high-resolution current recordings from cells and cell free membrane patches. Pflugers Arch 391:85–100.
- Hodgkin AL, Huxley AF (1952a) The components of membrane conductance in the giant axon of Loligo. J Physiol (Lond) 116:473–496.
- Hodgkin AL, Huxley AF (1952b) The dual effect of membrane potential on sodium conductance in the giant axon of *Loligo*. JPhysiol (Lond)116:497–506.

Book

- Hille B (1984) Ionic channels of excitable membranes. Sunderland, MA: Sinauer.

Chapter in a Book

- Stent GS (1981) Strength and weakness of the genetic approach to the development of the nervous system. In: Studies in developmental neurobiology: essays in honor of Viktor Hamburger (Cowan WM, ed), pp288–321. New York: Oxford UP.
- Abbreviations of journal titles should follow those listed in the *Index Medicus* [from the National Library of Medicine].

Figure Legends

Immediately following the reference list, provide the figure legends (starting on a new page).

Figures and Tables

Each figure or table is submitted on a separate page, following all other pages of the manuscript. Detailed information on the preparation and submission of figures and tables is available on the journal's website, but for a student report much of this information is unnecessary.

AMERICAN PSYCHOLOGICAL ASSOCIATION GUIDELINES

The American Psychological Association (APA) style guidelines for publication fill a manual that is currently more than 400 pages (see the suggested reading list at the end of this chapter). This manual is helpful, not just for the exact specification of format for publication used by APA-sponsored journals as well as many others. The APA's (2009) *Publication Manual* also contains chapters on writing style, grammar, preparing a thesis, and much more. Here, I will briefly summarize the major guidelines for preparing a manuscript.

Page Header

Identify each page of your manuscript with a manuscript page header, the first two to three words of the title. Place it in the upper right-hand corner, followed by the page number.

Title Page

The title page is page 1. It includes the title, as well as a short version of the title (no more than 50 characters and spaces), called the "running head." Do not confuse the running head with your manuscript page header. Put the manuscript page header, the first few words of the full title, on the pages of the manuscript you submit for publication. Once your manuscript is published, the running head will appear at the top of the pages. One double-spaced line below the title, list the authors and, on the next double-spaced line, the institutional affiliations. Place the title flush left and center both the authors and the institutions.

The APA's (2009) *Publication Manual* includes a few comments on determining authorship. The order of authorship generally should reflect the relative contributions of the persons involved with the research. If a multiple-authored paper is substantially based on a student's dissertation or thesis, the student is generally listed as the first author.

Abstract

Your completed manuscript should include an abstract, printed on a separate page immediately following the title page. The abstract is limited to 120 words. Head the abstract with the title "Abstract" centered at the top of the page. Type the abstract as a single block of text; do not use indentation.

Text

Begin the text on the page following the abstract. Type the title of the paper centered at the top of the page. The sections of the text follow each other without page breaks between them.

References

In-Text References

Cite references in the text as follows: "Another study finds the same effect (Cheng, 2009)," or "These results contrast with those of Martinez and Takahashi (2008) and of Grossman et al. (2007)," or with multiple references, in chronological order: "prior studies (Blake & Smith, 2007, 2008; Church et al., 2005; Smith, 2001, 2010)." When a reference has two authors, always include both names every time it is cited. When a reference has three to five authors, cite all authors the first time the reference appears in the text, and for all subsequent citations, use just the surname of the first author, followed by "et al." When a reference has six or more authors, cite it by the first author and "et al." Use an ampersand, instead of the word *and,* when the authors' names appear within parentheses.

Bibliography

References should start on a new page, with "References" typed centered at the top of the page. Use a hanging indent format, with the first line of the reference flush left and subsequent lines for the same reference indented. List references in alphabetical order by the surname of the author. One-author entries by the same author are listed chronologically, with the earliest reference appearing first. References with the same first author are listed alphabetically by the second author, or, if they also have the same second author, then by the third author, and so on.

Below are some examples for formatting references:

Periodical
Author, A. A., Author, B. B., & Author, C. C. (2010). Title of article. *Title of periodical, xx,* xxx–xxx.

Nonperiodical
Author, A. A. (2010). *Title of work.* Location: Publisher.

Book chapter
Author, A. A., & Author, B. B. (2010). Title of chapter. In A. Editor, B. Editor, & C. Editor (Eds.), *Title of book* (pp. xxx–xxx). Location: Publisher.

Figure Captions

Immediately following the reference list, provide the figure captions (starting on a new page). All figure captions should be typed together; do not put each figure caption on a separate page and do not put the caption on the same page as the figure itself. For each figure caption, put the word "Figure" and the number of the figure in italics, flush left.

Figures and Tables

Submit each figure or table on a separate page, following all other pages of the manuscript.

✓ CHECK YOUR UNDERSTANDING

1. Format a reference for three different journals. Use journals from the list below:

   Journal of Neuroscience: http://www.jneurosci.org

   Science: http://www.sciencemag.org

   Nature Neuroscience: http://www.nature.com/neuro

   Neuroscience Letters: http://www.elsevier.com/wps/find/authorshome .authors

   Brain Research: http://www.elsevier.com/wps/find/authorshome.authors

   Journal of Cognitive Neuroscience: http://intl-jocn.mitpress.org

2. Indicate which sentences require an in-text reference:

   a. My study provides the first attempt to measure the effect of marshmallows and chocolate on brain serotonin levels.

   b. Cells in the raphe nuclei have been shown to release serotonin when chocolate is visually detected.

   c. Marshmallows are often eaten in combination with chocolate.

   d. The computational model for combined activation of reward pathways predicted results opposite from ours.

   e. My hypothesis is that marshmallows and chocolate will have an additive effect on brain serotonin levels.

THINK ABOUT IT

1. Revise this "Results" section: The results of this study were probably meaningless. Mice in the experimental group showed increased time in the open arm as compared to mice in the control group. The mean time in the open arm for the mice in the control group was 6.789. The standard

deviation for the control mice was 3.234. The mean time in the open arm for the mice in the experimental group was 25.345. The standard deviation for the experimental group was 10.284. The two means were therefore different as is shown in the box plots in Figure 1. While the two means do look different, the statistics indicated that the groups were not different. The one-tailed t-test gave a t value of 4.5, and this was shown to be with 15 degrees of freedom, the p value was <0.05, which says that we cannot reject the null hypothesis, which was that the control mice would show increased time in the open arm.

SUGGESTIONS FOR FURTHER READING

American Psychological Association. (2009). *Concise rules of APA style* (6th ed.). Washington DC: Author.

Council of Science Editors. (2006). *Scientific style and format: The CSE manual for authors, editors and publishers*. Reston, VA: Rockefeller University Press.

Curran-Everett, D., & Benos, D. J. (2004). Guidelines for reporting statistics in journals published by the American Physiological Society. *American Journal of Physiology: Endocrinology and Metabolism, 287*, E189–191.

Houghton, P. M., Houghton, T. J., & Pratt, M. M. (2009). *APA: The easy way!* Flint, MI: Baker College.

Matthews J. R., & Matthews, R. W. (2008). *Successful scientific writing: A step-by-step guide for the biological and medical sciences*. Cambridge, UK: Cambridge University Press.

Strunk, Jr., W., & White, E. B. (2009). *The elements of style*. New York: Pearson Longman.

Tufte, E. R. (2007). *The visual display of quantitative information*. Cheshire, CT: Graphics Press.

Wainer, H. (2009). *Picturing the uncertain world: How to understand, communicate, and control uncertainty through graphical display*. Princeton, NJ: Princeton University Press.

Appendix C | A Sample Paper

This appendix includes a published paper. To help you work on your critical reading skills, I suggest you read the paper and attempt to answer the 12 questions from Table 3.1. I provide sample answers to those questions below. To help you prepare papers for publication, I provide the manuscript for this article prepared in the format for submitting to the *Journal of Neuroscience*.

12 Questions to Answer After Reading This Article

1. What report is this? (Use full reference citation, *Journal of Neuroscience* or APA format.)

2. What was the general purpose of the study? What questions does it address?

3. What was previously known about this question? How does answering the research question(s) add something new to what is already known?

4. Who or what was studied? (Cite number and key characteristics.) What was the experimental design? (See Chapter 8 for a list.)

5. In sequential order, what were the major steps in performing the study? (Record these in a flowchart.) Do not just repeat details from Items 1–4 and Items 6–9. Create an explanatory sketch that a year from now would help you recall how the study was done.

6. What data were recorded and used for analysis?

7. What kinds of data analysis were used?

8. What were the results? (Refer to figures.) (After analysis, what do the data from Item 6 say about the questions addressed in Item 2?)

9. What does the author conclude? (In light of both Item 8 and the entire study experience, what is said about Item 2?)

10. What cautions does the author raise about interpreting the study?

11. Were there any flaws in this study? How could the experimental design be improved?

12. What particularly interesting or valuable things did you learn from reading the report? (Consider results, method, discussion, references, and so on.)

Example Answers

1. Mitra R, Adamec R, Sapolsky R (2009) Resilience against predator stress and dendritic morphology of amygdala neurons. Behav Brain Res 205:535–543.

2. This study is most generally interested in understanding what is different in the brains of people who are differently affected by stress. What leads to some people developing PTSD and others not? Here they will use a model of rats exposed to cats, in which only some rats develop lasting anxiety, and will measure dendrites of neurons in the BLA. There are two hypotheses in response to stress: 1) Mal-adapted rats should show "neural expansion" in the BLA, and 2) well-adapted rats should show "neural retraction," and this response prevents the lasting anxiety.

3. What was already known was:

   a. The amygdala is implicated in some studies of humans increased reactivity to stress (amygdala reaction to threat is altered by a serotonin transporter alteration that is linked to a person's ability to cope with stress, changes in the amygdala are seen in people with PTSD).

   b. Rats vary in how stressed out they get after seeing a cat. This variability in behavior is linked with differences in the hippocampus.

   c. Mice without the serotonin transporter get more stressed out by a cat.

   d. Predator stress alters neurotransmission in the rat amygdala, possibly through changes in dendrite shape.

   e. Stress is associated with growth of dendrites in BLA and trimming dendrite length reduces anxiety.

4. They used 81 young adult male Long-Evans hooded rats. The experimental design was two-group, independent samples (IV: cat exposure or handled control) in some cases or a multiple-group, between-subjects, quasi-experiment (IV: mal-adapted, well-adapted, or handled control) in other cases. Also they used a correlational design, correlating variables related to dendrite morphology and behavior in EPM.

5. They randomly assigned rats to either 10 min cat exposure ($n = 71$) or 1 min handling ($n = 10$). Two weeks later, rats were tested in the hole board for 5 min, and then in the EPM for 5 min. Based on the EPM measures, they selected 4 well-adapted rats and 4 mal-adapted rats. Four handled rats were randomly selected from the 10 controls. These 12 rats were sacrificed one day after EPM testing and the right posterior BLA was processed for Golgi stain. Up to 10 neurons per rat were measured.

6. *During the cat exposure they measured:* (For the cat): latency to approach the rat, number of approaches, time spent near (within 1 ft) the rat; latency to sniff the rat and the time spent sniffing; latency to bite the rat, number of bites, and frequency of pawing. (For the rat): defensive behavior (active, passive, or escape).

   During the hole board test they measured: Time in motion, number of head dips, time near the walls (all 4 ft outside the center box).

   During the EPM test they measured: Ratio time (total time in open arms/total time in any arm), ratio entry (total entries in open arms/total entries in all arms), entries to closed arms, relative risk assessment (frequency of risk assessment/total time in closed arms).

   From the Golgi-stained neurons they measured: Dendritic length and branch points (Sholl's analysis).

7. They used means ± SEM, and ANOVA followed by post-hoc Fisher's LSD tests. They also used the Kolmogrov-Smirnov test, the Spearman correlation, and Sholl's analysis.

8. *From the measures taken during cat exposure:* No difference between mal-and well-adapted rats.

   From the hole board test measures: No difference between mal-and well-adapted rats. No difference in time in motion or number of head dips when comparing all stressed rats with all handled controls. Stressed rats spent more time near the walls than handled controls (see Table 1).

   From the EPM test: Mal-adapted rats differed from the other two groups, which did not differ from each other (see Figure 1), with the exception of ratio risk. When closed arm entries was used as a covariate, they still saw the original pattern of group difference (see Figure 2). When they compared all stressed rats with all handled controls, saw decreased ratio times and entries in the stressed group (see Table 1) and no difference in closed arm entries or risk assessment.

From the Golgi-stained neuron measures: No difference between mal-adapted versus handled controls in any measure. The well-adapted group differed from the other two groups in that they showed lower total dendrite length, higher total number branch points, higher branch packing (75–125 µm from the soma) and shorter dendritic extent (see Figures 3, 4, and 5). Within the four rats in the handled control group, two showed cells with longer dendrites than the others. No differences were seen in dendrite measures within the mal- and well-adapted groups.

Correlation of measures: Within the sample of stressed rats:

    a. The total dendritic length was negatively correlated with ratio time and entries (see Figure 6A).

    b. A similar correlation was seen for dendritic extent but this disappeared when controlled for effect of dendrite length.

    c. Branch packing was positively correlated with closed arm entries.

    d. Other variables were not correlated. When handled controls were included in the sample, the only variables that showed a correlation were branch packing and closed arm entries (see Figure 6B).

9. They conclude that predator stress experience did not differ between mal- and well-adapted rats. Mal-adapted rats are more anxious in the EPM than well-adapted and handled controls. Predator-stressed rats are more anxious in the EPM than handled controls, and locomotor activity did not contribute to these group differences. Well-adapted rats had retracted dendrites and increased packing density of dendrites in the BLA compared to both mal-adapted animals and unstressed controls. They tentatively conclude that the well-adapted rats came into this experiment with shorter dendrites and that longer dendrites might give a greater substrate for neuroplastic changes in response to stress. Different aspects of dendrites may contribute to different behaviors.

10. They caution that from these results one cannot precisely determine if well-adapted rats undergo dendritic retraction in response to stress, or if these rats came into the experiment with a less extensive dendritic tree.

11. (Answers may vary. Here is one possible answer.) They used each neuron as an independent data point (and they note that this is a widely accepted method), but these are not independent points given that several neurons were measured in each animal. They used both stellate and pyramidal cells, but did not indicate if results were different for these or if the cell types were balanced across the groups.

12. (Answers will vary.)

Journal Section: Behavioral/Systems/Cognitive

Resilience Against Predator Stress and Dendritic Morphology of Amygdala Neurons

Abbreviated title: Stress resilience and amygdale morphology

Rupshi Mitra*; Robert Adamec*; Robert Sapolsky (*Equal contributions)

Affiliations:

   Mitra, Sapolsky: Stanford University, Stanford, California, USA

   Adamec: Memorial University, St. John's, Newfoundland, Canada

Corresponding Author:

   Dr. Rupshi Mitra, Dept. of Biology Stanford University, Stanford, CA 94305

   Tel: 650 725 9898; email: rupshi@stanford.edu

Number of figures: 6

Number of tables: 1

5upplementary Material: None

Number of pages: 25

Total words in abstract, introduction, discussion: 238, 584, 1106

Key words: stress, anxiety, amygdala, neuron, morphology, plasticity.

Acknowledgements:

This work was supported by the CIHR (grant ROP 91548) to Dr. R. Adamec, and NIH R01 (AG020633) to Prof R M Sapolsky. Sincere gratitude is extended to Kim Pearcey and Chris Muir for their technical assistance.

ABSTRACT

Individual differences in coping response lie at the core of vulnerability to conditions like post traumatic stress disorder (PTSD). Like humans, not all animals exposed to severe stress show lasting change in affect. Predator stress is a traumatic experience inducing long-lasting fear, but not in all rodents. Thus, individual variation may be a cross species factor driving responsiveness to stressful events. The present study investigated neurobiological bases of variation in coping with severe stress. The amygdala was studied because it modulates fear and its function is affected by stress. Moreover, stress-induced plasticity of the amygdala has been related to induction of anxiety, a comorbid symptom of psychiatric conditions like PTSD. We exposed rodents to predator stress and grouped them according to their adaptability based on a standard anxiety test (the elevated plus maze). Subsequently we investigated if well-adapted (less anxious) and mal-adapted (extremely anxious) stressed animals differed in the structure of dendritic trees of their output neurons of the right basolateral amygdala (BLA). Two weeks after exposure to stress, well-adapted animals showed low anxiety levels comparable to unstressed controls, whereas mal-adapted animals were highly anxious. In these same animals, Golgi analysis revealed that BLA neurons of well-adapted rats exhibited more densely packed and shorter dendrites than neurons of mal-adapted or unstressed control animals, which did not differ. These data suggest that dendritic hypotrophy in the BLA may be a resilience marker against lasting anxiogenic effects of predator stress.

INTRODUCTION

Stress and trauma affect individuals differently. While traumatic experience leads to post traumatic stress disorder (PTSD) in some, others exposed to severe stressors are less affected (Kessler et al., 2005; Kessler et al., 1995; Stam, 2007a). Relatively little is known about molecular and neural substrates of such individual differences in coping (Stam, 2007a). However correlational behavioral research implicates a variety of possible factors, including personality traits (Heinrichs et al., 2005; McNally, 2003), interaction of genetic factors and experiential factors, such as reduced functioning polymorphisms in the serotonin transporter (5-HTTLPR), and life stress or social support at the time of stress (Adamec et al., 1998; Hariri et al., 2005; Kilpatrick et al., 2007). Moreover, reactivity of amygdala to environmental threat is modulated by 5-HTTLPR (Hariri et al., 2005) which has also been implicated in PTSD (Kilpatrick et al., 2007; Lee et al., 2005). So factors affecting functional amygdala reactivity may be important contributors to vulnerability to stress. In PTSD patients right amygdala activity is enhanced in response to both trauma reminder and general negative stimuli (Rauch et al., 2006; Shin et al., 2005).

These studies are suggestive, but being correlative, do not reveal causal factors (Stam, 2007a; Stam, 2007b). One way to identify putative causal substrates, however, is to study impact of stress on brain and behavior of more and less stress vulnerable animals. A useful paradigm in this regard is exposure of rodents to brief predator stress, a putative model of hyperarousal and generalized anxiety characteristics of PTSD (Adamec et al., 2006a).

Domesticated strains of laboratory rats retain the fear of predators like a cat, even if they have never been exposed to predators (Adamec et al., 1998; Blanchard and Blanchard, 1989). On exposure to a cat (predator stress) or cat stimuli (predator scent stress-PSS), laboratory rats and mice develop long-lasting (3 weeks or longer) anxiety

(Adamec and Shallow, 1993; Adamec et al., 2006c; Adamec et al., 2004; Cohen et al., 1996; Cohen et al., 2007; Cohen et al., 2003). However, not all stressed animals respond similarly. Some remain unaffected, showing little fear sensitization (Cohen et al., 2003; Cohen et al., 2004).

Reasons for these individual differences remain largely unknown, though there has been recent progress. In hippocampus (area CA1), up regulation of ARC gene expression (mRNA) was found in well-adapted rats unaffected by PSS (Kozlovsky, 2008), whereas down regulation of BDNF and up regulation of TrkB receptors was observed in mal-adapted rats made extremely fearful by PSS (Kozlovsky, 2007). In addition serotonin transporter gene knockout mice are more vulnerable to predator stress (Adamec et al., 2008; Adamec et al., 2006b), providing an interesting parallel to the human clinical literature, and in that context, implicating modulation of amygdala function in vulnerability to stress. Interestingly, predator stress induces a lasting enhancement of excitability of right rodent amygdala, detected as a potentiation of afferent and efferent transmission in basolateral (BLA) and central amygdala (Adamec et al., 2005a; Adamec et al., 2001). Furthermore, degree of anxiogenic effect of predator stress is tightly predicted by degree of potentiation in amygdala circuitry (Adamec et al., 2005b). Moreover, electrophysiological studies suggest that one mechanism mediating predator stress potentiation of amygdala circuitry could be changes in dendritic morphology (Adamec et al., 2001). Structural variation which alters neural transmission in BLA could alter fearful response which highly correlates with BLA transmission (Adamec et al., 2005b).

Indeed, variation in dendritic arbors of BLA neurons is related to the ability of restraint stress to generate anxiety (Vyas et al., 2002; Vyas et al., 2004). Anxiety generated by stress and stress hormone is accompanied by BLA hypertrophy (Mitra and Sapolsky, 2008; Vyas et al., 2002; Vyas et al., 2004), and experimental reduction of dendritic length results in reduction of anxiety (Mitra et al., 2009). Moreover, once generated, BLA hypertrophy is as long lasting as stress induced anxiety (Vyas et al., 2004).

Given the above considerations, it is timely to ask if neurons of the BLA and their plasticity are involved in individual differences in coping with predator stress. Two hypotheses can be proposed to explain individual differences. First, in mal-adapted animals, stress causes neural expansion in BLA related to the enhanced anxiety they experience. Second, stress causes neural retraction in well-adapted animals, and this plasticity prevents maladaptive effects of trauma. In this report, we attempted to test these two hypotheses.

METHODS AND MATERIALS

Subjects and Groups

A total of 81 adult male Long-Evans hooded rats were used. At arrival from Charles River Canada, rats were approximately 4 weeks of age and weighed between 76g and 100g. Rats were housed individually in standard clear polycarbonate cages. The animals were fed and watered ad lib, and were maintained on a 12 hour light-dark schedule (lights on at 07:00). Rats were first habituated to their home cage for one day, after which they were handled once per day for one minute over the following five days. Finally, rats were randomly assigned to either the predator stressed group (to be exposed to a cat, n = 71) or handled control (n = 10). Observations reported in this manuscript refer to young animals (5 weeks at start of experiment); an important variable because stress sensitivity can vary across lifespan of rodents.

Predator Stress and Handling

One week after arrival, predator stress group animals were exposed to one of two cats. Exposures were unprotected and occurred between the hours of 09:00 and 12:00. All exposures took place in a large enclosed room with a floor area of approximately 35 square feet as described elsewhere (Adamec and Shallow, 1993). Exposures lasted for ten minutes and were videotaped to capture the activities of both the rat and the cat. Cat response consisted of watching the rat from a distance, followed by several approaches, pawing, and the occasional mild attack. No rats were injured. Handled animals were handled for one minute on the day of cat exposure of predator stressed groups. Handled and predator stressed rats were housed in separate rooms and did not come into contact with each other. Time of treatment was counterbalanced among all groups. Following treatment, all rats were returned to their home cages and left unhandled until testing for lasting effects on rodent anxiety.

Behavioral Measures Taken From Cat Exposures

Behavior of both the rat and cat was analyzed from videotape. Cat behaviors consisted of latency to approach the rat, the number of approaches, and time spent near the rat; latency to sniff the rat and the time spent sniffing; latency to bite the rat, number of bites, and frequency of pawing. The cat was considered near the rat when it moved to within one foot of the rat determined from one foot square floor markings.

Rat behavior in response to the cat was also analyzed. Defensive behavior was categorized as frequency of active, passive, or escape as described elsewhere (Adamec and Shallow, 1993).

Post Treatment Behavioral Testing

Two weeks after handling or predator stress, anxiety-like behavior was examined using the hole board and elevated plus maze (EPM) tests. Such tests are commonly used to assess rodent exploration, activity, and anxiety (File, 1987; File and Wardill, 1975a; File and Wardill, 1975b). Behavior in all tests was video taped remotely for later blind analysis. All tests were 5 minutes in duration and conducted between 09:00 and 11:00 under normal room lighting. Rats were tested first in the hole board immediately followed by testing in the EPM.

Hole Board Testing

The hole board test provided independent measures of activity and exploratory tendency (File and Wardill, 1975b). The hole board apparatus was an open top square wooden box measuring $60 \times 60 \times 35$ cm (length $\times$ width $\times$ height). In addition four evenly spaced holes were drilled 14 cm from the walls in a floor that was raised 12 cm above the ground. Both floor and walls were painted with grey enamel. Tape marked a square inside the box, separating it into center (containing the 4 holes) and perimeter (near the wall) segments.

Rats were placed in the center of the hole board apparatus and allowed to explore freely for 5 minutes. Rats were then immediately transferred to the EPM located in the same room for a further 5 minutes of testing. After each test the box was cleaned with a 5% alcohol solution.

Measures of activity and exploratory behavior were taken from video taped records. Activity was recorded as time spent in motion of any kind. Exploratory tendency was scored as the number of head dips (placing the head or snout into one of the four holes drilled in the floor). In addition the amount of time spent near the walls of the box was measured. Rats were considered to be near the wall of the box when all four feet were outside the center square marked by tape.

Elevated Plus Maze (EPM)

Immediately following the hole board test, rats were placed in the EPM. The EPM was a wooden four armed platform with arms arranged in the shape of a plus. The platform was painted with gray enamel, and was raised 50 cm above the floor. All arms were 10 cm wide and 50 cm long and joined in the center to a 10 cm square platform. Two arms facing each other were closed arms, the other two were open. Closed arms were surrounded by 40 cm high wooden walls which were open at the top, while open arms were bounded by a 3 cm high edge only.

At the start of each test, rats were placed in the center square facing the same open arm, and were allowed to move freely for 5 minutes. At the conclusion of each test, rats were returned to their home cage and the maze was cleaned and wiped dry using a 5% alcohol solution.

A number of behavioral measures were taken from videotape. These included standard measures of rodent anxiety: ratio time and ratio entry. Ratio time refers to the total time spent in the open arms of the maze divided by the total time spent in any arm of the maze. Ratio entry refers to the total entries into the open arms of the maze divided by the total entries into any arm of the maze. Smaller ratios indicate less open arm exploration, or more "anxiety." A rat was considered within an arm of the maze when all four feet were within the arm.

In addition, entries into the closed arms of the maze were taken as a measure of activity/exploratory tendency. Finally, risk assessment was measured. Risk assessment was scored when a rat poked its head into the open arm of the maze with its hindquarters in one of the closed arms. Frequency of risk assessment was recorded. The frequency of risk assessment was divided by the total time spent in the closed arms of the maze to produce a relative frequency risk assessment measure.

Selection of Mal-Adapted and Well-Adapted Predator Stressed Rats and Handled Controls

On the day of EPM testing, ratio time measures were calculated for each rat. Inclusion into the mal-adapted group of predator stressed rats required a ratio time score of 0. Well-adapted predator stressed rats were identified as those with ratio time scores falling between .25 and .50. This was based on an extensive data base of handled hooded rat data in the Adamec laboratory and was considered characteristic of the range of handled control EPM response (95% confidence intervals around a mean of .375). From the 71 predator stressed rats it was possible to select four well-adapted rats; thus, four mal-adapted rats were also selected. Four handled rats were randomly selected from the 10 handled controls.

Morphological Studies and Analysis

Animals were sacrificed under deep (chloral hydrate, 1 ml, 1 g/ml) anesthesia one day after EPM testing and 15 days after predator exposure or handling. Fresh brain tissue was removed and cut into a block containing right posterior amygdala from approximately 2.80 mm posterior to bregma back. This was done to capture that part of the right posterior BLA in which potentiation of ventral hippocampal afferent transmission is produced by predator stress (Adamec et al., 2005a; Adamec et al., 2001). Dissected brain tissues containing posterior amygdala were processed for staining individual neurons using rapid Golgi method. Golgi-stained BLA tissue was sectioned (120 μm thick), mounted with cover slips and used for morphological analysis. Camera Lucida tracings (500 X) were obtained (Nikon, USA) from up to ten selected neurons per rat (a mix of stellate and pyramidal principle output cells) and were then scanned (8-bit grayscale TIFF images with 600 dpi resolution; HP Scan Jet 6200C) along with a calibrated scale for subsequent computerized image-analysis. Custom-designed macros embedded in 'Scion Image' software (http://www.scioncorp.com/) were used for morphometric analysis of digitized images. Using the center of the soma as the reference point, dendritic length and branch points were measured as a function of radial distance from the soma by adding up all values in each successive concentric segment (Sholl's analysis). Golgi analysis was done blind to the group assignment of the brain under study. A total of four brains from each group were processed except for the predator stressed well-adapted group, which for technical reasons had three brains with well enough stained sections to process.

Statistical Analysis

Values are reported as mean ± SEM. One way analysis of variance (ANOVA) tested differences between handled controls, mal- and well-adapted animals. Post-hoc Fisher's Least Significant Difference (LSD) test was used for mean contrasts. For the purpose of morphological studies each neuron was considered as a data point (Vyas et al., 2002), a widely accepted method of analysis in golgi studies of dendritic morphology similar to the present study (Chakravarty et al., 2006; Dolen et al., 2007; Quach et al., 2008; Sherren and Pappas, 2005; Spiga et al., 2005; Whitcher and Klintsova,2008; Zehr et al., 2006).

Ethical Approval

All procedures involving animals in this study adhered to the guidelines of the Canadian Council on Animal care, and were approved by the Institutional Animal Care committee of Memorial University. All efforts were made to minimize pain, stress, and the number of animals used.

RESULTS

Mal-Adapted Animals Are More Anxious in the EPM Than Well-Adapted and Handled Controls Two Weeks After Treatment

While rats in the mal- and well-adapted groups were selected based on ratio time criteria, handled controls were randomly selected from a larger group. It was therefore important to confirm the expected pattern of differences in open arm exploration (ratio time and ratio entry) among the groups. Moreover, it was necessary to compare groups on measures of activity and exploration in order to ensure that differences in ratio time could be interpreted as differences in anxiety (open arm avoidance due to fear) and not differences in activity/exploration.

As expected, one way ANOVA confirmed that mal-adapted animals exhibited reduced open arm exploration (reduced ratio time and entries) relative to the other groups (Figure 1 B,C, all $F(2,8) > 18.23$ all $p < .001$, mean contrasts $p < .05$ LSD), which did not differ ($p > .05$ LSD). Similar group differences were observed in closed arm entries (Figure 1 A, $F(2,8) = 6.56$, $p < .021$, mean contrasts $p < .05$ LSD), suggesting reduced locomotor activity in mal-adapted rats. To assess if locomotor activity contributed to group differences in anxiety (i.e., reduced open arm exploration), closed arm entries were used as a covariate in a reanalysis of ratio time and ratio entry. Reduced locomotor activity in the EPM did not contribute to reduced open-arm exploration, as the original pattern of group differences was preserved in the analysis of covariance (Figure 2 A,B, all $F(2,7) > 12.81$ all $p < .01$, mean contrasts $p < .05$ LSD). Consistent with this analysis, there were no group differences in the hole board measures of activity/ exploration (time active or head dips), nor did the groups differ in time near the wall (all $F(2,8) < 2.72$, all $p > .12$). These data support the conclusion that mal-adapted rats are selectively more anxious in the EPM than well-adapted rats and handled controls, which do not differ in anxiety.

Mal-adapted rats displayed less risk assessment in the EPM than well-adapted rats, and handled controls fell between these groups, differing from neither (Figure 1 D, $F(2,8) = 6.54$, $p < .03$; mean contrasts, $p < .05$, LSD). Though reduced risk assessment in mal-adapted rats is consistent with previous reports of effects of predator stress on this measure (Adamec and Shallow, 1993; Adamec et al., 2001), in the present study the group differences appear to reflect differences between groups in EPM activity (closed arm entries). Reanalysis of risk assessment data with closed arm entries as a covariate eliminated the group differences (Figure 2 C, $F(2,7) = 2.45$, $p < .16$).

The Predator Stress Experience

Well- and mal-adapted rats were compared with respect to cat response to them and their responses to the cat. There were no group differences (all $F(1,5) < .75$, $p > .43$).

Therefore the predator stress experience, as measured, did not differ between well and mal-adapted rats.

Predator Stressed Animals Per Se Are More Anxious in the EPM Than Handled Controls Two Weeks After Treatment

It is important to confirm that there was an overall anxiogenic effect of predator stress in the group from which mal-adapted and well-adapted rats were selected. Therefore, behavioral responses in the EPM and hole board of all handled (n = 10) and all stressed (n = 71) rats were compared. Stressed animals exhibited significantly reduced open arm exploration (reduced ratio times and entries) relative to handled animals (Table 1). Of interest, groups did not differ in closed arm entries ($F(1,79) = 0.50$, p>.48, means + SEM of handled, stressed respectively: 9.4 + .88, 8.7 + .33). These data suggest that locomotor activity did not contribute to group differences in anxiety, a conclusion drawn in the selected group analysis above. Consistent with this conclusion, there were no group differences in time active or head dips in the hole board (all $F(1,79) < 2.36$, all p > .12). Interestingly, stressed rats spent more time near the wall than handled controls (Table 1), consistent with increased EPM anxiety. Taken together the data support the conclusion that overall predator stressed rats were more anxious in the EPM than handled controls. Finally, consistent with the smaller group analyses above, groups did not differ in risk assessment ($F(1,79) = 2.20$, p < .15)

Predator Stress Well-Adapted Animals Show Differences From Other Groups in Dendritic Morphology of BLA Neuron

BLA stellate and pyramidal principle output neurons of the groups differed in dendritic length, number of branch points, branch packing (number of branches per 100 μm of dendrite length) and extent of dendritic tree (farthest distance from soma that any dendrite could be detected) (all $F(2,91) > 4.20$, p < .02). Mal-adapted animals did not differ significantly from handled controls in any dendritic parameter ($p > 0.25$). Total dendritic length was lowest in well-adapted animals compared to mal-adapted (26% reduction, $p < 0.001$ LSD, Figure 3 A) and to handled control animals (22% reduction, $p = 0.001$ LSD). In contrast, total number of branch points was highest in well-adapted animals compared to handled controls ($p < 0.01$ LSD, Figure 3 B) and to mal-adapted animals ($p < 0.05$ LSD). Thus, the number of branches per 100 µm of dendritic length (branch packing) was highest in animals well-adapted to predator stress (> 38 % increase over handled controls, $p < 0.001$ LSD, Figure 3 C). Additionally well-adapted animals exhibited the shortest dendritic extent, significantly differing from the other two groups ($p < 0.01$ LSD, Figure 3 D).

In summary, well-adapted animals showed retracted dendritic arbors with higher branch packing, compared to both handled controls and mal-adapted animals. Dendritic trees of mal-adapted animals, on the other hand, were not different from control animals. Representative neurons from the three groups and a typical golgi-stained BLA neuron are depicted in Figures 4 A and B respectively.

Well-Adapted Animals Show Maximum Branch Packing at Radial Distance 75–125 µm From the Soma

We conducted a segmental analysis of branch packing to qualitatively determine if dendritic changes were localized to certain parts of the arbor. Using the soma as the center, dendritic trees of individual neurons were sub-divided into successive concentric circles (25 µm successive increase in radius; Figure 5 B). Group means of dendritic length in each segment were divided by number of branch points of cells in a given group at that segment to generate a coefficient of packing for that group (Figure 5 A, no SEM plotted, none calculated since this is a ratio of a group mean to total group branch points at a given segment). Mal-adapted animals and handled controls exhibited sparser packing (more dendritic length per branch point) compared to well-adapted animals. These differences were evident between 75 μm to 125 μm distance from the cell soma. So well-adapted animals exhibited greater branch packing at a radial distance of 75 μm to 125 μm from the soma.

Total Dendritic Length Correlates
Selectively With EPM Anxiety

Total dendritic length, dendritic extent, total branch points and branch packing (branch points per 100 μm) were correlated with behavior in the EPM. Data consisted of dendritic parameter values averaged over cells for each rat in the different groups, as well as EPM measures that differed between groups: ratio time and entry and closed arm entries for each rat. Spearman non-parametric correlations were used since some variables were not normally distributed (Kolmogorov-Smirnov test > .304, p < .05). Correlations were calculated on stressed mal- and well-adapted rats as well as all three groups together (including handled controls).

Correlating BLA dendritic morphology and behavior in stressed rats revealed significant negative correlations between total dendritic length and ratio time and ratio entry only (all Spearman correlations or Spearman's rho— ρ <—0.865 all p < .012; see scatter plot example for ratio time vs length; Figure 6 A). The negative correlations indicate that the shorter the length and extent of dendrites, the larger the ratio time and entry, and the less the anxiety. In addition, dendritic extent correlated negatively with ratio time and entry (all ρ < −0.866 all p < .012). However this correlation was apparently mediated by total dendritic length as the correlation was not significant when the influence of total dendritic length was removed by partial correlation (p >.20). Total branch points and branch packing did not correlate with ratio time or ratio entry (all p > .05). In contrast, branch packing was positively related to closed arm entries (ρ = 0.873 p < .011), while closed arm entries did not correlate with total dendritic length, dendritic extent or total branch points (all p > .05).

When handled controls were included, dendritic morphology and behavior correlations broke down (all p > .13; see Figure 6 B), with one exception. Branch packing remained positively correlated with closed arm entries ($\rho = 0.626$, p < .040). Therefore total dendritic length is selectively predictive of EPM anxiety in stressed rats only. Moreover, a different aspect of dendritic morphology (branch packing) is selectively predictive of activity (closed arm entries) in stressed and unstressed rats.

Of importance to the interpretation is the apparent overlap of average total dendritic length of pairs of handled controls with that of well- and mal-adapted stressed rats (Figure 6 B). Handled rats segregated into pairs with cells of comparable total dendritic length (all p >.20), and the cells of the segregated pairs differed from each other in total dendritic length (t(28) = 3.26, p<.003). In addition similar comparisons of averages of the other dendritic parameters for each rat within each group showed no differences between rats within a given group. Thus, the segregation is particular to total dendritic length. Moreover the analysis also suggests that within groups, there were no outlier rats dominating a group's average, an important point, given the small group sizes.

DISCUSSION

Exposure to a cat induces long-lasting increases in anxiety in rats (Adamec and Shallow, 1993). Yet, not all animals show increased anxiety. A subset that we referred to here as well-adapted remains unaffected by the cat exposure. Thus, the same stress experience evokes different degrees of behavioral response. Here we report that animals showing these disparate behavioral outcomes differ in dendritic architecture of basolateral amygdala (BLA) neurons, which form part of the neural circuitry mediating stress-induced anxiety (Adamec et al., 2005b; Adamec et al., 2001; Mitra and Sapolsky, 2008; Vyas et al., 2002). Well-adapted animals exhibit retracted dendrites and increased packing density of dendrites compared to mal-adapted animals with high anxiety, and surprisingly, compared to unstressed handled controls. These findings point to a putative neurobiological substrate for resilience to the anxiogenic effects of severe (predator) stress. Interestingly, these resilient individuals do not differ from their less resilient counterparts in their interaction with the cat. Rather their differences are limited to the fact that these individuals do not generalize fear experienced during the trauma. Animal models have been successfully used to study key aspects of stress effects on anxiety and fear. We believe that this naturally occurring variation gives us an important animal model to study resilience.

There is significant interest in understanding resilience, that is, the process of adapting well in face of adversity or trauma (Charney, 2004; DeRijk and DeKloet, 2008; Freeman et al., 2006; McEwen, 2007; Nemeroff et al., 2006). Understanding mechanisms behind such resilience is important from the perspective of designing effective therapies. Our findings implicate variation in dendritic arbor of amygdala neurons as a candidate mechanism for variation in stress resilience. Correlation analysis suggests that dendritic length is particularly relevant to anxiety levels. Moreover, a reduced dendritic arbor as a mediator of resilience to stress makes functional sense. As reviewed in the introduction, the BLA is important in mediating anxiogenic effects of stress. The BLA can undergo structural reorganization in response to stressors as diverse as immobilization, maternal stress and external application of the stress hormone, corticosterone (Mitra et al., 2005; Mitra and Sapolsky, 2008; Vyas et al., 2002; Weinstock, 2008). A prominent feature of such structural reorganization is dendritic expansion (hypertrophy) of excitatory neurons of the BLA. Once evoked, BLA hypertrophy is as lasting as long-lasting anxiety (Vyas et al., 2004). Conversely, dendritic retraction, achieved by viral-mediated over expression of inhibitory SK2 potassium channels in BLA, results in reduction of anxiety (Mitra et al., 2009).

Based on a positive relationship between dendritic structure and anxiety, three hypothesis can be proposed to explain individual differences. First, mal-adapted animals showing greater anxiety undergo dendritic expansion, while well-adapted animals are resistant to such dendritic expansion. Second, well-adapted animals undergo dendritic retraction, thus countering anxiogenic effects of predator exposure. Third, preexisting differences in dendritic morphology in BLA cells predispose towards differences in the neuroplastic excitatory effect of stress on BLA response to afferent input, and towards differences in anxiety. Data presented here support the second and third possibilities. BLA dendritic trees of well-adapted animals either undergo dendritic retraction relative to mal-adapted animals and handled controls in response to stress, or well-adapted animals have a preexisting less extensive dendritic tree which works against the enhancement of anxiety by stress.

Variation in dendritic arbors can directly influence electrical properties of the neuron. Effects of a reduced arbor range from altered passive electrotonic properties to shorter surface area for receiving synaptic inputs. With regard to the latter possibility, reduced BLA response to excitatory input from the ventral hippocampus is associated with less EPM anxiety in predator stressed rats (Adamec et al., 2005b; Adamec et al., 2001). A working hypothesis requiring further testing is that reduced dendritic arbors in well-adapted rats reduces excitatory transmission in BLA circuitry and thereby counters the normal predator stress-induced potentiation in BLA afferent transmission. Interestingly, reduced dendritic length in hippocampal CA1 neurons is associated with impaired LTP (Champagne et al., 2008). Moreover, the concentration of dendritic branches near the soma might have inhibitory influences, which would be in agreement with a recent report (Muller et al., 2006).

In this study only a small number of animals (4 out of 71) showed resilience in the face of predator stress. From our present data, it is difficult to determine if morphometric differences between well- and mal-adapted animals were stress-induced, or were pre-existing differences. The segregation of handled controls into greater and lesser dendritic arbor lengths is suggestive of the latter, however. It is not possible to achieve paired measurements before and after stress, because of the post-mortem nature of Golgi staining. Nor is it yet possible to reliably predict mal- or well-adapted responses to predator stress, so a test of whether arbor retraction is induced by stress or is preexisting is difficult at this time. The fact that the correlations between dendritic length and behavior hold only for stressed rats, together with the finding that well-adapted stressed rats show smaller dendritic arbors than do handled controls with similar EPM anxiety, are consistent with a stress-induced retraction of dendritic arbor in well-adapted stressed rats.

Perhaps more compelling is the following: the pattern of findings point to total dendritic length as a critical neurostructural parameter underlying vulnerability to anxiogenic response to predator stress. It is likely that handled controls contain a mixture of dendritic length profiles akin to stress mal-adapted and stress well-adapted animals; thereby suggesting that dendritic length profiles are individual phenotypic differences. It is possible that smaller dendritic length prior to stress presents less of a substrate for the neuroplastic (LTP-like) changes in afferent inputs to the BLA shown to be induced by predator stress and to predict the degree of EPM anxiety (Adamec et al., 2005b). The opposite would apply to greater dendritic length profiles prior to stress. Animals with smaller total dendritic length profiles would be expected to show well-adapted responses to stress, whereas animals with greater total dendritic length would show mal-adapted stress responses. This logic is also consistent with the data showing anxiety-total dendritic length correlations only in stressed rats, since stress must act on the preexisting dendritic substrate to change neural response and behavior.

Finally, the present data also suggest that different aspects of dendritic morphology may contribute to different behaviors. A variety of studies, including the present study, point to differences in neural substrates mediating stress effects on EPM anxiety (open arm avoidance, ratio time/entry) and risk assessment and activity (closed arm entries) in EPM (Adamec, 2001; Adamec et al., 1999). Intriguingly, the present data suggest no relationship between BLA output, dendritic morphology and risk assessment, but a relationship between branch packing of BLA dendrites and EPM activity; while variation in dendritic length of the same cells may contribute to stress effects on EPM anxiety.

In conclusion, we show that well-adapted and mal-adapted animals systematically differ in terms of BLA dendritic arbors. Moreover, dendritic differences relate to disparate changes in anxiety exhibited by these animals. Thus different patterns of plasticity in BLA-neurons in response to stress could form the basis of widely reported individual differences observed in coping response to stress and trauma.

FINANCIAL DISCLOSURES

Dr. Mitra has no biomedical financial interests or potential conflicts of interest.

Dr. Adamec has no biomedical financial interests or potential conflicts of interest.

Dr. Sapolsky has no biomedical financial interests or potential conflicts of interest.

REFERENCES

Adamec R (2001) Does long term potentiation in periacqueductal gray (PAG) mediate lasting changes in rodent ALB produced by predator stress? Effects of low frequency stimulation (LFS) of PAG on place preference and changes in ALB produced by predator stress. Behav Brain Res 120:111–135.

Adamec RE, Shallow T (1993) Lasting effects on rodent anxiety of a single exposure to a cat. Physiol Behav 54:101–109.

Adamec R, Kent P, Anisman H, Shallow T, Merali Z (1998) Neural plasticity, neuropeptides and anxiety in animals—implications for understanding and treating affective disorder following traumatic stress in humans. Neurosci Biobehav Rev 23:301–318.

Adamec RE, Burton P, Shallow T, Budgell J (1999) Unilateral block of NMDA receptors in the amygdala prevents predator stress-induced lasting increases in anxiety-like behavior and unconditioned startle—Effect on behavior depends on the hemisphere. Physiol Behav 65:739–751.

Adamec RE, Blundell J, Collins A (2001) Neural plasticity and stress induced changes in defense in the rat. Neurosci Biobehav Rev 25:721–744.

Adamec R, Walling S, Burton P (2004) Long-lasting, selective, anxiogenic effects of feline predator stress in mice. Physiol Behav 80:401–410.

Adamec R, Blundell J, Burton P (2005a) Role of NMDA receptors in the lateralized potentiation of amygdala afferent and efferent neural transmission produced by predator stress. Physiol Behav 86:75–91.

Adamec RE, Blundell J, Burton P (2005b) Neural circuit changes mediating lasting brain and behavioral response to predator stress. Neurosci Biobehav Rev 29:1225–1241.

Adamec R, Blundell J, Strasser K, Burton P (2006a) Mechanisms of lasting change in anxiety induced by severe stress. In: PTSD: Brain mechanisms and clinical implications (Sato N, Pitman R, eds), pp61–81. Tokyo: Springer-Verlag.

Adamec R, Burton P, Blundell J, Murphy DL, Holmes A (2006b) Vulnerability to mild predator stress in serotonin transporter knockout mice. Behav Brain Res 170:126–140.

Adamec R, Head D, Blundell J, Burton P, Berton O (2006c) Lasting anxiogenic effects of feline predator stress in mice: Sex differences in vulnerability to stress and predicting severity of anxiogenic response from the stress experience. Physiol Behav 88:12–29.

Adamec R, Holmes A, Blundell J (2008) Vulnerability to lasting anxiogenic effects of brief exposure to predator stimuli: Sex, serotonin and other factors-Relevance to PTSD. Neurosci Biobehav Rev 32:1287–1292.

Blanchard RJ, Blanchard DC (1989) Antipredator defensive behaviors in a visible burrow system. J Comp Psych 103:70–82.

Chakravarthy S, Saiepour MH, Bence M, Perry S, Hartman R, Couey JJ, Mansvelder HD, Leveit CN (2006) Postsynaptic TrkB signaling has distinct roles in spine maintenance in adult visual cortex and hippocampus. Proc Natl Acad Sci U S A, 103:1071–1076.

Champagne DL, Bagot RC, van Hasselt F, Ramakers G, Meaney MJ, de Kloet ER, Joels M, Krugers H (2008) Maternal care and hippocampal plasticity: Evidence for experience-dependent structural plasticity, altered synaptic functioning, and differential responsiveness to glucocorticoids and stress. J Neurosci 28:6037–6045.

Charney DS (2004) Psychobiological and vulnerability: Implications for successful adaptation to extreme stress. Am J Psychiatry 161:195–216.

Cohen H, Friedberg S, Michael M, Kotler M, Zeev K (1996) Interaction of CCK-4 induced anxiety and post-cat exposure anxiety in rats. Depress Anxiety 4:144–145.

Cohen H, Zohar J, Matar M (2003) The relevance of differential response to trauma in an animal model of posttraumatic stress disorder. Biol Psychiatry 53:463–473.

Cohen H, Zohar J, Matar MA, Zeev K, Loewenthal U, Richter-Levin G (2004) Setting apart the affected: The use of behavioral criteria in animal models of post traumatic stress disorder. Neuropsychopharmacology 29:1962–1970.

Cohen H, Geva B, Matar MA, Zohar J, Kaplan Z (2008) Post-traumatic stress behavioural responses in inbred mouse strains: can genetic predisposition explain phenotypic vulnerability? Int J Neuropsychopharmacol 11:331–349.

DeRijk RH, DeKloet ER (2008) Corticosteroid receptor polymorphisms: Determinants of vulnerability and resilience. Eur J Pharmacol 583:303–311.

Dolen G, Osterweil E, Rao BS, Auerbach BD, Chattarji S, Bear MF (2007) Correction of fragile X syndrome in mice. Neuron 56:955–962.

File SE (1987) The contribution of behavioural studies to the neuropharmacology of anxiety. Neuropharmacology 26:877–886.

File SE, Wardill AG (1975a) The reliability of the hole-board apparatus. Psychopharmacologia 44:47–51.

File SE, Wardill AG (1975b) Validity of head-dipping as a measure of exploration in a modified hole-board. Psychopharmacologia 44:53–59.

Freeman T, Kimbrell T, Booe L Myers M, Cardwell D, Lindquist DM, Hart J, Komoroski RA (2006) Evidence of resilience: Neuroimaging in former prisoners of war. Psychiatric Research: Neuroimaging 146:59–64.

Hariri AR, Drabant EM, Munoz KE Kolachana BS, Mattay VS, Egan MF, Weinberger DR (2005) A susceptibility gene for affective disorders and the response of the human amygdala. Arch Gen Psychiatry 62:146–152.

Heinrichs M, Wagner D, Schoch W, Soravia LM, Hellhammer DH, Ehlert U (2005) Predicting posttraumatic stress symptoms from pretraumatic risk factors: A 2-year prospective follow-up study in firefighters. Am J Psychiatry 162:2276–2286.

Kessler RC, Sonnega A, Bromet E, Hughes M, Nelson CB (1995) Posttraumatic stress disorder in the National Comorbidity Survey. Arch Gen Psychiatry 52:1048–1060.

Kessler RC, Berglund P, Demler O, Jin R, Merikangas KR, Walters EE (2005) Lifetime prevalence and age-of-onset distributions of DSM-IV disorders in the National Comorbidity Survey Replication. Arch Genl Psychiatry 62:593–602.

Kilpatrick DG, Koenen KC, Ruggiero KJ, Acierno R, Galea S, Resnick HS, Roitzsch J, Boyle J, Gelernter J (2007) The serotonin transporter genotype and social support and moderation of posttraumatic stress disorder and depression in hurricane-exposed adults. Am J Psychiatry 164:1693–1699.

Kozlovsky N, Matar MA, Kaplan Z, Kotler M, Zohar J, Cohen H (2007) Long-term down-regulation of BDNF mRNA in rat hippocampal CA1 subregion correlates with PTSD-like behavioural stress response. Int J Neuropsychopharmacol 10:741–758.

Kozlovsky N, Matar MA, Kaplan Z, Kotler M, Zohar J, Cohen H (2008) The immediate early gene Arc is associated with behavioral resilience to stress exposure in an animal model of posttraumatic stress disorder. European Neuropsychopharmacology 18:107–116.

Lee HJ, Lee MS, Kang RH, Kim H, Kim SD, Kee BS, Kim YH, Kim YK, Kim JB, Yeon BK, Oh KS, Oh BH, Yoon JS, Lee C, Jung HY, Chee IS, Paik IH (2005) Influence of the serotonin transporter promoter gene polymorphism on susceptibility to posttraumatic stress disorder. Depress Anxiety 21:135–139.

McEwen BS (2007) Physiology and neurobiology of stress and adaptation: Central role of the brain. Physiol Rev 87:873–904.

McNally RJ (2003) Psychological mechanisms in acute response to trauma. Biol Psychiatry 53:779–788.

Mitra R, Sapolsky RM (2008) Acute corticosterone treatment is sufficient to induce anxiety and amygdaloid dendritic hypertrophy. Proc Natl Acad Sci U S A 105:5573–5578.

Mitra R, Jadhav S, McEwen BS, Vyas A, Chattarji S (2005) Stress duration modulates the spatiotemporal patterns of spine formation in the basolateral amygdala. Proc Natl Acad Sci U S A 102:9371–9376.

Mitra R, Ferguson D, Sapolsky R (2009) SK2 potassium channel overexpression in basolateral amygdala reduces anxiety, stress-induced corticosterone secretion and dendritic arborization. Molecular Psychiatry 14: 847–855.

Muller JF, Mascagni F, McDonald AJ (2006) Pyramidal cells of the rat basolateral amygdala: Synaptology and innervation by parvalbumin-immunoreactive interneurons. J Comp Neurol 494:635–650.

Nemeroff CB, Bremner JD, Foa EB, Mayberg HS, North CS, Stein MB (2006) Posttraumatic stress disorder: a state-of-the-science review. J Psychiatr Res 40:1–21.

Quach TT, Massicotte G, Berlin MF, Honnorat J, Glasper ER, DeVries AC (2008) CRMP3 is required for hippocampal CA1 dendritic organization and plasticity. FASEB J 22:401–409.

Rauch SL, Shin LM, Phelps EA (2006) Neurocircuitry models of posttraumatic stress disorder and extinction: Human neuroimaging research—Past, present, and future. Biol Psychiatry 60:376–382.

Sherren N, Pappas BA (2005) Selective acetylcholine and dopamine lesions in neonatal rats produce distinct patterns of cortical dendritic atrophy in adulthood. Neuroscience 132:445–456.

Shin LM, Wright CI, Cannistraro PA, Wedig MM, McMullin K, Martis B, Macklin ML, Lasko NB, Cavanagh SR, Krangel TS, Orr SP, Pitman RK, Whalen PJ, Rauch SL (2005) A functional magnetic resonance imaging study of amygdala and medial prefrontal cortex responses to overtly presented fearful faces in posttraumatic stress disorder. Arch Gen Psychiatry 62:273–281.

Spiga S, Puddu MC, Pisano M, Diana M (2005) Morphine withdrawal-induced morphological changes in the nucleus accumbens. Eur J Neurosci 22:2332–2340.

Stam R (2007a) PTSD and stress sensitisation: A tale of brain and body Part 1: Human studies. Neurosci Biobehav Rev 31:530–557.

Stam R (2007b) PTSD and stress sensitisation: A tale of brain and body Part 2: Animal models. Neurosci Biobehav Rev 31:558–584.

Vyas A, Mitra R, Rao BSS, Chattarji S (2002) Chronic stress induces contrasting patterns of dendritic remodeling in hippocampal and amygdaloid neurons. J Neurosci 22:6810–6818.

Vyas A, Pillai AG, Chattarji S (2004) Recovery after chronic stress fails to reverse amygdaloid neuronal hypertrophy and enhanced anxiety-like behavior. Neuroscience 128:667–673.

Weinstock M (2008) The long-term behavioural consequences of prenatal stress. Neurosci Biobehav Rev 32:1073–1086.

Whitcher LT, Klintsova AY (2008) Postnatal binge-like alcohol exposure reduces spine density without affecting dendritic morphology in rat mPFC. Synapse 62:566–573.

Zehr JL, Todd BJ, Schulz KM, McCarthy MM, Sisk CL (2006) Dendritic pruning of the medial amygdala during pubertal development of the male Syrian hamster. J Neurobiol 66:578–590.

FIGURE LEGENDS

Figure 1. Plotted across handled and stressed mal- and well-adapted groups in Figures A–D are mean + SEM of behaviors measured in the EPM. Within a given behavioral plot, means marked with the same letter do not differ, means marked differently differ, and means marked with two letters fall between and do not differ from means marked with either letter.

Figure 2. Plotted across handled, and stressed mal- and well-adapted groups in Figures A–C are mean + SEM of measures of open arm exploration (ratio time/entry) and risk in the EPM after covarying closed arm entries from them. Within a given behavioral plot, means marked with the same letter do not differ, means marked differently differ. Unmarked means in C do not differ.

Figure 3. Plotted across handled, and stressed mal- and well-adapted groups in Figures A–D are mean + SEM of dendritic morphological measures taken from BLA neurons ($n = 30$ neurons for well-adapted [10 cells from each of 3 rats], $n = 25$ for handled [6 cells from each of 3 rats and 7 cells from the fourth] and $n = 39$ [10 cells from each of 3 rats and 9 cells from the fourth] for mal-adapted groups of animals). Within a given plot, means marked with the same letter do not differ, means marked differently differ.

Figure 4. Qualitative representation of neurons from each group of animals. A. Schematic diagram of neuronal tracing from handled (left), well-adapted (middle) and mal-adapted (right) animals. Scale bar = 100 mm. B. A typical BLA field stained with Golgi, showing a stellate neuron at 500X.

Figure 5. Segmental analysis showing packing density (length per branch). A. Well-adapted animals show highest packing density compared to other two groups at a radial distance 75–125 mm from cell soma. B. Sholl's analysis (with a typical tracing of a golgi-stained neuron) used for determination of segmental branch-packing in all groups; each concentric circle with 25 mm radial distance away from inner one.

Figure 6. Scatter plots illustrating the variation of EPM ratio time with total dendritic length—A. scatter plot of predator stressed rats (well- and mal- adapted) only; B. scatter plot including all groups (handled and well- and mal- adapted).

Figure 1

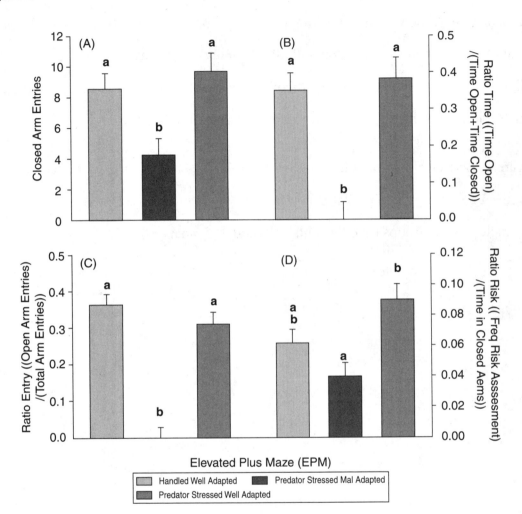

Figure 2

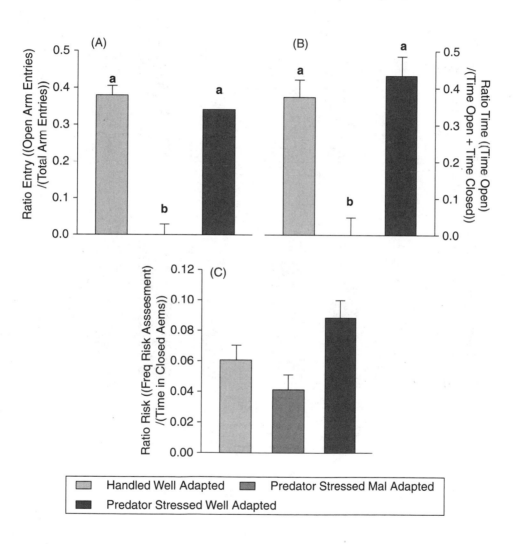

Figure 3

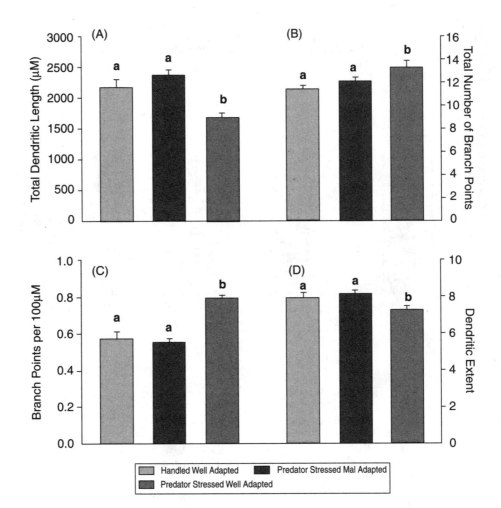

Figure 4

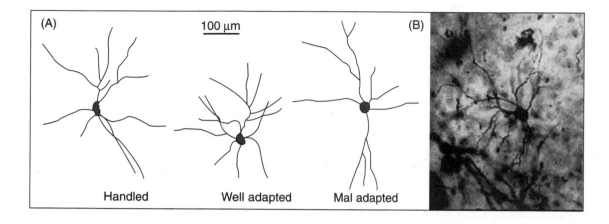

Figure 5

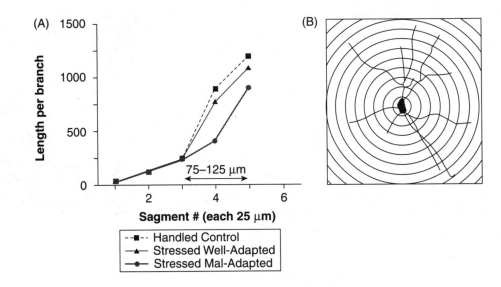

Figure 6

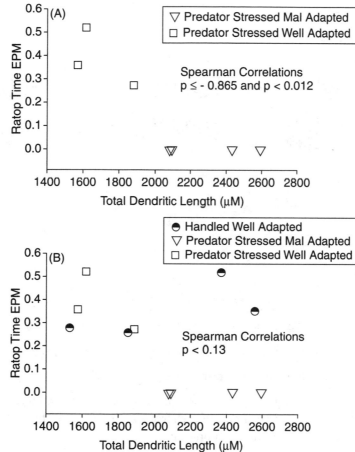

Appendix D | Review Questions and Exercises

1. What is science? (p. 6)

2. How can you distinguish science from pseudoscience? (pp. 6–7)

3. Distinguish experimental from nonexperimental science. (pp. 8–9)

4. Explain how epistemology is relevant to science. (p. 9)

5. Define empiricism, rationalism, paradigm, and interfield theories, and give an example of each from neuroscience, different from the examples used in the textbook. (pp. 9–14)

6. Give an example of a question within our currently accepted paradigm for neuroscience research and a question that is outside our current paradigm. (p. 13)

7. List three good habits for data analysis and three rules for keeping a laboratory notebook that can help to protect you from suspicions of fraud. (p. 19)

8. Describe the "three Rs" used to guide the ethical use of nonhuman animals in research. (pp. 23–24)

9. Contrast the Animal Welfare Act to the *PHS Policy on Humane Care and Use of Laboratory Animals*. Address the researchers and animals they apply to as well as how they are enforced. (pp. 25–26)

10. Define and give examples of the three major ethical principles in the Belmont Report. (pp. 29–30)

11. How might bias affect your choice of a research question in neuroscience? (pp. 38–40)

12. Describe how a model is different from a theory. (p. 48)

13. By what criteria would you judge a theory within neuroscience? Give at least three criteria and no more than five. (p. 48)

14. What criteria might you use to choose among competing scientific theories? (p. 50)

15. Design a test of locomotor function that uses an ordinal scale of measurement. Contrast with one that uses a ratio scale. (pp. 56–57)

16. Define and give an example of a null hypothesis, research hypothesis, operationalized hypothesis, alternative hypothesis, and straw-man hypothesis. (pp. 46–47)

17. Distinguish naturalistic observations from structured observations. (p. 58)

18. Contrast a multiple case design with a case control design. (p. 61)

19. Contrast an independent-samples design with a within-subjects design. (pp. 63, 78–79)

20. Define experiment, independent variable, dependent variable, controlled variable, confounding variable, randomization, and replication. (pp. 62–65)

21. Contrast descriptive statistics with inferential statistics. (pp. 66, 142)

22. What is a Type I error? What is a Type II error? How can you decrease the chances of making each of these different errors? (pp. 68–69)

23. Describe how you could use a matched-samples design to control for serotonin levels. (p. 79)

24. Contrast a single-blind to a double-blind study. (pp. 87–88)

25. Describe what procedures you would follow for: a vehicle control group, a sham surgery control group, and a placebo control group. (pp. 86, 88–89)

26. Using an example fMRI experiment, contrast a blocked design to an event-related design. (p. 92)

27. How is a quasi-experiment different from a true experiment? (pp. 131, 70)

28. Your lab wants to assess the anxiolytic properties of a benzodiazepine (for example, Valium) on mouse behavior using an elevated plus maze. List two potential confounding variables that could affect your study, and state briefly how you would avoid their influence in your experimental design. (pp. 64–65)

29. Describe two different studies on Parkinson's disease, with one study high on internal validity and the other study high on external validity. Describe what features make them high in that type of validity. (p. 50)

30. How can you use convergent methods to approach a research problem with studies high in both external validity and internal validity? (p. 52)

31. In a $2 \times 8 \times 4$ design, how many independent variables are there? How many groups are there? (pp. 99–101)

32. In a $3 \times 5 \times 2$ experimental design, how many independent variables are there? How many groups are there? If each group had $n = 10$ subjects, how many total subjects would you need (assume all conditions are between subjects)? (pp. 99–101)

33. Draw a sample plot that demonstrates a 2×2 factorial experiment with one main effect and no interaction. Draw a graph with two main effects and a significant interaction. (pp. 102–107)

34. A transcranial magnetic stimulator can inactivate a brain area, while fMRI can show activity in a brain area. Describe a hypothetical experiment where you used both of these techniques to determine if activity in a particular area is both necessary and sufficient for a particular behavior. (p. 72)

35. Be able to interpret a correlation value. (pp. 114–118)

36. What are several problems common to correlational studies? (pp. 118–122)

37. Draw a scatterplot that shows: a strong positive correlation, a moderate negative correlation, and no correlation. Identify the properties of each graph that indicate the type of correlation illustrated. (pp. 114–117)

38. Be able to construct a frequency histogram, a box plot, a scatterplot, and a bar graph with error bars. (Appendix A)

39. Know how to calculate the mean, median, and mode. (Appendix A)

40. Describe the shape, center, and spread of a distribution using appropriate measures. (Appendix A)

41. What is an outlier? What is one quantitative way you might define an outlier? (Appendix A)

42. Contrast descriptive statistics with inferential statistics. (Appendix A)

43. When would you use a *t*-test? When would you use an ANOVA? (Address both the experimental design and the assumptions behind the test.) (Appendix A)

44. What is the ratio underlying the *F* statistic for an ANOVA? (Appendix A)

45. Why are multiple comparison tests required after an ANOVA? (Appendix A)

46. The following analysis was reported: $t(120) = 2.00$, $p < 0.05$. What do these numbers mean? (Appendix A)

Appendix E | Glossary

alpha (α): The cutoff value of a probability of a Type I error (rejecting the null hypothesis when it is true) that you will accept; typically, alpha is set to 0.05.

alternative hypothesis: A hypothesis that will be supported if your results do not support your experimental hypothesis; in well-designed studies, the experiment tests two equally strong hypotheses.

analysis of variance (ANOVA): A parametric inferential statistical test used for making inferences about the means of multiple populations; used to determine if any of the groups sampled are statistically different from any of the other groups; based on comparisons of variation *within* the groups versus *between* the groups.

Animal Welfare Act: The first legislation to set standards for the use of animals in laboratories in the United States. The Animal Welfare Act currently covers all warm-blooded animals used in research and teaching, except for rats, mice, birds, and farm animals used in agricultural research.

Association for Assessment and Accreditation of Laboratory Animal Care (AAALAC): An organization that certifies that the very highest standards of animal care are being applied to all vertebrate animal use in teaching and research at a particular institution.

attrition: The loss of subjects before or during your experiment.

authority: An expert or an especially respected person who serves as a source of knowledge.

Belmont Report: A report first published in 1979 that provides the basis of current ethical guidelines for research with human participants.

beta (β): The probability of making a Type II error (failing to reject the null hypothesis when it is false).

between-subjects design: An experimental study in which each subject experiences only one level of each independent variable.

bimodal: A distribution that has two major peaks.

blind analysis: A procedure of coding samples before analysis so that the researcher conducting the analysis is unaware of prior treatments.

blocked design: A study in which the experimental conditions occur in an alternating order, with each level of the independent variable presented for an extended time, in blocks.

box plot: A graphical representation using the five-number summary to provide a display of the distribution of data.

case control design: A study in which the researcher selects controls for each case in the sample.

case study: A study based on the description and analysis of one particular individual, group, or event.

central tendency: The typical score in a distribution. Common statistical measures of central tendency are the mean, median, and mode.

Common Rule: A policy that governs study of humans in research across a wide range of U.S. federal agencies.

confounding variable: A variable that changes with the independent variable but is not intended by the experimenter to vary with the independent variable.

controlled variables: Variables explicitly eliminated or made identical for two or more groups.

convergent evidence: Results from experiments using widely divergent techniques that converge on the same conclusion.

correlation coefficient: A statistic that indicates the strength and direction of the relationship between two variables; can vary between $n-1.0$ and $+1.0$.

correlational design: A research study that allows you to measure the relationship between two or more measured variables.

counterbalance: A method to control for order effects, varying the order of the conditions so that an equal number of subjects experience the various possible orders of the conditions.

critical value: The minimum value for a statistic in an inferential test (such as a *t* or *F*) that you would accept to reject the null hypothesis at a given level of alpha; the minimum value for the results to be considered statistically significant; depends on the sample size and the level of risk you will accept for making a Type I error.

debriefing: The session following completion of an experiment, where the experiment is fully explained to each participant, including information on the rationale for the experiment and the person's specific contribution to the research.

degrees of freedom: The number of independent elements when a sample statistic is computed.

dependent (or outcome) variable: The measured variable, the tool by which the experimenter will assess the effects of the independent variable.

descriptive statistics: Numbers summarizing characteristics of a sample such as the central tendency or the variability.

descriptive study: Research designed to describe a phenomenon in a careful and replicable manner.

directional hypothesis: A prediction that explicitly states the direction of an effect.

dissociation: A situation that occurs in cases of brain damage, in which the damage causes a problem in one function while not affecting other functions.

distribution: A collection of values for a variable.

double-blind procedure: A method of conducting a study in which neither the participants nor the experimenters administering the treatments know who is in the experimental group and who is in the control group.

double dissociation: A situation in which a single dissociation can be demonstrated in one person, and the opposite type of dissociation can be demonstrated in another person. For example, the presentation of a patient with damage to one area of the brain, who demonstrates the ability to carry out one task but not another, and another patient with damage to a different brain area, who cannot complete the first task but can easily complete the second task.

ecological validity: How well your research mirrors the conditions in the natural world.

empiricism: The idea that all knowledge arises from experience through the senses.

epistemology: The study of how we know what we know.

euthanasia: A "gentle death," generally by overdose with an anesthetic or some other approved humane means.

event-related design: A research study in which brain activity is measured following short-duration presentations of stimuli in discrete events or trials.

event sampling: Counting the number of times a particular behavior or event occurs during the observation period.

experiment: Research where the investigator gains new information by observing results after manipulating at least one independent variable, controlling other variables.

experimental hypothesis: The hypothesis that the independent variable will have an effect on the dependent variable.

experimenter effects: Influence of the experimenter on the outcome of the experiment, due to bias in treating subjects or recording data.

external validity: The extent to which a research study generalizes to other populations or other settings.

***F* ratio:** The ratio of between-groups variability to within-groups variability.

fabrication: The creation of false data with an intent to deceive.

factorial design: A research study that includes more than one independent variable; described by the number of independent variables and the number of levels of each independent variable (for example, a 3×4 factorial has two independent variables, one with three levels and the other with four levels).

falsifiability: A property of a theory, model, or hypothesis possessing some specific predictions, which, if verified, will demonstrate that the theory, model, or hypothesis is wrong.

five-number summary: The minimum, the first quartile, the median, the third quartile, and the maximum.

fMRI: Functional magnetic resonance imaging.

frequency histogram: A graphical representation in which the range of values of the variable is divided into intervals of equal size. These intervals are placed on the x axis, and the frequency or number of occurrences is plotted using the y axis.

hypothesis: A prediction regarding the outcome of a study, often involving the relationship between two variables.

independent-samples design: A study in which the experimenter varies one independent variable across two groups.

independent (or predictor) variable: The manipulated variable, the variable the experimenter changes across the experimental groups; has at least two levels.

inferential statistics: Statistics that are based on the laws of probability and that allow us to judge if samples are from different populations, if differences between groups are larger than would be expected based on chance alone.

informed consent: The agreement of a person to participate in a research study, after having been fully informed of the risks and benefits of the proposed research before beginning participation; generally documented by a signed form.

Institutional Animal Care and Use Committee (IACUC): A group of individuals who review any proposed use of vertebrate animals at a U.S. institution.

institutional review boards (IRBs): Groups of individuals who review any proposed use of human research participants at a U.S. institution.

interaction: Mutual or reciprocal action when the effect of one independent variable depends on the level of another independent variable.

interfield theories: Theories within an interdisciplinary field that may consist of links between different levels of explanation for the same phenomenon.

internal validity: The extent to which the results of an experiment can be attributed to the manipulation of the independent variable; a reflection of the quality of the research design and the success of the experimenter in controlling extraneous and confounding variables.

interquartile range: The distance between the first and the third quartile.

interval scale: A scale of measurement with equal intervals between the points on the scale, but with no meaningful zero; a scale on which equal distances between scores represent equal differences in the property being measured.

knockin: An organism with a gene inserted at a targeted site in the genome, allowing more reliable over-expression of the protein product of that gene.

knockout: An organism with a particular gene inactivated or disrupted, so that the protein product of that gene is no longer produced or is produced in a truncated form and thus is no longer functional.

levels: The different values of the independent variable.

main effect: The overall effect of one independent variable in a factorial design, ignoring the level of the other independent variable.

matched-samples design: A research study of independent groups where a variable associated with the experimental units is controlled by measuring that variable and then matching subjects in the experimental and control group for that variable.

mean (average): The sum of all the observations divided by the number of observations; the mathematical average.

measures of central tendency: Statistical descriptions of the center of a distribution; estimates of the typical score in that sample.

measures of variability: Descriptions of the spread of a distribution.

median: The number in the middle of a rank-ordered list of numbers.

meta-analysis: Collation and statistical analysis of results from multiple studies on the same topic.

minimal risk: A level of risk that does not exceed the risk expected from ordinary daily life or routine physical or psychological examinations or tests.

mixed design: A research study with one or more independent variables varied within subjects, while one or more other independent variables are between subjects.

mode: The most commonly occurring number.

model: A description of a process or phenomenon; an explanation of how a particular process occurs.

multiple case studies: Analysis of several cases with similar performance deficits or similar areas of brain damage.

multiple-group experiment: A study that measures the effect of one independent variable, with more than two levels, on a dependent variable.

naturalistic observations: Observations that occur in the natural environment, without an attempt by the experimenter to intervene.

negative control: A sample that should demonstrate a negative reaction.

neuron doctrine: The belief that the neuron is the fundamental unit of the nervous system.

nominal scale: A categorical scale, with the categories not in any obvious ranked position relative to one another.

nonparametric inferential statistics: Statistics that are based on fewer assumptions, generally requiring only that the samples are independent, and that do not assume the underlying population has a normal distribution.

null hypothesis (H_0): The hypothesis that there is no difference between any of the groups in the experiment, that the independent variable had no effect.

Nuremberg Code: Ten-point statement setting the limits of permissible medical experimentation on humans, drafted in 1947 by the judges of the Nazi war criminals.

observational studies: Careful observations of a phenomenon.

Office for Human Research Protections (OHRP): Office within the U.S. Department of Health and Human Services concerned with the protection of human participants in research and the oversight of institutional review boards (IRBs).

one-factor ANOVA: An analysis of variance to evaluate an experiment with one independent variable.

one-tailed test: A statistical test used to evaluate a directional hypothesis. In a one-tailed test, the area of the distribution allowing rejection of the null hypothesis is at only one extreme of the distribution.

operational definition: A concept defined solely in terms of the procedures to produce and measure it.

operationalized hypothesis: A hypothesis defined in terms of the operations or procedures a researcher will perform to test it.

order effect: The influence of the order of the experimental conditions on the results; always a concern for within-subject designs.

ordinal scale: A ranked ordering of instances.

outliers: Extreme scores; points well out of the range of the other points; individual data points that deviate strikingly from the overall distribution. An outlier is commonly defined as scores either more than ±3 standard deviations from the mean or more than 1.5 times the interquartile range beyond the first or third quartile.

paradigm: The current agreed-upon facts and accepted approaches in a scientific field at any one time in history.

parametric inferential statistics: Statistics based on several assumptions about the design of the study, most notably the assumption of randomly chosen, independent samples and an underlying normal distribution of the population parameters. Examples of such statistics are the t test and the analysis of variance (ANOVA).

Pearson product correlation coefficient: A summary of the strength and the direction of the linear relationship between two variables; summarized as r. The value of r lies between -1 and 1. An $r = 0$ result indicates no linear relationship between the two variables. An $r = -1$ result indicates a perfect negative linear relationship. An $r = +1$ result indicates a perfect positive relationship.

placebo: A pill with no biochemical action (from the Latin for "to please"); originally, inert pills that physicians gave to patients with a malady for which the physicians had no other treatment.

placebo control group: Participants who receive only an ineffective treatment used to measure the placebo effect.

placebo effect: A physiological or psychological change that occurs as a result of the mere suggestion that a change will occur.

plagiarism: Presenting someone else's words or ideas without clearly identifying the source.

population: The entire collection of cases of interest.

positive control: A sample that should definitely demonstrate a positive reaction.

post hoc tests: Statistical tests that follow an ANOVA to determine which means differ; also called "multiple comparisons."

power: The probability that a statistical test will reject the null hypothesis when the null hypothesis is false; defined as $(1-\beta)$.

predictive validity: How well your measures can predict outcomes of key importance.

primary research articles: Direct reports of experiments conducted by the authors.

proximate causation: An explanation of a phenomenon at the level of "how" (as opposed to "why") questions.

pseudoscience: Nonscientific information masquerading as science.

quartiles: In a rank-ordered set of numbers, the first quartile is the point where 25% of the distribution falls at or below it, the second quartile is the point of the 50th percentile (the median), and the third quartile is the point where 75% of the distribution falls at or below it.

quasi-experiment: A study that is as close to a true experiment as possible but that lacks one or more of the key characteristics of true experiments, often because subjects cannot be randomly assigned to groups.

random assignment: Assigning subjects to conditions in an experiment in such a way that each subject has an equal probability of being chosen for any condition.

randomization: Placement of items in an order or sample from a population such that the selection of the next item in the order or sample does not depend on the prior item selected and all items have the same chance of being selected.

random sample: A sample created by choosing cases from the entire population, with each case selected independently from the next.

rationalism: The idea that truth and knowledge are attainable through reason, not experience.

ratio scale: A scale of measurement with a nonarbitrary origin and equal intervals between its points; a measurement scale on which scores possess all of the characteristics of real numbers.

reduce: One of the "three Rs"; to decrease the number of animals used to the minimum necessary to achieve statistically meaningful results.

refine: One of the "three Rs"; to improve research procedures to ensure the animals are treated as humanely as possible.

relative frequency: The proportion of participants who scored within a certain range in a frequency histogram.

reliable: Giving similar results on subsequent trials under the same conditions.

replace: One of the "three Rs"; to substitute research animals with nonanimal alternatives, such as computer simulations, or to substitute "higher" animals, such as nonhuman primates, with those from "lower" orders, such as invertebrates.

replicable: A result that can be confirmed by conducting a duplicate experiment.

replication: Observation of the same phenomena under the same conditions multiple times.

restricted range: A term used to describe a data set obtained when the researcher did not examine data from a wide enough span of scores.

sample: A smaller subset drawn from a larger population, used to represent the population.

scatterplot: A graphical representation of participants' scores on two variables, with each of the two variables of interest shown on the x and y axes and each individual case shown as a point.

science: "An interconnected series of concepts and conceptual schemes that have developed as a result of experimentation and observation and are fruitful of further experimentation and observation" (Conant, 1951, p. 5).

scientific methodology: A collection of logical rules, experimental designs, theoretical approaches, and laboratory techniques accumulated throughout history. Each field has slightly different scientific methods.

secondary sources: Reviews of research, the primary report of which is published elsewhere.

sham surgery: A control group that is anesthetized for surgery, placed in any special apparatus necessary for surgery, and treated exactly as the experimental group except for the step that is thought to alter the critical variable.

shape: The overall pattern of a distribution.

single-blind procedure: A method of conducting a study in which participants do not know if they are in the experimental group or the control group.

skewed: A term used to describe a distribution in which the bulk of the values fall to the right or the left of the midpoint.

spatial conditional knockout: Animal with a target gene inactivated only in certain brain regions.

Spearman rank correlation coefficient: A measure of the strength and direction of a correlation between two variables that researchers use if they have measured a variable using the ordinal scale of measurement.

spread: The amount that a distribution is scattered away from the most typical value.

standard deviation: A measure of how much the observations vary from the mean; the square root of the sum of the squared deviations from the mean divided by one less than the total number of observations ($n-1$).

standard error of the mean: The standard deviation divided by the square root of n, the number of observations.

statistically significant: When the probability of a difference between groups in an experiment is larger than you would expect based on laws of probability; determined on the basis of inferential statistics.

statistical significance: The risk you take that you will reject the null hypothesis when it is actually true.

stratified random sampling: A method for producing a sample from a population in which cases are randomly selected from within subpopulations (or strata) of an entire population.

straw-man hypothesis: An assumption that is not plausible at all and that no one would really support.

structured observations: Observations taken under conditions where the researcher has intervened in some way to structure the situation.

subject variables: Variables associated with personal characteristics of each subject or participant in an experiment, such as the age, prior experience, or body weight of the participant. When an independent variable is a subject variable, the researcher may be restricted to doing a quasi-experiment.

symmetric: Having a similar shape on either side of the midpoint of the distribution.

temporal conditional knockout: Animal with a target gene inactivated only at certain times in development.

theory: A set of logical propositions that explains relationships among events and the occurrence of events; can be used to guide research; incorporates diverse phenomena and describes general organizing principles.

third variable: An unmeasured variable that is related to each of the other two variables and that, by this association, makes the two variables measured appear to be correlated.

three Rs: Principles for improving the humane use of animals in research (see *reduce, refine,* and *replace*).

time sampling: Observation of behavior within a certain time frame—for example, for 1 minute every 15 minutes.

time-series design: A within-subjects design that involves measures of the dependent variable taken at different times, with the experimental or control treatment applied between the measures.

transgenic: Relating to an organism with a segment of artificially constructed DNA (a transgene) incorporated into its genome that may cause that organism to produce the protein coded for by the transgene.

_t_-test: A parametric inferential statistic used for making generalizations about either the mean of a population or a comparison of two means.

Tuskegee Study: An infamous study of the natural course of the disease syphilis conducted between 1932 and 1972 by the U.S. Public Health Service.

two-factor ANOVA: An analysis of variance to assess an experiment with two independent variables.

two-group experiment: A design to measure the effect of one independent variable, with two levels, on a dependent variable.

two-tailed test: A statistical test used to determine if two groups differ, without making a directional hypothesis. In a two-tailed test, the area of the distribution allowing rejection of the null hypothesis is at both the positive and negative extremes of the distribution.

Type I error: Rejecting the null hypothesis and concluding that the groups differ when, in fact, the null hypothesis is true and the groups do not actually differ.

Type II error: Accepting the null hypothesis when, in fact, it is false.

ultimate causation: An explanation of a phenomenon at the level of answering "why" (as opposed to "how") questions.

unimodal: A distribution with one major peak.

variability: The dispersion of scores in a sample; the measure of a distribution's spread.

variance (s^2): A measure of how much observations vary from the mean; the sum of the squared deviations from the mean divided by one less than the total number of observations ($n-1$). The square root of the variance is the standard deviation.

vehicle-control group: Animals that are treated exactly the same as the animals getting the experimental drug except that no drug is dissolved in the solution, which may be saline or artificial cerebrospinal fluid.

whiskers: Lines extending from the central box of a box plot to the largest and smallest observations that are not suspected outliers.

wildtype: Organisms without any particular mutation that are chosen for an experiment because they are littermates of mutant animals or are from the same strain as mutant animals.

within-subjects design: A study in which each participant in the experiment experiences all the experimental conditions.

zoonotic: An infectious disease that can be transmitted from nonhuman animals to humans.

Appendix F | Answers to End-of-Chapter Questions

CHAPTER 1

Check Your Understanding

True or False?

1. False

2. False

3. True

4. False

5. True

Select the best answer

1. C

2. B

3. B

Think About It

1. Answers will vary.

2. Answers will vary. This could be considered one piece of evidence challenging the neuron doctrine. Scientists would require more evidence to be convinced that neurons are not the fundamental units of the nervous system. But they certainly would be interested to know if glial cells play an equally important role.

CHAPTER 2

Check Your Understanding

1. E

2. C

3. B

4. C

5. Respect for persons, Beneficence, Justice

6. a. Visual sexual stimuli create a greater response in the amygdala and hypothalamus of men than of women, as measured by fMRI (Hamann, Herman, Nolan, & Wallen, 2004).

   b. Here is a close paraphrase of the entire paragraph, which would be considered plagiarism: Men have a greater interest in and show a greater response to visual sexual stimuli. Through the use of fMRI, Hamann, Herman, Nolan, and Wallen (2004) demonstrated that the amygdala and hypothalamus are more greatly responsive in men as compared to women, in response to the same sexual stimuli. The finding held up even when women said they were more aroused. Differences were found across genders only when the stimulus was sexual in nature, mostly in limbic regions, and were more noticeable in the left rather than the right amygdala. The activation patterns of men and women were similar across several brain regions, such as ventral striatal regions implicated in reward. They found that the amygdala is responsible for gender differences in reaction to biologically important stimuli. In humans, it is possible that the amygdala also is responsible for the larger function of visual stimuli in the sexual behavior of men, similar to what was found in previous animal studies.

7. At least five people, qualified to evaluate the research in question but not directly involved in it, must sit on the institutional review board. When vulnerable populations are part of the research, an individual familiar with that population's needs must sit on the committee.

8. Participants were not given sufficient information to decide whether they wished to participate. Those with syphilis were not told they were not being treated; they were not even informed they had the disease. When better treatments for the disease became available, no one told participants in the study about the availability of these treatments.

9. Potential participants must know the purpose of the study, the procedure, the risks and benefits to society and especially to the participants, and the possible alternatives to the study. The participants also must be informed that they are free to leave the study at any time.

10. None. The researcher should never directly harm the participants. Societal benefit never outweighs harm to a participant.

11. *Reduce*: Use as few animals as possible. *Replace*: Use models or computers instead; use lower animals instead of higher-order animals. *Refine*: Go the extra mile to ensure humane treatment of the animals in the experimental procedure.

12. No, yes.

13. Scientists, nonscientists, lab animal veterinarians, unaffiliated members.

14. First talk to your teaching assistant or instructor. If not satisfied, talk to the director of the animal facility, perhaps anonymously. If still not satisfied, talk to the institutional officer to whom the IACUC reports.

Think About It

1. Prisoners might have elected to participate due to explicit or implicit pressures or incentives. Hopelessness may have driven them to believe that the risks of the research did not matter. Researchers may have been drawn to this population because prisoners are in a tightly regulated environment, which means fewer uncontrolled variables. Prisoners are also unlikely to be absent when the researchers want access to them. One possible safeguard would be to provide incentives to attract members of all classes; only the poor are likely to be drawn by money incentives, for example. Another safeguard would be to encourage medical researchers to seek out participants from communities, rather than from people already in treatment, because disproportionate numbers of

those in treatment are likely to be affluent. Studies appropriate for the prison population would be studies from which this population in particular is likely to benefit most.

2. Informed consent requires that the participants be able to understand the purpose, possible risks, and the procedure of the study. In the case of children, guardians should be asked to give informed consent. Who would be available to speak for the interests of the institutionalized orphans? You can read the results of a study that provided the basis for this question (Nelson et al., 2007) and associated commentary pointing to this and other ethical concerns (Rudan, 2008).

3. Some of the arguments of a PETA member: Animals are unable to give their informed consent. We often cannot tell whether and to what degree an animal is in pain. Animal life/freedom is not necessarily less valuable than human life/freedom. Research should be conducted on those whom it will benefit, and for many research questions, humans will benefit more than animals. Some of the biomedical researcher's arguments: Animals lack consciousness or a sense of self and therefore are unable to "mind" being used in research. They are more readily available than human subjects. They protect humans from being subjected to dangerous treatments. This policy ensures that human subjects will only be used in research that is very likely to be productive. Animals cannot be used to study higher cognitive functions (such as language), cannot provide feedback (such as self-reports), and are of limited use in the study of diseases only present in humans.

4. One concern might be harming a person's self-concept by telling them their responses were in the pattern the researchers labeled "dishonest." The researchers in fact did not do this, and they were also careful in their paper to note that "these labels describe these subjects' present behavior only and that we make no claims concerning more general behavioral tendencies" (Greene & Paxton, 2009, p. 12506).

5. Answers may vary, but it could be difficult for an individual researcher to hold different ethical standards when working in different settings.

CHAPTER 3

Check Your Understanding

1. a. This is a poor hypothesis because it is not operationally defined. "Behaving oddly" and "animals" need to be specified. For example, the animals could be mice or chimpanzees, and the variable measured

could be performance on a motor task or grooming behaviors. Second, good hypotheses are based on previous research, and bring a meaningful addition to existing knowledge. Additionally, testing this hypothesis may not be feasible due to the availability of MDMA and the ethics of administering a potentially dangerous drug to animals.

b. This is a good hypothesis because it makes sense in the context of previous research. Other strengths are that it tests a prediction of an accepted model and that it is directed toward possibly falsifying the model. However, a problem with the hypothesis is that there are other possible explanations for the results. The method of testing for increased neurotransmitter release could be faulty, and other variables could account for a change in level of neurotransmitter.

c. This represents an instructional laboratory exercise rather than a real research question because there is virtually no doubt that the researcher will confirm the hypothesis.

d. This is a good hypothesis because testing between two realistic theories is valuable no matter what the result.

2. Defining a hypothesis operationally is necessary because it ensures precision and makes the study replicable. However, it also means that studies may not be widely generalized. Small changes in a study, such as the ages of the subjects or the form of a drug used, will likely affect the results. Other animals may react differently to estrogen, or the same mice may show changes in circadian rhythms following administration of a different form of the hormone. "Estrogen" could be operationalized as "administration of an intravenous injection of 30% estradiol benzoate," and "mice" could be defined as "129s female, 7-month-old mice that have been individually housed since birth."

3. B

Think About It

1. Answers will vary.

CHAPTER 4

Check Your Understanding

1. a. Ratio
   b. Ratio
   c. Nominal

    d. Nominal

    e. Ordinal

    f. Ordinal

    g. Ratio

2. a. DV: Performance on radial arm maze

      IV: Hippocampal damage

   b. DV: Presence of action potentials

      IV: Application of sodium blocker

   c. DV: Improvement on memory task

      IV: Which sleep stage was deprived

   d. DV: Dopamine release

      IV: Pattern of electrical stimulation

3. a. There is no control group of rats not given the drug.

   b. Time after training was a confounded variable. For example, maybe waiting 24 hours improves performance, regardless of whether you sleep during that time.

   c. The researcher would need to replicate this observation from one rat, and would need to experimentally manipulate levels of dopamine and measure cocaine motivation to determine if dopamine causes cocaine motivation.

   d. The control mice were different in a crucial way from the experimental mice. Perhaps the experimental mice showed less reaction to the anesthesia because they were young and not fully developed, not because they lacked the portion of the GABA receptor.

4. a. If x is necessary for y, then when I remove x, y does not occur.

   b. If x is sufficient for y, then when I add x, and hold all other variables constant, y occurs.

Think About It

1. Answers may vary. Some may argue that the experimenters were biased against separate memory systems, whereas other students may not label this tendency as a bias. Scientists are conservative for two reasons. First, if scientists overhauled their theories every time a study's result failed to agree with them, then science would be too chaotic to be useful. An observation inconsistent with a theory can be due to a problem with the theory, but it could also be due to a misinterpretation of the observation.

Even if the observation did point out a flaw in the theory, an otherwise sound theory that still allows its adherents to produce fruitful findings might be better than no theory at all. Second, it can be heart wrenching to be forced to give up an otherwise useful theory due to a few examples of its failings when it seems to work so well in many other ways. Changing a theory often entails the daunting task of rethinking much of the work that has been done on the basis of that theory and finding new explanations for findings that the old theory had previously explained. Experienced scientists may prefer to ignore an observation inconsistent with their accepted theory rather than be forced to reconsider their life's work.

2. You would need to find a way to induce the transcription of the *per1* gene without using light. If the only important effect of light was to stimulate transcription of *per1*, its transcription alone would be enough to reset circadian rhythms. On the other hand, it is possible that light has more global effects, the triggering of *per1* transcription being only one of them.

3. Answers will vary.

4. a. A population is the entire group of subjects you want to know about. A sample is a subset of the population, small enough so that you actually could test it. You use information gained from testing the subjects in the sample to make generalizations about the population.

   b. The null hypothesis is the hypothesis that the groups in a study are drawn from the same population and have no significant difference. This is the hypothesis that statistical tests either confirm or reject.

   c. The significance level (alpha) is chosen to be the level of Type I error you will accept. If alpha is chosen as $p<.05$, that means you will accept a 5% chance of concluding that there is a statistically significant difference between the groups when, in fact, there is none. This would be a Type I error.

CHAPTER 5

Check Your Understanding

1. a. IV: Recalling words (true memories from list/false memories from similar words)

   DV: Brain activity measured by PET

    b. IV: Brain injury (none/mild)

       DV: Selective and sustained attention, verbal and nonverbal fluency, verbal memory

    c. IV: Signaling of hedgehog

       DV: Development and structure of pituitary

2. C

3. C

4. B

5.

Subject	First treatment	Second treatment	Third treatment	Fourth treatment
1	A	B	C	D
2	B	C	D	A
3	C	D	A	B
4	D	A	B	C

Think About It

1. One major flaw in this study was that the researcher was likely biased and may have omitted data points to gain results that support her hypothesis. There are other flaws; students may mention ethical issues about confidentiality, definition of terms (for example, "took drugs"), and the lack of a control group.

2. The effect of time is a major confounded variable.

3. Causation cannot be conclusively inferred from this study because the independent variable (presence of an integrin) was a subject variable, which means that any differences in the dependent variables between the groups could be due to other variables associated with the presence or absence of the integrin. Littermate controls are required.

4. The analysis was biased due to experimenter effects.

CHAPTER 6

Check Your Understanding

1. A factorial design is an experiment with more than one independent variable.

2. Two independent variables

3. Twelve groups

4. One independent variable has four levels, and the other one has six levels. Thus, there are 24 groups in this experiment.

5. 120

6. See Figure 6.5.

Think About It

1. Main effect of aspirin

   Main effect of time

   Interaction between time and aspirin

	Aspirin	*Control*
T1	450	100
T2	275	150

2. Main effect of serum

   Main effect of amyloid peptide

   Interaction between serum and amyloid peptide

	Serum	*No Serum*
1–40	No change	More receptors
1–42	No change	More receptors
40–1	No change	No change
No treatment	No change	No change

3.

Figure 6.4 | Two Potential Outcomes of a 2 × 2 Factorial Design

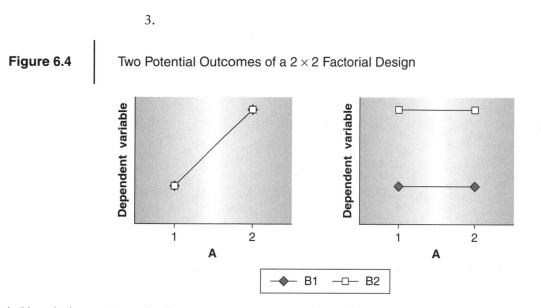

In this and subsequent examples, the row and column means are given adjacent to the table to allow comparisons for the main effect of each independent variable. In the example shown on the left, there is no main effect of independent Variable A, as indicated by the overall means for groups A1 and A2 being identical (7). There is a main effect for independent Variable B, indicated by the overall mean for the B1 sample (4) being less than the overall mean for the B2 sample (10). There is no interaction between A and B. On the right, there is a main effect of Variable A but no main effect of Variable B and no interaction between A and B.

Figure 6.5 | Other Possible Outcomes of a 2 × 2 Factorial Design

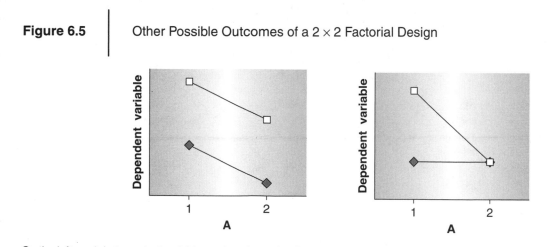

On the left, each independent variable produced a main effect, but there is no interaction between the two independent variables. On the right, there is similarly a main effect for each independent variable, and there is an interaction between the two independent variables. The effect of Variable A on the dependent variable depends on the level of the other independent variable, Variable B. When B is at level one, A has no effect on the dependent variable; however, when B is at level two, A has a large effect on the dependent variable. This is an interaction.

Figure 6.6   Possible Outcomes of a 2 × 2 Factorial Design

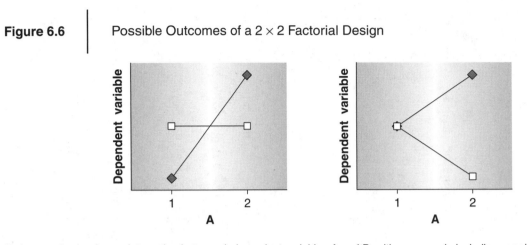

Both examples involve an interaction between independent variables A and B, with an example including a main effect for A shown on the left and a main effect for B shown on the right.

Figure 6.7   Interaction but No Main Effects

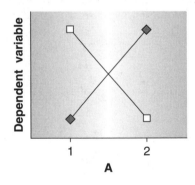

Example of a 2 × 2 factorial design that yielded no main effects for either independent variable, but an interaction between the two independent variables.

CHAPTER 7

Check Your Understanding

1. D
2. C
3. C

4. B

5. D

6. C

Think About It

1. Studies of twins assume that monozygotic and dizygotic twins are raised in the same environment. Therefore, the study results support the conclusions of the authors, that environmental factors did not cause the correlation between general intelligence and brain volume seen in the sample of monozygotic twins. It is possible that the assumption of similar environments for the two types of twins is somehow invalidated, if, for example, growing up as a monozygotic twin alters the manner in which your parents treat you, thus altering your environment. You could use this point to argue against the conclusion of the authors.

2.

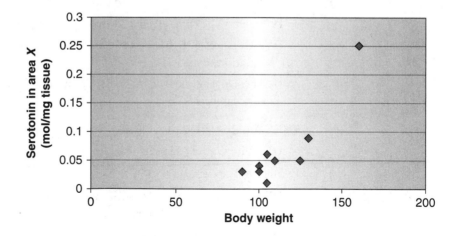

Body weight was positively correlated with serotonin levels in Area X ($r5.9$), but an outlier may have a strong influence on the data.

3. Answers will vary.

CHAPTER 8

Check Your Understanding

1. This is a correlational study. The two variables correlated are severity of symptoms of posttraumatic stress syndrome and volume of the hippocampus.

2. IV: Prior exposure (five levels): 2 days of torpor, 7 days of torpor, 1 hour after arousal, 8 hours after arousal, no hibernation

   DV: Phosphorylation of the microtubule-associated protein tau

   Design: Multiple-group experiment, independent-samples design (between subjects)

3. IV: Treatment: Infusion of either Schwann cells, olfactory ensheathing glia, a mixture of Schwann cells and olfactory ensheathing glia, or culture medium

   DV: Assessment of use of hindlimbs once a week for 12 weeks

   DV2: Evidence for spinal cord nerve regrowth

   Design: Multiple-group experiment, independent-samples design (between subjects)

4. IV: Sex (two levels): Male and female

   IV2: Genotype (two levels): Over-expressing Bcl-2 or wildtype control

   DV: Measures of hypothalamic and spinal cord areas important for regulation of sexual behavior

   Design: Quasi-experiment, 2 × 2 factorial design, both IVs are between subjects

5. IV: Auditory input (two levels): Present or absent

   DV: Rate of glucose use in the primate auditory cortex

   Design: Case study, within-subjects design

   DVs: Cell grouping, levels of hair-cell-specific proteins and in the number of characteristic stereocilia

   Design: Descriptive observational study

6. IV: Growth factor (three levels)

   DV: Motor neuron degeneration in mice with mutation in the gene for superoxide dismutase-1

   Design: Three-group experiment, independent-samples (between subjects)

7. IV: Timing of opening within a burst of openings

   DV: Duration of single-channel openings

   Design: Time-series design

8. IV: What is paired with novel taste (two levels): Leptin or lithium chloride

   DV: Later avoidance of the taste

   Design: Two-group experiment, independent samples (between subjects)

9. IV: Type of item (with three levels): Animals, fruits, and vegetables/ furniture, tools, and articles of clothing/ musical instruments

   DV: Ability to name the item

   Design: Case study

   B. *Abstract 1:* IVs: Social isolation, exercise. DV: Proliferation of dentate gyrus progenitor cells. Controlled variable: sex. Design: 2×2 factorial design

   Abstract 2: IVs: suicide, history of childhood abuse DVs: Glucocorticoid receptor mRNA, mRNA transcripts bearing the glucocorticoid receptor 1_F splice variant, cytosine methylation of an *NR3C1* promoter. Controlled variables: Humans, hippocampus. Design: 3 groups, between subjects, quasi-experiment

   C. a. C

      b. Alzheimer's disease

      c. Astrocyte activity, amyloid plaques, intracellular calcium in neurons and astrocytes

      d. C

      e. A

      f. B

      g. a. No control group; the necessary control group is wildtype and Alzheimer's disease brains without tetrodotoxin

      h. C

Think About It

Only one example is given for the further questions in Chapter 8.

1. Vaiva et al. (2003). Immediate treatment with propranolol decreases posttraumatic stress disorder two months after trauma. *Biological Psychiatry 54,* 947–949.

2. To test the effect of administering propranolol following trauma exposure. More generally, it addresses the issue of developing a treatment to ease the severity of PTSD.

3. Previous studies have shown that adrenergic activation is partially responsible for symptoms of PTSD, particularly tachycardia and overconsolidation of memory of the trauma. An adrenergic antagonist such as propranolol would therefore probably reduce the likelihood of developing PTSD. This study differs from others because the researchers were assured that all the participants had been subjected to trauma of similar severity.

4. Trauma victims ages 21 to 30 presenting with tachycardia, 11 in experimental group and 8 in control group. Single-blind, two-group, quasi-experiment, between-subjects design.

5. Recruit participants → Assess severity of distress and physical injury → Administer propranolol (40 mg, 33 daily) for 7 days to experimental group → Administer drug every 4 days for 8 to 12 days (tapering) → Assess participants for PTSD.

6. Scores on the following tests: Peritraumatic Distress Inventory (for level of distress following trauma), Trauma Score (level of physical injury), Treatment Outcome PTSD scale (PTSD symptoms), DSM-IV criteria (PTSD diagnosis), Mini International Neuropsychiatric Interview (baseline mental health and history).

7. Wilcoxon rank test and Fisher exact test.

8. Three of out 8 control-group subjects and 1 out of 11 experimental-group subjects were diagnosed with PTSD 2 months following trauma exposure. The mean PTSD score of the control group was higher than that of the experimental group.

9. Administration of propranolol following trauma exposure helps reduce PTSD symptoms and diagnosis.

10. Small sample size, lack of randomization, and short duration of the study.

11. First, this study used only a very small number of subjects, limited in age and level of trauma exposure. Second, because the subjects chose which group to be in (self-selection), the researchers could not control for placebo effects and they could not discount the possibility that uncontrolled variables were responsible for the difference between the groups.

12. Answers will vary.

APPENDIX A

Check Your Understanding

1. False. First, it is easy to miss important information when you begin summarizing your data immediately. Looking at the distribution of the data gives you a broad overview of your results and helps you determine how to proceed. Second, an average might not be the best way to summarize the data, depending on what the distribution looks like. If there are outliers, for example, the median is a more accurate description of the data than the mean (average).

2.

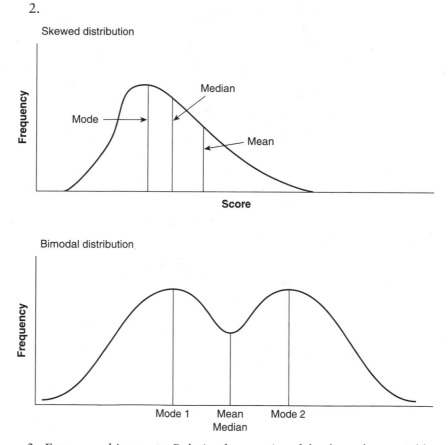

3. Frequency histogram: Relative frequencies of the dependent variable

4. Bar graph: Dependent variable

5. An outlier

6. More than 1.5 times the interquartile range away from the central box

7. The minimum, the first quartile, the median, the third quartile, and the maximum of a data set

8. Hypothetical box plot comparing the speed of two mouse strains:

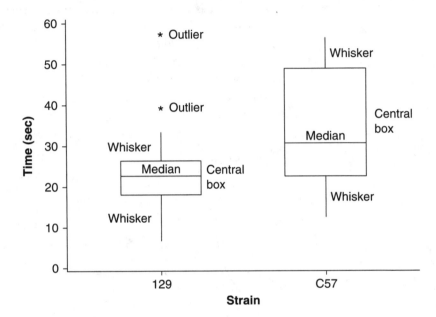

9. The independent-samples *t*-test assumes that the two samples are, in fact, independent (randomly chosen) and that the data is normally distributed.

10. Descriptive statistics give information about the sample, while inferential statistics allow us to use samples to make inferences about the population.

11. For example: The two groups did not differ, $t(6) = 2.05$, $p > .05$.

12. The *F*-ratio is a ratio of the variability between groups to the variability within groups.

13. C

14. B

15. A

Think About It

1. The first study could have had less variability around the mean in the two groups.

2. Because you are concerned with the health of the babies and would prefer to err on the side of safety, you would be more concerned with minimizing the possibility of making a Type I error. You would rather determine that the plastic is dangerous and not expose the babies to it even though it is safe. In the second study, it would be a shame to halt further research into a potentially useful compound because you wrongly determined that it had no effect (accepting the null hypothesis). Safety and effectiveness issues can be worked out later; it would be better to study useless compounds than not to study useful compounds. Therefore, you would be more concerned with minimizing the possibility of a Type II error.

3. No. A scientist can only support or refute an experimental hypothesis. Hypotheses are made about populations, but experiments can never test entire populations, only samples. Statistical tests such as *t*-tests only suggest whether or not it is possible to assume that information from the samples accurately reflects the truth about the populations they come from. The tests do not provide certainty. There is always a very unlikely possibility that the sample does not accurately represent the population.

APPENDIX B

Check Your Understanding

1. *Journal of Neuroscience:*

   Lall GS, Biello SM (2003) Neuropeptide Y, GABA and circadian phase shifts to photic stimuli. Neuroscience 120:915–921.

   Science:

   G. S. Lall, S. M. Biello, *Neuroscience* 120, 915 (2003).

   Nature Neuroscience:

   Lall, G.S. & Biello, S.M. Neuropeptide Y, GABA and circadian phase shifts to photic stimuli. *Neuroscience* 120, 915–921 (2003).

   Neuroscience Letters:

   G.S. Lall, S.M. Biello, Neuropeptide Y, GABA and circadian phase shifts to photic stimuli, Neuroscience 120 (2003) 915–921.

   Brain Research:

   G.S. Lall, S.M. Biello, Neuropeptide Y, GABA and circadian phase shifts to photic stimuli, Neuroscience 120 (2003) 915–921.

   Journal of Cognitive Neuroscience (APA format):

   Lall, G. S., & Biello, S. M. (2003). Neuropeptide Y, GABA, and circadian phase shifts to photic stimuli. *Neuroscience, 120,* 915–921.

2. a. No in-text reference required because the information comes from the researcher's own discoveries.

   b. In-text reference required: Who demonstrated this?

   c. No in-text reference required: Common knowledge.

   d. In-text reference needed if the computational model that predicted the results is not included in the current paper.

   e. No in-text reference necessary because the hypothesis is the researcher's own; however, references showing how the researcher arrived at this hypothesis would be helpful (for example, maybe others have found that certain stimuli have an additive effect on neurotransmitter levels).

Think About It

1. The problems in this Results section include the following:

   - It is unlikely that the results were meaningless. Results such as "the groups did not differ significantly" or "the results did not support the hypothesis" are meaningful.
   - Numbers need to have units (e.g., seconds). It is unnecessary to report the number of seconds the mice spent in the open arm down to the nearest hundredth second; these numbers can probably be rounded down.
   - Numerical results should be included in a way that minimizes the wordiness of the sentence.

     "The mean time in the open arm for the mice in the control group was 6.789. The standard deviation for the control mice was 3.234. The mean time in the open arm for the mice in the experimental group was 25.345. The standard deviation for the experimental group was 10.284."

   You could rewrite this as: "The mice in the control group spent less time in the open arms ($M = 6.8$ s, $SD = 3.2$ s) than the experimental group ($M = 25.3$ s, $SD = 10.3$ s)."

   Since the groups do not differ significantly, one sentence would suffice. For example, "The control group did not spend significantly more time on the open arms, $t(15) = 4.5$, $p > .05$." Note that the experimental group may have spent significantly more time on the open arms than the control group, but the author states that the hypothesis was directional, with the prediction that the control group would spend more time on those arms. It would be appropriate to comment on the unexpected direction of the group trends.

References

Abizaid, A., Mezei, G., Sotonyi, P., & Horvath, T. L. (2004). Sex differences in adult suprachiasmatic nucleus neurons emerging late prenatally in rats. *European Journal of Neuroscience, 19,* 2488–2496.

Akiyama, M., Kouzu, Y., Takahashi, S., Wakamatsu, H., Moriya, T., Maetani, M., et al. (1999). Inhibition of light- or glutamate-induced mPer1 expression represses the phase shifts into the mouse circadian locomotor and suprachiasmatic firing rhythms. *Journal of Neuroscience, 19,* 1115–1121.

Alzheimer's Association. (2010). *Alzheimer's disease facts and figures.* Retrieved from http://www.alz.org/documents_custom/report_alzfactsfigures2010.pdf

Amateau, S., & McCarthy, M. M. (2004). Induction of PGE2 by estradiol mediates developmental masculinization of sex behavior. *Nature Neuroscience, 7,* 643–650.

American Psychological Association. (2009). *Publication manual of the American Psychological Association* (6th ed.). Washington, DC: Author.

Angrosina, M. V. (2007). *Naturalistic observation.* Walnut Creek, CA: Left Coast Press.

Arendt, T., Stieler, J., Strijkstra, A. M., Hut, R. A., Rudiger, J., Van der Zee, E. A., et al. (2003). Reversible paired helical filament-like phosphorylation of tau is an adaptive process associated with neuronal plasticity in hibernating animals. *Journal of Neuroscience, 23,* 6972–6981.

Bandettini, P. A. (2009). What's new in neuroimaging methods? *Annals of the New York Academy of Science, 1156,* 260–293.

Bannon, A. W., Seda, J., Carmouche, M., Francis, J. M., Norman, M. H., Karbon, B., et al. (2000). Behavioral characterization of neuropeptide Y knockout mice. *Brain Research, 868,* 79–87.

Barja, I., Silvan, G., & Illera, J. C. (2008). Relationships between sex and stress hormone levels in feces and marking behavior in a wild population of Iberian wolves (Canis lupus signatus). *Journal of Chemical Ecology, 34,* 697–701.

Barker, K. (2004). *At the bench: A laboratory navigator.* New York: Cold Spring Harbor Laboratory Press.

Barker, K. (2005). *At the bench: A laboratory navigator* (Updated ed.). Woodbury, NY: Cold Spring Harbor Laboratory Press.

Bartlett, P. C., Bartlett, A., Walshaw, S., & Halstead S. (2005). Rates of euthanasia and adoption for dogs and cats in Michigan animal shelters. *Journal of Applied Animal Welfare Science, 8*, 97–104.

Barlow D. H., Nock, M., & Hersen, M. (2009). *Single case experimental designs: Strategies for studying behavior for change.* Boston: Allyn & Bacon.

Barry, S. R. (2009). *Fixing my gaze: A scientist's journey into seeing in three dimensions.* New York: Basic Books.

Benzer, S. (2004, October). *Adventures in neurogenetics.* Peter Gruber lecture delivered at the meeting of the Society for Neuroscience, San Diego, CA.

Bernard, A., Sorensen, S. A., & Lein, E. S. (2009). Shifting the paradigm: New approaches for characterizing and classifying neurons. *Current Opinion in Neurobiology, 19,* 530–536.

Beyer, W. H. (1960). *Handbook of tables for probability and statistics* (2nd ed.). Cleveland, OH: The Chemical Rubber Co.

Bianchi, L. M., Person, A. L., & Penney, E. B. (2002). Embryonic inner ear cells reaggregate into specific patterns in vitro. *Journal of the Association for Research in Otolaryngology, 3,* 418–429.

Bikei-Gorzo, A., Racz, I., Michel, K., & Zimmer, A. (2002). Diminished anxiety- and depression-related behaviors in mice with selective deletion of the Tac1 gene. *Journal of Neuroscience, 22,* 10046–10052.

Birner, P., Piribauer, M., Fischer, I., Gatterbauer, B., Marosi, C., Ambros, P. F., et al. (2003). Vascular patterns in glioblastoma influence clinical outcome and associate with variable expression of angiogenic proteins: Evidence for distinct angiogenic subtypes. *Brain Pathology, 13,* 133–143.

Bolton, P. A. (2002). Scientific ethics. In *Management benchmark study* (chap. 16). Washington, DC: U.S. Department of Energy, Office of Science, Office of Planning & Analysis.

Bremer, M. (2010). *Statistics at the bench: A step-by-step handbook for biologists.* Cold Spring Harbor, NY: Cold Spring Harbor Laboratory Press.

Brodmann, K. (1909). *Vergleichende Lokalisationslehre der Grossnirnrinde in ihren prinzipien dargestellt auf Grund des Zellenbaues.* Leipzig, Germany: Barth.

Buckley, C. A., & Schneider, J. E. (2001). Leptin treatments that decrease food intake do not support a conditioned taste aversion in Syrian hamsters. *Hormones and Behavior, 39,* 326.

Cajal, S. (1999). *Advice for a young investigator.* Cambridge, MA: MIT Press. (Original work published 1897)

Carter, M., & Shieh, J. (2010). *Guide to research techniques in neuroscience.* New York: Academic Press.

Castelli, L., Zibetti, M., Rizzi, L., Caglio, M., Lanotte, M., & Lopiano, L. (2008). Neuropsychiatric symptoms three years after subthalamic DBS in PD patients: A case-control study. *Journal of Neurology 255,* 1515–1520.

Cernansky, R. (2009, March 19). Stay-awake drug popular with college kids has addictive potential [Blog]. *Discover Magazine.* Retrieved from http://blogs.discovermagazine.com/80 beats/2009/03/18/stay-awake-drug-popular-with-college-kids-has-addictive-potential

Chiao, J. (2009). Cultural neuroscience: Cultural influences on brain function, Vol. 178 (*Progress in brain research* series). New York: Elsevier.

Coates, J. M., & Herbert, J. (2008). Endogenous steroids and financial risk taking on a London trading floor. *PNAS USA 105,* 6167–6172.

Cohen, N. J. (1984). Preserved learning capacity in amnesia: Evidence for multiple memory systems. In L. R. Squire & N. Butters (Eds.), *Neuropsychology of memory* (pp. 83–103). New York: Guilford Press.

Committee on Science, Engineering, & Public Policy (COSEPUP). (1995). *On being a scientist: Responsible conduct in research.* Washington, DC: National Academy Press. Retrieved February 8, 2010, from http://books.nap.edu/catalog/4917.html

Conant, J. B. (1951). *Science and common sense.* New Haven, CT: Yale University Press.

Coolidge, F. L. (2006). *Statistics: A gentle introduction.* Thousand Oaks, CA: Sage.

Council of Science Editors. (2006). *Scientific style and format: The CSE manual for authors, editors and publishers.* Reston, VA: Rockefeller University Press.

Cowell, R. A., Bussey, T. J., & Saksida, L. M. (in press). Functional dissociations within the ventral object processing pathway: Cognitive modules or a hierarchical continuum? *Journal of Cognitive Neuroscience.*

Crawley, J. N. (1997). *Current protocols in neuroscience.* New York: Wiley.

Cumming, G., Fidler, F., & Vaux, D. L. (2007). Error bars in experimental biology. *Journal of Cell Biology, 177,* 7–11.

Curran-Everett, D., & Benos, D. J. (2004). Guidelines for reporting statistics in journals published by the American Physiological Society. *American Journal of Physiology—Endocrinology and Metabolism, 287,* E189–191.

Darden, L. (2006). *Reasoning in biological discoveries: Essays on mechanisms, interfield relations, and anomaly resolution (Cambridge studies in philosophy and biology).* New York: Cambridge University Press.

Darden, L., & Maull, N. (1977). Interfield theories. *Philosophy of Science, 43,* 44–64.

Desai, S. S., Ali, H., Lysakowski, A. (2005). Comparative morphology of rodent vestibular periphery: I. Saccular and utricular maculae. *Journal of Neurophysiology, 93,* 251–266.

De Zeeuw, C. I., Chorev, E., Devor, A., Manor, Y., Van Der Giessen, R. S., De Jeu, M. T., et al. (2003). Deformation of network connectivity in the inferior olive of connexin 36-deficient mice is compensated by morphological and electrophysiological changes at the single neuron level. *Journal of Neuroscience, 23,* 4700–4711.

DiMasi, J. A., Hansen, R. W., & Grabowski, H. G. (2003). The price of innovation: New estimates of drug development costs. *Journal of Health Economics, 22,* 151–185.

Dixon, M. J., Piskopos, M., & Schweizer, T. A. (2000). Musical instrument naming impairments: The crucial exception to the living/nonliving dichotomy in category-specific agnosia. *Brain Cognition, 43,* 158–164.

Eastman, C. I., Young, M. A., Fogg, L. F., Liu, L., & Meaden, P. M. (1998). Bright light treatment of winter depression: A placebo-controlled trial. *Archives of General Psychiatry, 55,* 883–889.

Erwin, E., Gendin, S., & Kleiman, S. (Eds.). (1994). *Ethical issues in scientific research: An anthology* (Garland studies in applied ethics). New York: Routledge.

Estabrooke, I. V., McCarthy, M. T., Ko, E., Chou, T. C., Chemelli, R. M., Yanagisawa, M., et al. (2001). Fos expression in orexin neurons varies with behavioral state. *Journal of Neuroscience, 21,* 1656–1662.

Fanelli, D. (2009). How many scientists fabricate and falsify research? A systematic review and meta-analysis of survey data. *PLoS ONE 4*(5), e5738. doi:10.1371/journal.pone.0005738

Farah, M. J. (2002). Emerging ethical issues in neuroscience. *Nature Neuroscience, 5,* 1123–1129.

Finger, S. (2000). *Minds behind the brain: A history of the pioneers and their discoveries.* New York: Oxford University Press.

Foundation for Biomedical Research. (2008). *Fact vs. myth: About the essential need for animals in medical research* [Brochure]. Retrieved April 26, 2010, from http://www.fbresearch.org/Portals/9/docs/FactMyth.pdf

Gavériaux-Ruff, C., & Kieffer, B. L. (2007). Conditional gene targeting in the mouse nervous system: Insights into brain function and diseases. *Pharmacology Therapy, 113,* 619–634.

Gazzaniga, M. S. (2008). *Essay: Arts and cognition: Findings hint at relationships* (The 2008 progress report on brain research). Available from the Dana Foundation website: http://www.dana.org/news/publications/detail.aspx?id=10768

Genn, R. F., Tucci, S., Edwards, J. E., & File, S. E. (2003). Dietary restriction and nicotine can reduce anxiety in female rats. *Neuropsychopharmacology, 28,* 1257–1263.

Geschwind, D. H., & Konopka, G. (2009). Neuroscience in the era of functional genomics and systems biology. *Nature, 461,* 908–915.

Gilbertson, M. W., Shenton, M. E., Ciszewski, A., Kasai, K., Lasko, N. B., Orr, S. P., et al. (2002). Smaller hippocampal volume predicts pathologic vulnerability to psychological trauma. *Nature Neuroscience, 5,* 1242–1247.

Gonzalez, R. (2009). *Data analysis for experimental design.* New York: Guilford Press.

Gould, S. J. (1981). *The mismeasure of man.* New York: W. W. Norton.

Grashow, R., Brookings. T., & Marder. E. (2009). Reliable neuromodulation from circuits with variable underlying structure. *Proceedings of the National Academy of Science, 106,* 11742–11746.

Greene, J. D., & Paxton, J. M. (2009). Patterns of neural activity associated with honest and dishonest moral decisions. *Proceedings of the National Academy of Sciences, 106,* 12506–12511.

Griffiths, D. (2009). *Head first statistics: A brain friendly guide.* Sebastopol, CA: O'Reilly Media.

Gross, C. G. (1999). *Brain, vision, memory: Tales in the history of neuroscience.* Cambridge, MA: MIT Press.

Gross, C. G. (2010). *A hole in the head: More tales in the history of neuroscience.* Cambridge, MA: MIT Press.

Haag, J., & Borst, A. (2004). Neural mechanism underlying complex receptive field properties of motion-sensitive interneurons. *Nature Neuroscience, 7,* 628–634.

Hall, A. C., & Harrington, M. E. (2003). Experimental methods in neuroscience: An undergraduate neuroscience laboratory course for teaching ethical issues, laboratory techniques, experimental design and analysis. *Journal of Undergraduate Neuroscience Education, 2,* A1–A7.

Hall, A. C., Turcotte, C. M., Betts, B. A., Yeung, W-Y., Agyeman, A. S., & Burk, L. A. (2004). Modulation of human GABA-A and glycine receptor currents by menthol and related monoterpenoids. *European Journal of Pharmacology, 506,* 9–16.

Hamann, S., Herman, R. A., Nolan, C. L., & Wallen, K. (2004). Men and women differ in amygdala response to visual sexual stimuli. *Nature Neuroscience, 7,* 411–416.

Hamilton, D. (1986). *The monkey gland affair.* London, UK: Chatto & Windus.

Hebert, L. E., Scherr, P. A., Bienias, J. L., Bennett, D. A., & Evans, D. A. (2003). Alzheimer disease in the U.S. population: Prevalence estimates using the 2000 census. *Archives of Neurology, 60,* 1119–1122.

Heiman, G. W. (2001). *Understanding research methods and statistics*. Boston: Houghton Mifflin.

Hoffman, G. E., & Lyo, D. (2002). Anatomical markers of activity in neuroendocrine systems: Are we all "fos-ed out"? *Journal of Neuroendocrinology, 14*, 259–268.

Hogan, T. P. (2011). *Bare-bones R: A brief introductory guide*. Thousand Oaks, CA: Sage.

Hornblum, A. M. (1997). They were cheap and available: Prisoners as research subjects in twentieth-century America. *British Medical Journal, 315*, 1437–1441.

Houghton, P. M., Houghton, T. J., & Pratt, M. M. (2009). *APA: The easy way!* Flint, MI: Baker College.

Huettel, S. A., Song, A. W., & McCarthy, G. (2008). *Functional magnetic resonance imaging*. Sunderland, MA: Sinauer Press.

Journal of Neuroscience. Retrieved June 15, 2004, from http://www.jneurosci.org/misc/ifa_organization.dtl

Kandel, E. R. (2007). *In search of memory: The emergence of a new science of mind*. New York: W. W. Norton.

Kaspar, B. K., Llado, J., Sherkat, N., Rothstein, J. D., & Gage, F. H. (2003). Retrograde viral delivery of IGF-1 prolongs survival in a mouse ALS model. *Science, 301*, 839–842.

Kevles, D. (1998). *The Baltimore case: A trial of politics, science, and character*. New York: W. W. Norton.

Kirkpatrick, L. A., & Feeney, B. C. (2006). *A simple guide to SPSS for Windows for versions 12.0 and 13.0*. Belmont, CA: Wadsworth.

Kleckner, N. W., & Pallotta, B. S. (1995). Burst kinetics of single NMDA receptor currents in cell-attached patches from rat brain cortical neurons in culture. *Journal of Physiology, 486*, 411–426.

Kolb, B., & Wishaw, I. (1996). *Fundamentals of human neuropsychology* (4th ed.). New York: Worth Publishing.

Koolschijn, P. C., van Haren, N. E., Lensvelt-Mulders, G. J., Hulshoff Pol, H. E., & Kahn, R. S. (2009). Brain volume abnormalities in major depressive disorder: A meta-analysis of magnetic resonance imaging studies. *Human Brain Mapping, 30*, 3719–3735.

Kuchibhotla, K.V., Lattarulo, C. R., Hyman, B. T., & Bacskai, B. J. (2009). Synchronous hyperactivity and intercellular calcium waves in astrocytes in Alzheimer mice. *Science, 323*, 1211–1215.

Kuhn, T. S. (1975). *The structure of scientific revolutions*. Chicago: University of Chicago Press.

Lall, G. S., & Biello, S. M. (2003). Neuropeptide Y, GABA and circadian phase shifts to photic stimuli. *Neuroscience, 120*, 915–921.

Lathe, R. (2004). The individuality of mice. *Genes, Brain and Behavior, 3*, 317–327.

Lazic, S. E. (2010). The problem of pseudoreplication in neuroscientific studies: Is it affecting your analysis? *BMC Neuroscience 11*(5). doi:10.1186/1471-2202-11-5

Leary, M. R. (2001). *Introduction to behavioral research methods* (3rd ed.). Boston: Allyn & Bacon.

Leasure, J. L., Decker, L. (2009). Social isolation prevents exercise-induced proliferation of hippocampal progenitor cells in female rats. *Hippocampus, 19*, 907–912.

Lindvall, O., & Kokaia, Z. (2010). Stem cells in human neurodegenerative disorders: Time for clinical translation? *Journal of Clinical Investigation, 120*, 29–40.

Locke, L. F., Silverman, S. J., & Spirduso, W. W. (1998). *Reading and understanding research* (form 5.2, pp. 94–96). Thousand Oaks, CA: Sage.

Lu, L., Hope, B. T., Dempsey, J., Liu, S. Y., Bossert, J. M., & Shaham, Y. (2005). Central amygdala ERK signaling pathway is critical to incubation of cocaine craving. *Nature Neuroscience, 8*, 212–219.

Mathias, J. L., Beall, J. A., & Bigler, E. D. (2004). Neuropsychological and information processing deficits following mild traumatic brain injury. *Journal of International Neuropsychology Society, 10*, 286–297.

McCutcheon, J. E., & Marinelli, M. (2009). Age matters. *European Journal of Neuroscience, 29*, 997–1014.

McGowan, P. O., Sasaki, A., D'Alessio, A. C., Dymov, S., Labonté, B., Szyf, M., et al. (2009). Epigenetic regulation of the glucocorticoid receptor in human brain associates with childhood abuse. *Nature Neuroscience, 12*, 342–348.

McLeod, P. J., Moger, W. H., Ryon, J., Gadbois, S., & Fentress, J. C. (1996). The relation between urinary cortisol levels and social behaviour in captive timber wolves. *Canadian Journal of Zoology, 874*, 209–216.

Milner, B., Corkin, S., & Teuber, H. L. (1968). Further analysis of the hippocampal amnesic syndrome: 14-year follow-up study of H. M. *Neuropsychologia, 6*, 215–234.

Monory, K., Blaudzun, H., Massa, F., Kaiser, N., Lemberger, T., Schütz, G., et al. (2007). Genetic dissection of behavioural and autonomic effects of Delta(9)-tetrahydrocannabinol in mice. *PLoS Biology, 5*, e269.

Monory, K., Massa, F., Egertova, M., Eder, M., Blaudzun, H., Westenbroek, R., et al. (2006). The endocannabinoid system controls key epileptogenic circuits in the hippocampus. *Neuron, 51*, 455–466.

National Institutes of Health. (1979). *The Belmont report: Ethical principles and guidelines for the protection of human subjects of research*. Retrieved February 8, 2010, from http://ohsr.od.nih.gov/guidelines/belmont.html

National Institutes of Health. (n.d.). NIH image software, developed at the U.S. National Institutes of Health. Available at http://rsb.info.nih.gov/nih-image

National Research Council. (1996). *Guide for the care and use of laboratory animals* (7th ed.). Washington, DC: National Academy Press, Office of Laboratory Animal Welfare. Available at http://www.nap.edu/openbook.php?record_id=5140

Nelson, C. A., 3rd, Zeanah, C. H., Fox, N. A., Martshall, P. J., Smyke, A.T., & Guthrie, D. (2007). Cognitive recovery in socially deprived young children: The Bucharest Early Intervention Project. *Science, 318*, 1937–1940.

Office of Laboratory Animal Welfare. (2002). *PHS policy on humane care and use of laboratory animals*. Retrieved April 26, 2010, from National Institutes of Health website: http://grants.nih.gov/grants/olaw/references/phspol.htm

Committee on Science, Engineering and Public Policy. National Academy of Sciences, National Academy of Engineering, Institute of Medicine. (1995). *On being a scientist*. Washington, DC: National Academy Press. Available from http://www.nap.edu

Owen, A. M., Schiff, N. D., & Laureys, S. (2009). A new era of coma and consciousness science. *Progress in Brain Research, 177*, 399–411.

Pace, T. W., Negi, L. T., Adame, D. D., Cole, S. P., Sivilli, T. I., Brown, T. D., et al. (2009). Effect of compassion meditation on neuroendocrine, innate immune and behavioral responses to psychosocial stress. *Psychoneuroendocrinology, 34*, 87–98.

Pangalos, M. N., Schechter, L. E., & Hurko, O. (2007). Drug development for CNS disorders: Strategies for balancing risk and reducing attrition. *Nature Reviews Drug Discovery, 6*, 521–532.

Parkin, A. (1987). *Memory and amnesia: An introduction*. Oxford, UK: Blackwell.

Pinker, S. (2002). *The blank slate: The modern denial of human nature*. New York: Penguin Books.

Platt, J. R. (1964). Strong inference. *Science, 146*, 347–353.

Plaut, D. C. (1995). Double dissociation without modularity: Evidence from connectionist neuropsychology. *Journal of Clinical and Experimental Neuropsychology, 17,* 291–321.

Pollo, A., & Benedetti, F. (2009). The placebo response: Neurobiological and clinical issues of neurobiological relevance. *Progress in Brain Research, 175,* 283–294.

Poremba, A., Saunders, R. C., Crane, A. M., Cook, M., Sokoloff, L., & Mishkin, M. (2003). Functional mapping of the primate auditory system. *Science, 299,* 568–572.

Posthuma, D., De Geus, E. J., Baare, W. F., Hulshoff Pol, H. E., Kahn, R. S., & Boomsma, D. I. (2002). The association between brain volume and intelligence is of genetic origin. *Nature Neuroscience, 5,* 83–84.

Price, D. D., Finniss, D. G., & Benedetti, F. (2008). A comprehensive review of the placebo effect: Recent advances and current thought. *Annual Review of Psychology, 59,* 565–590.

Purves, D., & Lotto, R. B. (2003). *Why we see what we do: An empirical theory of vision.* Sunderland, MA: Sinauer.

Raizada, R. D. S., & Kishiyama, M. M. (2010). Effects of socioeconomic status on brain development, and how cognitive neuroscience may contribute to leveling the playing field. *Frontiers in Human Neuroscience, 4,* 1–11. doi:10.3389/neur0.09.003.2010

Ramachandran, V. S., & Blakeslee, S. (1998). *Phantoms in the brain: Probing the mysteries of the human mind.* New York: Morrow.

Rattenborg, N. C., Voirin, B., Vyssotski, A. L., Kays, R. W., Spoelstra, K., Kuemmeth, F., et al. (2008). Sleeping outside the box: Electroencephalographic measures of sleep in sloths inhabiting a rainforest. *Biology Letters, 4,* 402–405.

Ray, W. J. (2003). *Methods: Toward a science of behavior and experience.* Belmont, CA: Wadsworth.

Ricaurte, G. A., Yuan, J., Hatzidimitriou, G., Cord, B. J., & McCann, U. D. (2002). Severe dopaminergic neurotoxicity in primates after a common recreational dose regimen of MDMA ("Ecstasy"). *Science, 297,* 2260–2263.

Ricaurte, G. A., Yuan, J., Hatzidimitriou, G., Cord, B. J., & McCann, U. D. (2003). Retraction. *Science, 301,* 1479.

Riggs, T. L. (2004). Research and development costs for drugs. *The Lancet, 363,* 184.

Rodrigue, K. M., & Raz, N. (2004). Shrinkage of the entorhinal cortex over five years predicts memory performance in healthy adults. *Journal of Neuroscience, 24,* 956–963.

Rosenbaum, P. R. (2002). *Observational studies.* New York: Springer.

Rosenzweig, M. R., Leiman, A. L., & Breedlove, S. M. (1999). *Biological psychology.* Sunderland, MA: Sinauer.

Rossner, M., & Yamada, K. M. (2004). What's in a picture? The temptation of image manipulation. *Journal of Cell Biology, 166,* 11–15.

Rudan, I., et al. (2008). Preventing inequity in international research [Letter to editor with author response]. *Science, 319,* 1336–1337.

Russell, W. M. S., & Burch, R. L. (1959). *The principles of humane experimental technique.* London: Metheun.

Ryan, B. C., & Vandenbergh, J. G. (2002). Intrauterine position effects. *Neuroscience and Biobehavioral Reviews, 26,* 665–678.

Salkind, N. J. (2002). *Exploring research.* Upper Saddle River, NJ: Prentice-Hall.

Salkind, N. J. (2004). *Statistics for people who (think they) hate statistics.* Thousand Oaks, CA: Sage.

Salkind, N. J. (2010). *Excel statistics: A quick guide.* Thousand Oaks, CA: Sage.

Santarelli, L., Saxe, M., Gross, C., Surget, A., Battaglia, F., Dulawa, S., et al. (2003). Requirement of hippocampal neurogenesis for the behavioral effects of antidepressants. *Science, 301,* 805–809.

Sbrogna, J. L., Barresi, M. J. F., & Karlstrom, R. O. (2003). Multiple roles for hedgehog signaling in zebrafish pituitary development. *Developmental Biology, 254,* 19–35.

Schummers, J., Yu, H., & Sur, M. (2008). Tuned responses of astrocytes and their influence on hemodynamic signals in the visual cortex. *Science 320,* 1638–1643.

Schwartz, M. A. (2008). The importance of stupidity in scientific research. *Journal of Cell Science, 121,* 1771.

Schwartzkroin, P. A. (2009). *So you want to be a scientist?* New York: Oxford University Press.

Scoville, W. B., & Milner, B. (1957). Loss of recent memory after bilateral hippocampal lesions. *Journal of Neurology, Neurosurgery and Psychiatry 20,* 11–12.

Seidman, L. J., Faraone, S. V., Goldstein, J. M., Kremen, W. S., Horton, N. J., Makris, N., et al. (2002). Left hippocampal volume as a vulnerability indicator for schizophrenia: A magnetic resonance imaging morphometric study of nonpsychotic first-degree relatives. *Archives of General Psychiatry, 59,* 839–849.

Shaywitz, B. A., Shaywitz, S. E., Blachman, B. A., Pugh, K. R., Fulbright, R. K., Skudlarski, P., et al. (2004). Development of left occipitotemporal systems for skilled reading in children after a phonologically-based intervention. *Biological Psychiatry, 55,* 926–933.

Sheline, Y. I., Gado, M. H., & Kraemer, H. C. (2003). Untreated depression and hippocampal volume loss. *American Journal of Psychiatry, 160,* 1516–1518.

Shepherd, G. M. (1991). *Foundations of the neuron doctrine.* New York: Oxford University Press.

Shepherd, G. M. (2010). *Creating modern neuroscience: The revolutionary 1950s.* New York: Oxford University Press.

Skinner, M. K., Anway, M. D., Savenkova, M. I., Gore, A. C., & Crews, D. (2008). Transgenerational epigenetic programming of the brain transcriptome and anxiety behavior. *PLoS One, 3*(11), e3745.

Smith, M. T., Perlis, M. L., Park, A., Smith, M. S., Pennington, J., Giles, D. E., & Buysse, D. J. (2002). Comparative meta-analysis of pharmacotherapy and behavior therapy for persistent insomnia. *American Journal of Psychiatry, 159,* 5–11.

Society for Neuroscience. (1998). *Responsible conduct for scientific communication.* Available at http://web.sfn.org/skins/main/pdf/Guidelines/Responsible Conduct.pdf

StatSoft, Inc. (2003). *Electronic statistics textbook.* Tulsa, OK: StatSoft. Available at http://www.statsoft.com/textbook/stathome.html

Stevens, C. F. (2000). Models are common; good theories are scarce. *Nature Neuroscience Supplement, 3,* 1177.

Strunk, W., Jr., & White, E. B. (1999). *The elements of style.* New York: Pearson Longman.

Szuchman, L. T. (2002). *Writing with style: APA style made easy.* Belmont, CA: Wadsworth.

Takahashi, H., Kato, M., Matsuura, M., Mobbs, D., Suhara, T., & Okubo, Y. (2009). When your gain is my pain and your pain is my gain: Neural correlates of envy and schadenfreude. *Science, 323,* 937–939.

Takami, T., Oudega, M., Bates, M. L., Wood, P. M., Kleitman, N., & Bunge, M. B. (2002). Schwann cell but not olfactory ensheathng glia transplants improve hindlimb locomotor performance in the moderately contused adult rat thoracic spinal cord. *Journal of Neuroscience, 22,* 6670–6681.

Taub, E., Uswatte, G., & Pidikiti, R. (1999). Constraint-induced movement therapy: A new family of techniques with broad application to physical rehabilitation—a clinical review. *Journal of Rehabilitation Research and Development, 36,* 237–251.

Thilo, K. V., Santoro, L., Walsh, V., & Blakemore, C. (2004). The site of saccadic suppression. *Nature Neuroscience 7*, 13–14.

Tillerson, J. L., Cohen, A. D., Philhower, J., Miller, G. W., Zigmond, M. J., & Schallert, T. (2001). Forced limb-use effects on the behavioral and neurochemical effects of 6-hydroxydopamine. *Journal of Neuroscience, 21*, 4427–4435.

Tobin, V. A., Hurst, G., Norrie, L., Dal Rio, F. P., Bull, P. M., & Ludwig, M. (2004). Thapsigargin-induced mobilization of dendritic dense-cored vesicles in rat supraoptic neurons. *European Journal of Neuroscience, 19*, 2909–2912.

Tsuzuki, K., Xing, H., Ling, J., & Gu, J. G. (2004). Menthol-induced Ca2+ release from presynaptic Ca2+ stores potentiates sensory synaptic transmission. *Journal of Neuroscience, 24*, 762–771.

Tufte, E. R. (1983). *The visual display of quantitative information.* Cheshire, CT: Graphics Press.

Tufte, E. R. (2006). *The cognitive style of PowerPoint.* Cheshire CT: Graphics Press.

Tufte, E. R. (2007). *The visual display of quantitative information.* Cheshire, CT: Graphics Press.

USDA Animal Care Annual Report. (2008). *Animal care annual report of activities: Fiscal year 2007.* Retrieved April 26, 2010, from http://www.aphis.usda.gov/publications/animal_welfare/content/printable_version/2007_AC_Report.pdf

U.S. National Library of Medicine. *PubMed.* Retrieved March 2, 2005, from http://www.nlm.nih.gov

Vaiva, G., Ducrocq, F., Jezequel, K., Averland, B., Lestavel, P., Brunet, A., & Marmar, C. R. (2003). Immediate treatment with propranolol decreases posttraumatic stress disorder two months after trauma. *Biological Psychiatry, 54*, 947–949.

Van Someren, E. J. W., Kessler, A., Mirmiran, M., & Swaab, D. F. (1997). Indirect bright light improves circadian rest-activity rhythm disturbances in demented patients. *Biological Psychiatry, 41*, 955–963.

Volkow, N. D., Fowler, J. S., Logan, J., Alexoff, D., Zhu, W., Telang, F., et al. (2009). Effects of modafinil on dopamine and dopamine transporters in the male human brain: Clinical implications. *JAMA, 301*, 1148–1154.

Wainer, H. (2009). *Picturing the uncertain world: How to understand, communicate, and control uncertainty through graphical display.* Princeton, NJ: Princeton University Press.

Wilson, E. O. (1998). *Consilience: The unity of knowledge.* New York: Knopf.

Woodbury-Harris, K. M., & Coull, B. M. (2009). *Clinical trials in the neurosciences.* New York: Karger.

Yannielli, P. C., Brewer, J. M., & Harrington, M. E. (2004). Blockade of the NPY Y5 receptor potentiates circadian responses to light: complementary in vivo and in vitro studies. *European Journal of Neuroscience, 19*, 891–897.

Yannielli, P. C., & Harrington, M. E. (2000). Neuropeptide Y applied in vitro can block the phase shifts induced by light in vivo. *NeuroReport, 11*, 1587–1591.

Zhang, Y., Hong, Y., Bounhar, Y., Blacker, M., Roucou, X., Tounekti, O., et al. (2003). p75 neurotrophin receptor protects primary cultures of human neurons against extracellular amyloid beta peptide cytotoxicity. *Journal of Neuroscience, 23*, 7385–7394.

Zhou, Z., Zhu, G., Hariri, A. R., Enoch, M. A., Scott, D., Sinha, R., et al. (2008). Genetic variation in human NPY expression affects stress response and emotion. *Nature, 452*, 997–1001.

Zup, S. L., Carrier, H., Waters, E. M., Tabor, A., Bengston, L., Rosen, G. J., et al. (2003). Overexpression of Bcl-2 reduces sex differences in neuron number in the brain and spinal cord. *Journal of Neuroscience, 23*, 2357–2362.

Index

Supporting researchers for more than 40 years

Research methods have always been at the core of SAGE's publishing program. Founder Sara Miller McCune published SAGE's first methods book, *Public Policy Evaluation*, in 1970. Soon after, she launched the *Quantitative Applications in the Social Sciences* series—affectionately known as the "little green books."

Always at the forefront of developing and supporting new approaches in methods, SAGE published early groundbreaking texts and journals in the fields of qualitative methods and evaluation.

Today, more than 40 years and two million little green books later, SAGE continues to push the boundaries with a growing list of more than 1,200 research methods books, journals, and reference works across the social, behavioral, and health sciences. Its imprints—Pine Forge Press, home of innovative textbooks in sociology, and Corwin, publisher of PreK–12 resources for teachers and administrators—broaden SAGE's range of offerings in methods. SAGE further extended its impact in 2008 when it acquired CQ Press and its best-selling and highly respected political science research methods list.

From qualitative, quantitative, and mixed methods to evaluation, SAGE is the essential resource for academics and practitioners looking for the latest methods by leading scholars.

For more information, visit **www.sagepub.com**.